Sport in the Global Society

General Editor: J.A. Mangan

CRICKET AND ENGLAND

SPORT IN THE GLOBAL SOCIETY

General Editor: J.A. Mangan

ISSN 1368-9789

The interest in sports studies around the world is growing and will continue to do so. This unique series combines aspects of the expanding study of *sport in the global society*, providing comprehensiveness and comparison under one editorial umbrella. It is particularly timely, with studies in the political, cultural, social, economic, geographical and aesthetic elements of sport proliferating in institutions of higher education.

Eric Hobsbawm once called sport one of the most significant practices of the late nineteenth century. Its significance is even more marked in the late twentieth century and will continue to grow in importance into the next millennium as the world develops into a 'global village' sharing the English language, technology and sport.

Other Titles in the Series

CRICKET AND ENGLAND

A Cultural and Social History of
the Inter-war Years

JACK WILLIAMS
John Moores University

FRANK CASS
LONDON • PORTLAND, OR

First published in 1999 in Great Britain by
FRANK CASS PUBLISHERS
Newbury House, 900 Eastern Avenue
London, IG2 7HH

and in the United States of America by
FRANK CASS PUBLISHERS
c/o ISBS, 5804 N.E. Hassalo Street
Portland, Oregon 97213-3644

Website: http://www.frankcass.com

British Library Cataloguing in Publication Data

Williams, Jack, 1940–
    Cricket and England : a cultural and social history of the
    inter-war years. – (Sport in the global society; no. 8)
    1. Cricket – Social aspects – England 2. England – Social
    conditions – 20th century
    I. Title
    796.3'58'0942

                ISBN 0-7146-4861-2 (cloth)
                ISBN 0-7146-4418-8 (paper)
                ISSN 1368-9789

Library of Congress Cataloging-in-Publication Data

Williams, Jack, 1940–
    Cricket and England: a cultural and social history of the
    inter-war years / Jack Williams.
        p. cm. – (Sport in the global society, ISSN 1368-9789;
    vol. 8)
    Includes bibliographical references and index.
    ISBN 0-7146-4861-2 (cloth). – ISBN 0-7146-4418-8 (pbk.)
    1. Cricket – England – History – 20th century. 2. Cricket –
    Social aspects – England – History – 20th century. I. Title.
    II. Series: Cass series – sport in the global society; 8.
    GV928.G7W54   1999
    796.358'0942 – dc21   98-47285
                                                            CIP

Printed in Great Britain by
Bookcraft (Bath) Ltd, Midsomer Norton, Somerset

Contents

List of Illustrations

Acknowledgements

Thanks are due to many individuals and institutions for their help with this book. It has grown out of a PhD thesis and I was more than fortunate to have such enthusiastic and stimulating research supervisors as Steve Constantine and John Walton. The Liverpool John Moores University and in particular Dave McEvoy of the School of Social Science arranged travel and accommodation grants essential for undertaking research in different parts of the country. Officials of many cricket clubs and cricket organisations have been most kind in allowing me access to their archives. I hope that those whom I interviewed enjoyed our conversations as much as I did. The staffs of many libraries and record offices have been of immeasurable assistance, but a special mention must be made of Stephen Green and Glenys Williams of the MCC library whose courtesy and friendliness always made visits to Lord's so pleasurable. Mr R.D.V. Knight, secretary of the MCC, was most generous in permitting me to consult such a wide range of archives at Lord's. The Inter-library Loans Unit of the JMU was able to provide me with materials from the most obscure locations. With his typical benevolence Don Ambrose loaned many items from his private collection of cricket books and memorabilia and allowed me to draw upon his encyclopaedic knowledge of cricket history. Like all who have studied sport history I have learned much from the writings of Tony Mason, Tony Mangan, Jeff Hill, Dick Holt, Grant Harvie, John Lowerson, Wray Vamplew and Gareth Williams, but equally important have been the conversations with them over the years about sport history. Mary and John Lowerson must also be thanked for their hospitality while I was researching in Sussex. The bibliographic researches of Richard Cox have been of immense help, while Dave Terry and Tony Collins have drawn my attention to items which otherwise would have escaped my attention. Thanks must also be extended to those who granted permission to quote from printed works and for the reproduction of photographs. My greatest debt is to my wife Pat for her unfailing encouragement, patience and understanding.

Jack Williams
September 1998

Series Editor's Foreword

Lord Mancroft, the politician, who came to manhood in the 1930s, described cricket in his biography *Bees in Some Bonnets* (1979) as 'a game which the English, not being a spiritual people, have invented in order to give themselves some conception of eternity' (p.185). Americans, of course, whether spiritual or otherwise, frequently claim that watching cricket seems like an eternity. In this analysis of English cricket in the inter-war years Jack Williams may help Americans to understand both the game and the 'Anglo-Saxon' better. It is more likely, however, that the book will serve to reinforce their claim that they know us rather well.

Some little time ago, William Arens, an American sociologist, wrote a short article to the effect that if you want to know the Americans watch their football: through football they reveal themselves. Williams would make a similar claim for cricket and the English in the 1920s and 1930s. He demonstrates that those in power invested the game with a unique moral worth which, fortunately for them, was inculcated in both them and their sons by means of frequent exposure to cricket in their privileged schools, thus providing them with a precious 'cultural capital' which allowed them to lay claim to political, cultural and social leadership. This fact underlines the logic of the game's class and gender privileges, prejudices and parameters. 'Few other cultural institutions', in his words, 'made the social inequalities surrounding gender and class so obvious' (p.xi).

The attraction of this book is its chosen time-scale – the inter-war years – when, Williams would assert, the image of cricket, as a fused symbol of Englishness and Stability created by the Victorians, saw its 'Golden Age', was diffused successfully through all layers of English society, and helped to sustain a relatively placid and acquiescent social order. Derek Birley, in his elegantly readable *Playing the Game: Sport and British Society, 1910–45* (1995), may well have gone to the heart of the matter: 'the idea of cricket probably appealed to the average Englishman more than the actual game' (p.184). This appeal, it would seem, was as much a feature of the English working class as any other class, and goes some way to explain E.A. Nordlinger's observation in his *The Working Class Tories: Authority, Deference and Stable Democracy* (1967) that 'the characteristic dimension of the English working class culture is the diffusion of acquiescient attitudes towards authority' (p.210).

No less an academic heavyweight than Asa Briggs is clearly on the side of Williams. In his *A Social History of England* (1983) he remarked: 'There were so many forces making for collaboration rather than confrontation that the General Strike has been seen in retrospect not as the high watermark of class warfare, but as the moment when the class war ceased to shape the pattern of British industrial relations at least for several decades' (p.266). It would be interesting to know what significance, as a consolidating force, Lord Briggs would give to cricket.

Williams' challenging assertion that 'cricket made social distinctions and economic inequalities so obvious [that] responses to the forms of social privilege and exclusion found in cricket, provide an unusual yet highly illuminating perspective upon class mentalities between the wars' (p.xiii) should stimulate lively discussion in the Groves of Academe. The statement certainly makes the point with force that sport is integral, not marginal, to culture. Williams goes further, linking, perhaps daringly, cricket specifically to the debate about British cultural attitudes and associated economic decline – another opportunity for strenuous reflection in academia. In fact, Williams could now well become one of a provocative quartet. With Correlli Barnett, *The Collapse of British Power* (1972), Martin Weiner, *English Culture and the Decline of the Industrial Spirit 1850–1980* (1972) and David Rubinstein, *Capitalism, Culture and Decline in Britain* (1993) he has committed views on Englishness, economic survival and cultural tradition. It is surely not contentious for Williams to suggest that a consideration of English cricket as part of English culture offers the possibility of a deeper understanding of the cultural assumptions and values that fashioned social and economic relations.

In fact, Williams raises a number of fascinating points for discussion – not least, incidentally, that in the light of the pending break-up of the United Kingdom cricket could come to represent uniquely English qualities since in the past it has been a vital part of those 'narratives' through which the English have told themselves what Englishness is, and just what it means to them. Village cricket may yet become a symbol for a new Nationalism arising out of an old Nationalism.

And what of his suggestion that the support of women for men's cricket in this period provides an explanation for the absence of challenge to male social power on the part of the post-Great War 'new feminism'? He also has fascinating points to make about the role of church cricket in delaying secularisation, distracting the militant socialists and promoting social co-operation, and about the morality attributed to cricket which kept commercialism, which might undermine sportsmanship and fair play, at arm's length.

Bertrand Russell, who certainly should have known, claimed in *Sceptical Essays* in 1928 that 'Every man, wherever he goes, is encompassed by a cloud of comforting convictions, which move with him like flies on a summer day.' Williams is a writer of strong convictions and firm conclusions. He is in no doubt that cricket between the wars was as much the social cement of Britain as it was of the Empire. Between the wars, in his words, 'the belief that cricket was a distillation of English morality was related to the association of cricket with the Christian churches, assumptions about the Empire being a moral trust, the English pastoral idyll, the limited degree of commercialisation within cricket, reverence for tradition and respect for accepted forms and manners' (p.183).

Throughout the book Williams delivers his firmly held views in a continuous series of fluid assertions. England, of course, was not without its troubles in the 1920s and 1930s – militant industrial action in the 1920s, severe economic depression in both the 1920s and the 1930s and the first successful challenges to the Empire in the period – yet England eschewed extremism and embraced moderation. It was an unequal nation largely at ease with itself. And cricket played its part in this. *In nuce*, cricket held up a mirror to society; it reflected its essential inequalities, snobberies and its essential harmony: but it did more, it successfully sustained all three.

This is a book full of marvellous debating points. Let the debate begin in class, seminar, tutorial and bar rooms. There is much to discuss.

Jack Williams expresses the hope that he has filled a gap. He has.

J. A. Mangan
International Research Centre for Sport, Socialisation, Society,
Strathclyde University
November 1998

Introduction

This book explores the cultural and social significance of cricket in England between the wars. It reflects a conviction that explaining the status accorded to cricket is essential for an understanding of English society in the 1920s and 1930s. Cricket was celebrated as far more than a game. The social groups with economic and political power esteemed cricket as an expression of a distinctively English sense of moral worth and cricket had a key role in how they imagined themselves and their fitness to exercise authority. They believed that cricket encouraged and reflected a sense of social harmony which extended beyond the world of cricket. Yet many levels of cricket in the 1920s and 1930s were riddled with privilege and social distinction. Few other cultural institutions made the social inequalities surrounding gender and class so obvious. Accounting for the importance attached to cricket and assessing the responses among the English to the social distinctions of cricket provide crucial insights into how the English perceived themselves and their social world.

Culture has been an area of growing interest among historians in the 1980s and 1990s, but differing meanings have been attached to the term 'culture'. For some 'culture' and the 'high arts' are used interchangeably. 'Popular culture' may mean those forms of artistic expression which are not considered high-brow or elitist but it is also used as catch-all description for the various forms of mass entertainment. For the purposes of this book, 'culture' is used in its more anthropological sense of being those assumptions and values which shape how groups define themselves and imagine the social order. Such an approach to culture is very much influenced by the writings of Raymond Williams who did so much to stimulate the study of culture. Williams defined culture as 'a whole body of practices and expectations, the whole of living; ... our shaping perceptions of ourselves and of our world. It is a lived system of meanings and values'.[1] Culture in this sense is very much concerned with what has been called 'collective subjectivity', which has been designated as a rejection of the notion that 'culture' refers to 'the best and most glorious achievements of a people or civilization',[2] though cricket writers have often stressed the aesthetic appeal of cricket and have described playing cricket, and especially batting with style, as a form of artistic expression. As cricket was a sport with which males from all classes were involved and as those with political and economic power placed such emphasis upon the moral value of cricket, the approach to culture adopted in this book has also been informed by the contentions of Pierre Bourdieu that the differing values which different social groups ascribe to the same cultural practices act as forms of social distinction and can provide elite groups with cultural capital which reinforces their social prestige.[3] Regarding culture as those processes which govern how groups perceive the social world and their place within it is very much involved with notions of identity and the narratives through which these are expressed and constructed. It is through narratives, and narratives taken as more than the written and spoken word, that people make sense of the world and shape their perception of themselves. Cricket can be seen as narrative through which the English expressed their cultural values and their sense of who they were. In order to analyse the narrative power of cricket it is necessary to examine cricket discourses. Some advocates of the 'linguistic turn' in historical study such as Patrick Joyce appear to use the words 'culture' and 'language' as synonyms and maintain that the social order or, rather, perceptions of the social order are determined by language.[4] Whilst this book is concerned with culture and with cricket discourses, it does not reflect acceptance of an extreme linguistic determinism and a rejection of economic factors as causes of social change. Material circumstances do seem to have had an impact on cricket. Economics, for instance, did much to determine who was able to play or watch cricket in its more socially exclusive settings.

In order to appraise what can be inferred from cricket about culture and social relations, this book considers the values underlying the representations of cricket and the extent to which such representations of cricket were a myth. It discusses how and why cricket had come to be regarded as such a powerful symbol of England and of English moral worth and goes on to examine what cricket reveals about attitudes in England to gender identities, class distinction, the exercise of authority, the social role of the churches and the acceptance of commercialism. Assumptions about cricket being an expression of English morality were not restricted to the inter-war period, though they were probably no stronger at any other time. The image of cricket as a symbol of England was very much a creation of the Victorians yet even at the close of the twentieth century, when the social milieu and ethos of cricket are very different from the 1920s and 1930s, cricket is still used to create an immediately recognisable vision of England. The main reason why this book concentrates on the inter-war decades is that an appraisal of what cricket reveals about culture and social relations has to consider all forms and levels of cricket. Much can be learned from first-class cricket about snobbery and privilege within cricket, but village cricket was very often portrayed as representing the true heart of cricket. The support provided by women for men's cricket was often most apparent in recreational cricket. Playing cricket at whatever level was often seen as the most effective means of encouraging the moral lessons of cricket. With a longer time span it would not have been possible to consider all levels and forms of cricket. It is not being suggested that cricket between the wars did not change. The playing of cricket among women became more widespread and more organised. More people watched county cricket in the early 1920s than in the late 1930s. England started to play test matches against the West Indies, New Zealand and India. But the changes within cricket were gradual and moderate rather than radical. Perceptions of cricket in 1939 remained very much what they had been in 1918.

The importance accorded to cricket means that an exploration of cricket can make a crucial contribution to debates among historians about the nature of English society and cultural values between the wars. The growth in recent years in the political expression of Scottish and Welsh nationalism has led to more consideration of English identity and the nature of Englishness. Because cricket was played and watched to a far greater extent in England rather than in Scotland or Wales, but more particularly because cricket discourses emphasised that cricket expressed uniquely English qualities, cricket can be seen as a vital part of those narratives through which the English told themselves what being English meant to them. Yet at the same time, as Jeffrey Richards has pointed out, many in England used the terms England and English as synonyms for Britain and British.[5] The rise of post-modernist and post-structuralist forms of social analysis has led to a questioning of how far social class, and class identities based on convictions that the interests of different classes were in conflict, were the dominant form of social identity in England between the wars. Establishing how far perceptions of the social order were characterised by a sense of animosity and conflict is related to the question of why support for Labour was not sufficient for it to have won a clear majority at any inter-war general election and to the issue of why support for political extremism was so limited in England in the 1920s and 1930s.[6] Because cricket made social distinctions and economic inequalities so obvious, responses to the forms of social privilege and exclusion found in cricket provide an unusual yet highly illuminating perspective upon class mentalities between the wars. The role of women in cricket deepens understanding of gender relations in inter-war England, and in particular why there were not more demands from women for greater equality with men. The expansion of cricket playing among women can be seen as a form of emancipation for women, but the degree of support from women for men's cricket does much to explain why what has been called the 'new feminism' of the period from 1918 until the 1960s did not so much challenge male social power as call for greater recognition of those areas of social activity which were thought to be forms of feminine expertise.[7]

There has been debate among historians and social analysts about how far English cultural values, and especially those cultivated by the public schools, have contributed to Britain's relative decline as one of the world's major economic powers. This debate was originally concerned with how far English culture had discouraged industrial growth, but it has been broadened into a discussion of how far cultural assumptions in England inhibited respect for commercialism and discouraged a spirit of unbridled acquisitivism which has been seen as a prerequisite for economic expansion.[8] Because of the enormous significance accorded to cricket, especially among those with inherited wealth, and because county cricket was so often financially ailing and characterised by respect for the amateur, cricket can help to determine how far English culture reflected a sympathy for aggressive commercialisation. It has often been asserted that English society was becoming more secularised between the wars, but as secularisation is very much involved with attitudes and assumptions, tracing with precision any decline in the influence of religious teachings over everyday life and conduct is difficult.[9] The frequent claims that cricket expressed Christian morality, the involvement of clerics with cricket and the high number of cricket teams based on churches and Sunday schools in some regions all suggest that cricket can help to register how the social role of the churches was perceived between the wars. It cannot be claimed, of course, that the study of cricket in itself can resolve all debate about the nature of English society between the wars, but it does deepen understanding of those cultural assumptions and values which fashioned social relations.

Interest in sport among academics has grown rapidly in the 1980s and 1990s. Much of this concern with sport has stemmed from Tony Mason's *Association Football and English Society, 1863–1915*,[10] which appeared in 1980, and from Tony Mangan's *Athleticism in the Victorian and Edwardian Public School*,[11] published a year later. Mason examined the social and economic factors which had attracted a mass following to football before the First World War, whilst Mangan analysed the rise of the games cult at the public schools and the part that this played in the mind-set of the Victorian and Edwardian elite. These seminal works were followed by a steady stream of books and articles on the history of sport in Britain. At the same time, sport has also been a site of increasing concern for sociologists. In 1979 *Barbarians, Gentlemen and Players: A Sociological Study of the Development of Rugby Football* by Dunning and Sheard[12] provided a figurationist explanation for the development of rugby union football in nineteenth- and twentieth-century Britain. In the 1980s concern over football hooliganism stimulated a burgeoning sociological literature into its nature and causes. Perhaps because of its recent growth, many gaps remain in historical and sociological writing on sport. Far more has been written about football than other sports, which possibly reflects the vast following for football in contemporary society. The chronological range of historical studies on sport is also uneven. Much has now been written about the development of sport in the Victorian period and in the last three decades of the present century, but less attention has been devoted to the period from the end of the First World War until the 1960s.

Given the importance attached to cricket as symbol of England, surprisingly few academic studies of cricket in England between the wars have been published. *The Willow Wand* by Sir Derek Birley, though concerned with a time-span much longer than the inter-war period, has examined many of the myths surrounding cricket and reveals that cricket practice often failed to match the ideals of its apologists.[13] *Cricket and Empire: The 1932–33 Bodyline Tour of Australia* by Ric Sissons and Brian Stoddart has shown that the significance accorded to cricket as an expression of the morality assumed to underlie British imperialism meant that England's employment of bodyline bowling had ramifications in the world of high politics.[14] Eric Midwinter has related the rise of W.G. Grace as the first English 'super-star' of team ball sports to the social and cultural climate of Victorian England, whilst Jeffrey Hill and Richard Holt have discussed the cultural connotations of cricket stars in the 1920s and 1930s.[15] The biographies of Lord Harris by J.D. Coldham and of Sir Pelham Warner by Gerald Howat[16] have uncovered much about how power was exercised at the highest levels of first-class cricket. Ric Sissons' *The Players: A Social History of the Professional Cricketer* has looked at the pay and employment conditions of county cricketers.[17] Michael Marshall's *Gentlemen & Players*[18] and David Lemmon's *The Crisis of Captaincy: Servant and Master in English Cricket* and *For the Love of the Game*[19] were probably not intended primarily for an academic readership but their interviews with retired county cricketers contain a wealth of fascinating detail about the social gulfs between amateurs and professionals. The vast number of autobiographies, mainly ghosted, and biographies of first-class cricketers are primarily concerned with the playing exploits of their subjects, but David Foot's studies of Charlie Parker, Cecil Parkin, Jack MacBryan and Walter Hammond indicate much about the personal and social tensions of first-class cricket.[20] Mike Marqusee's *Anyone but England* is written with great polemical verve and demonstrates how throughout the twentieth century, cricket, but especially first-class cricket, can provide penetrating insights into the outlook of those from privileged backgrounds.[21]

More has been written about cricket before 1914 and after 1945 than in the inter-war period. Many key areas of the inter-war cricket scene have been largely ignored. No study equivalent to Keith Sandiford's appraisal of the social and economic factors which shaped cricket in the Victorian period has been published.[22] The relations between professional and amateur cricketers in first-class cricket are discussed in Christopher Brookes' *English Cricket: The Game and Its Players through the Ages*,[23] but the years 1873 to 1962 are covered in only one chapter. Little has been published about social backgrounds and numbers of those who played or watched cricket between the wars. *Sporting Females: Critical Issues in the History and Sociology of Women's Sports*,[24] the admirable examination of sport and female identity in twentieth-century Britain by Jennifer Hargreaves, shows how little is known about the growth of cricket playing among women between the wars or about the support from women for men's cricket. Wray Vamplew's detailed comparison of the financial structure of county cricket with that of association football, horse racing and rugby league does not extend beyond 1914.[25] A number of studies have discussed aspects of sport and working-class identity between the wars,[26] though little has been written about sports often thought to have a strong working-class ambience such as rugby league, whippet racing or speedway, and there is no examination of middle-class involvement with sport in the twentieth century which approaches the breadth of John Lowerson's *Sport and the English Middle Classes, 1878–1914*.[27] Jeffrey Hill and Jack Williams have made exploratory forays, but no more than these, into the social history of league cricket between the wars.[28] *Beyond a Boundary* by C.L.R. James has acquired the status of a classic study into the history and sociology of cricket. It was one of the first works to show how cricket had been invested with a cultural significance which had close links with imperialism and race, but its discussion of cricket in England between the wars concentrates on the reactions in the town of Nelson to the West Indian cricketer Learie Constantine. In many ways James' book is more a personal memoir than an analysis of empirical data. Club cricket and village cricket, especially in the south of England, have been very largely neglected in academic studies of cricket. Christopher Brookes' biography of Neville Cardus,[29] the journalist whose writings on cricket helped to bolster the belief that cricket stimulated 'great literature', in itself helps to draw attention to the surprising fact that few studies have concentrated on cricket writing. There is no published history of the development of cricket between the wars in any region which has the thoroughness of Andrew

Hignell's study of the rise of cricket in South Wales before 1914[30] though two doctoral theses have considered the inter-war social history of cricket in different parts of Lancashire.[31] Hopefully this book will help to remedy the omissions from the historiography of cricket between the wars.

NOTES

1. R. Williams, *Marxism and Literature* (Oxford: Oxford UP, 1977), p. 110.
2. P. Alasuutari, *Researching Culture: Qualitative Method and Cultural Studies* (London: Sage, 1996), p. 25.
3. P. Bourdieu, *Distinction: A Social Critique of the Judgement of Taste* (Cambridge: Harvard UP, 1984).
4. See, for instance, P. Joyce, *Visions of the People: Industrial England and the Question of Class, 1840–1914* (Cambridge: Cambridge UP, 1991), and *Democratic Subjects: The Self and the Social in Nineteenth-century England* (Cambridge: Cambridge UP, 1994).
5. *Guardian,* 15 Aug. 1997.
6. For conflicting views of whether class was the dominant form of social identity see P. Joyce, *Visions of the People* and *Democratic Subjects*, and M. Savage and A. Miles, *The Remaking of the British Working Class 1840–1940* (London: Routledge, 1994). N. Kirk, ed., *Social Class and Marxism: Defences and Challenges* (Aldershot: Scolar, 1996), discusses whether class should be seen as the dominant form of social consciousness in modern Britain. P. Joyce, *Class* (Oxford: Oxford UP, 1995), reviews how the responses of historians and social analysts to the concept of social class have changed in the nineteenth and twentieth centuries.
7. For an overview of feminism in Britain since 1918, see M. Pugh, *Women and the Women's Movement in Britain* (London: Macmillan, 1992).
8. B. Collins and K. Robbins, eds., *British Culture and Economic Decline* (London: Weidenfeld and Nicolson, 1990), chapter one reviews the course of the debate over culture and industrialisation. J. Raven, 'Viewpoint; British History and the Enterprise Culture', *Past & Present,* 129 (Nov., 1989), shows how the debate became broadened into a discussion of whether British culture had inhibited enterprise in general.
9. For a discussion of the nature of secularisation and of the possible connections between secularisation and theories of modernisation, see R. Wallis and S. Bruce, 'Secularization: The Orthodox Model' in S. Bruce, ed., *Religion and Modernization: Sociologists and Historians Debate the Secularization Thesis* (Oxford; Oxford UP, 1992). J. Stevenson, *British Society 1914–45* (Harmondsworth: Penguin, 1984) considers the growth of secularisation in Britain between the wars.
10. T. Mason, *Association Football and English Society, 1863–1915* (Brighton: Harvester, 1980).
11. J.A. Mangan, *Athleticism in the Victorian and Edwardian Public School* (Cambridge: Cambridge UP, 1981).
12. E. Dunning and K. Sheard, *Barbarians, Gentlemen and Players: A Sociological Study of the Development of Rugby Football* (Oxford: Martin Robertson, 1979).
13. D. Birley, *The Willow Wand: Some Cricket Myths Explored* (London: Queen Anne, 1979).
14. R. Sissons and B. Stoddart, *Cricket and Empire: The 1932–33 Bodyline Tour of Australia* (London: Allen and Unwin, 1984).
15. E. Midwinter, *W.G. Grace: His Life and Times* (London: Allen and Unwin, 1981);

J.Hill, 'Reading the Stars: A Post-modernist Approach to Sports History', *Sports Historian*, 14 (May, 1994), discusses Cecil Parkin and Learie Constantine as cricket stars of the inter-war period; R. Holt, 'Cricket and Englishness: The Batsman as Hero', *International Journal of the History of Sport*, 13, 1 (Mar. 1996).

16. J.D. Coldham, *Lord Harris* (London: Allen and Unwin, 1983); G. Howat, *Plum Warner* (London: Unwin Hyman, 1987).

17. R. Sissons, *The Players: A Social History of the Professional Cricketer* (London: Kingswood, 1988).

18. M. Marshall, *Gentlemen & Players; Conversations with Cricketers* (London: Grafton, 1987).

19. D. Lemmon, *For the Love of the Game: An Oral History of First-class Cricket* (London: Michael Joseph, 1993) and *The Crisis of Captaincy: Servant and Master in English Cricket* (London: Christopher Helm, 1988).

20. D. Foot, *Cricket's Unholy Trinity* (London: Stanley Paul, 1985) and *Wally Hammond: The Reasons Why: A Biography* (London: Robson, 1996).

21. M. Marqusee, *Anyone but England: Cricket and the National Malaise* (London: Verso, 1994).

22. K.A.P. Sandiford, *Cricket and the Victorians* (Aldershot: Scolar, 1994).

23. C. Brookes, *English Cricket: The Game and Its Players through the Ages* (London: Weidenfeld and Nicolson, 1978).

24. J. Hargreaves, *Sporting Females: Critical Issues in the History and Sociology of Women's Sports* (London: Routledge, 1994).

25. W. Vamplew, *Pay Up and Play the Game: Professional Sport in Britain* (Cambridge: Cambridge UP, 1988).

26. See particularly, R. Holt, ed., *Sport and the Working Class in Modern Britain* (Manchester: Manchester UP, 1990) and J. Hill and J. Williams, eds., *Sport and Identity in the North of England* (Keele: Keele UP, 1996). S.G. Jones, *Sport, Politics and the Working Class: Organised Labour and Sport in Inter-war Britain* (Manchester: Manchester UP, 1988) considers the attitudes of socialist organisations to sport and the appraises how far working-class interest in commercialised sport supported bourgeois hegemony. J. Hargreaves, *Sport, Power and Culture: A Social and Historical Analysis of Popular Sports in Britain* (Cambridge: Polity, 1986), discusses the how far sport has discouraged working-class support for socialism, but says very little about the inter-war period.

27. J. Lowerson, *Sport and the English Middle Classes, 1878–1914* (Manchester: Manchester UP, 1993).

28. J. Hill, '"First Class" Cricket and the Leagues: Some Notes on the Development of English Cricket, 1900–40', *International Journal of the History of Sport*, 4, 1 (May 1987); J. Hill, 'League Cricket in the North and Midlands, 1900–1940' and J. Williams, 'Recreational Cricket in the Bolton Area between the Wars', in R. Holt. ed., *Sport and the Working Class in Modern Britain* (Manchester: Manchester UP, 1990); J. Williams, 'The Economics of League Cricket: Lancashire League Clubs and Their Finances since the First World War', *British Society of Sports History Bulletin*, 9 (1990).

29. C. Brookes, *His Own Man: The Life of Neville Cardus* (London: Methuen, 1985).

30. A. Hignell, *A 'Favourit' Game: Cricket in South Wales before 1914* (Cardiff: University of Wales Press, 1992).

31. A.J. Ross, 'Cricket and the Establishment: A Social History of Cricket in Lancashire with Specific Reference to the Liverpool Competition, 1775–1935', Ohio State University PhD thesis (1987); J.A. Williams, 'Cricket and Society in Bolton between the Wars', Lancaster University PhD thesis (1992).

1

Images of Cricket

REPRESENTATIONS OF CRICKET

Between the wars cricket was celebrated as a metaphor for England and for Englishness. Cricket was seen as an expression of English moral worth and had a key role in how the economically and socially privileged imagined themselves and their place in the world. Much was written about how cricket encapsulated the spirit of England. In his book entitled *The Heart of England* which sought to establish the essential nature of the English character whilst stressing its diversity, Ivor Brown wrote in 1935 that 'cricket remains at the heart of England'.[1] In 1928 an editorial in *The Times* claimed that for Englishmen abroad, nothing pulled so hard at the heart strings as memories of Lord's and went on to state that cricket was 'English as nothing else, perhaps, is English: the greatest of all games played in the best of settings and in the finest spirit'.[2] Looking back upon his education at Oxford in the 1920s, Christopher Hollis, an Etonian, former Conservative MP, writer and publisher, recalled in 1976 that 'cricket still had its prestige as the chief and most English of games. At Oxford it was honoured alike by undergraduates – even by those who did not play themselves – and by Dons.'[3] Foreign observers of England emphasised that cricket was quintessentially English. For the German Rudolph Kircher writing in 1928 cricket was 'pre-eminently English … a phase of English mentality, a key to the Englishman's soul, a product of English temperament' and 'the most typical of all English games'.[4]

Cricket was seen as much more than a game. It was invested with a special moral worth. Cricket discourses stressed that it was permeated by a spirit of sportsmanship and fair play which expressed English character and extended to other areas of life. Assumptions about its encouragement of sportsmanship caused the playing of cricket to be seen as an education in morality. Lord Harris, probably the most powerful figure within the administration of first-class cricket in the 1920s, argued that 'We cricketers … are something more than mere participants in a game, we are the

1

ministers of a high moral and educational medium'.[5] In 1929, Frank Sugg, a sporting journalist who had been a professional county cricketer in the 1880s and 1890s and who played twice for England, wrote that for a century cricket had stood for 'the very essence of sportsmanship, tolerance and fair play'.[6] In the introduction to an anthology of cricket writings, Samuel Looker claimed in 1925 that 'Cricket remains the King of Games, with its specially English appeal and standard of honour'.[7] Besides encouraging a sense of fair play, the nature of cricket, it was believed, stimulated other moral qualities. Hesketh Pritchard, a noted big game hunter, thought that cricket combined collective effort with the courage needed to face physical danger.[8] In the 1933 issue of the Lancashire County Elementary Schools' Cricket Association Handbook, Herbert Sutcliffe, the Yorkshire and England professional batsman, wrote that cricket was

> a contest calling for courage, skill, strategy and self-control. It is a contest of temper – a trial of honour and a revealer of character. Above all, it teaches one team spirit, the spirit of comradeship which is so necessary for success in every game and in every branch of life …The very spirit of cricket is sportsmanship. A recognised axiom in life, in whatever sphere of labour one finds oneself, is that it is 'not cricket' to take a mean advantage of another.

Much was said and written about how the playing of cricket was an antidote to selfishness because its spirit encouraged players to place the team before the individual. Comments such as those of Major Weekes, a Lancashire industrialist and enthusiastic club cricketer, who spoke of cricket teaching more than anything how 'to play for one's side instead of trying to shine individually' and of how it brought out 'the value of team work', are found frequently in inter-war newspapers.[9] The sportsmanship of cricket was seen to have produced a distinctively national character. An editorial in *The Times* in 1920 declared that 'cricket has probably had a greater share than any other of our national sports in making England what it is'.[10] In a talk at a grammar school in 1935 Herbert Sutcliffe said that 'nothing had contributed more to the British character and games than cricket'.[11]

The degree of sportsmanship in cricket, and consequently its moral worth, were perceived as far stronger than those found in other sports. An American writing in *The Sunday Chronicle* in 1934 described cricket as 'the flywheel or governor of British sport, a kind of standard according to which the spirit of other sports are attuned', as *Punch* set the standard for comic writing and Rolls Royce for motor cars.[12] Bob Wyatt, a captain of England, wrote in 1936 'that so long as an umpire *is* an umpire, his decisions must be accepted without question. It is partly in this last respect that the spirit of cricket differs so materially from that of other games.'[13] Lord Harris believed that the need for a cricketer to put the team's needs before his own meant that cricket taught self-denial, giving it a moral superiority over 'the selfish game of golf', a view shared by Hesketh Pritchard who also stressed that golf lacked the element of physical danger found in cricket.[14] Samuel Looker believed that football and tennis could not compete with the standard of honour found in cricket.[15]

The discourses which presented cricket as an expression of English moral worth emanated primarily but far from exclusively from those who belonged to economically and socially privileged groups. Jack Hobbs and Frank Woolley were two professional cricketers from relatively humble backgrounds whose ghosted autobiographies contained passages about cricket having high moral standards, though it could be claimed that by the time their autobiographies were issued their earnings had reached the level of the middle class. Cecil Parkin of Lancashire and Fred Root of Worcestershire were two professionals who both played for England but on occasions were criticised by those who controlled first-class cricket, yet in their ghosted books they did not challenge the view that cricket was superior to other sports or that standards of fair play in cricket were high. In his ghosted defence of 'bodyline' bowling which was published in 1933, Harold Larwood, who had been a miner before becoming a professional cricketer, was at pains to show that this form of bowling was not unfair and that it did not represent a break with cricket's tradition of sportsmanship. The discourses which emphasised that cricket was pervaded with a spirit of sportsmanship and fair play were predominantly male. Probably no woman was employed to write regularly upon men's cricket for a national newspaper, but Marjorie Pollard, one of the leading women cricketers in England, edited *Women's Cricket*, the monthly journal of the Women's Cricket Association and in the 1930s wrote on women's cricket for *The Morning Post*, was probably the woman who wrote most about women's cricket. Pollard always took the view that women's cricket should observe the standards of sportsmanship which were supposed to characterise men's cricket.

Not all accepted that cricket was a distillation of English moral worth. Writing in 1948 about his inter-war playing career with Oxford and as an amateur with Somerset, the cricket journalist R.C. Robertson-Glasgow claimed to have never regarded cricket as a branch of religion and that

> I have met, and somehow survived, many of its blindest worshipers. I have staggered, pale and woozly, from the company of those who reject the two-eyed stance as Plymouth Brethren reject all forms of pleasure except money-making …

The air of holy pomp started from the main temple at Lord's, and it breathed over the Press like a miasma … Sometimes I look back at reports of games in which I took part, and I have thought: 'And are these arid periphrases, these formal droolings, these desiccated shibboleths really supposed to represent what was done and how it was done? What has become of that earthly striving, that comic, tragic thing which was our match of cricket?'[16]

Expressions of such sentiments were very rare and far outnumbered by writings praising cricket as the epitome of English moral worth. Newspapers occasionally, and only occasionally, mentioned instances of unsporting behaviour in cricket and surrounded them with calls to maintain the moral nature of cricket. Robertson-Glasgow would not have felt the need to make the above comments had he not believed that cricket was so often perceived to have a special moral significance. It is not possible to establish how many of those who wrote about cricket being the distillation of Englishness and English moral worth may not have believed such sentiments. But the fact that they did describe cricket in such a way, whether stemming from the instructions of editors or a feeling that cricket ought to have been so described, indicates that it was widely believed that cricket was permeated with a high level of sportsmanship and was a reflection of essentially English qualities.

CRICKET, THE VICTORIAN INHERITANCE AND THE FIRST WORLD WAR

The esteem in which cricket was held by the Victorians does much to explain why cricket was so often taken to be a metaphor for English moral worth between the wars. Keith Sandiford has shown how the Victorians, and especially those educated at public schools, had come to view cricket as an expression of a distinctively English form of Christian morality and of the English character. Many of cricket's dominant personalities between the wars had passed their most impressionable years in the Victorian and Edwardian eras. Lord Harris was born in 1851. Lord Hawke, another powerful figure at Lord's and at the Yorkshire county club was born in 1860. Sir Edwin Stockton, who was president and chairman of Lancashire was born in 1873. Among cricket journalists, Neville Cardus of *The Manchester Guardian* had been born in 1887, Colonel Philip Trevor of *The Daily Telegraph* in 1863, H.J. Henley of *The Daily Mail* in 1862. Sir Theodore Cook, who remained editor-in-chief of *The Field,* a weekly sports magazine which gave extensive coverage to cricket, until his death in 1928,

4

was born in 1867. C.B. Fry and Pelham Warner, England captains who turned to cricket journalism, were both born in 1873. Several of the most famous county and England cricketers whose careers stretched into the 1930s had been born in the Victorian period. Hobbs was born in 1882, Woolley in 1887, and Hendren, Ernest Tyldesley and Mead in 1889. The emphasis in Victorian cricket discourses upon cricket as a symbol of England and of English moral worth had been made so often and so insistently that such notions were ingrained in the consciousness of many between the wars. Even in the 1990s cricket is perceived as being distinctively English. John Bale has shown how cricket figures prominently in advertisements and other areas to create immediately recognisable images of England.[17]

Beliefs that cricket expressed Christian values had been inherited from the Victorians and did much to explain why cricket between the wars was so often held to be a distillation of English moral worth. The level of clerical involvement with cricket among the Victorians was high. Nearly a third of all Victorian Oxbridge cricket blues became ordained.[18] Tony Mason has shown that muscular Christian clergymen encouraged the playing of football among working men in the industrial North and Midlands[19] and it seems likely they had a similar role in the spread of cricket playing. By 1914 most towns and large industrialised villages in the north of England had church or Sunday school cricket leagues and in this region the numbers of teams based upon churches and the men's sections of Sunday schools far exceeded those based upon other social institutions. By the end of the Victorian period it was most unusual in the North for cricket clubs to be openly associated with pubs, though it is possible but almost impossible to verify that the players of clubs based upon a locality may have used pubs as unofficial club headquarters. Evidence about the origins of Victorian and Edwardian church cricket clubs is very scanty but the sheer scale of the numbers of church teams suggests that clerics did not feel that cricket was in any way inimical to Christian teachings and indicates a widespread acceptance among the laity that it was natural for the churches to have a strong presence within cricket. Sunday school cricket leagues were less common in the South and fewer clubs had formal links with churches, but Gerald Howat has shown that clerics often encouraged the formation of cricket clubs in their parishes.[20] Between the wars cricket discourses placed less emphasis upon cricket as an expression of Christian morality. Fewer clerics played first-class cricket. In most parts of the North, the number of teams based upon churches and Sunday schools fell in the late 1930s after reaching a peak in the early 1920s. Yet local newspapers show that clerics were often the presidents of cricket clubs and attended

5

cricket club functions where they spoke of cricket encouraging Christian virtues. Similar statements were often made at such gatherings by laymen. Impressionistic evidence suggests that for the overwhelming majority of English people, Christianity and morality were synonymous and as a result, the associations of cricket with churches and Sunday schools, and the approval of cricket by clerics, bolstered perceptions of cricket as an expression of morality.

The First World War strengthened associations of cricket with Englishness. Surprisingly wartime propaganda rarely used images of cricket and England as a symbolic recreation of the England being fought for or to stimulate support for the war, but cricket was portrayed as having made a greater contribution to the war effort than other sports and association football in particular. When the war began, the cricket season of 1914 was more than half over and several counties cancelled some of their remaining fixtures. No decision had to be taken immediately about whether a county championship would be held in 1915 and so cricket avoided much of the obloquy which was heaped upon association football's authorities for permitting the FA Cup competition and a full Football League programme to be held in the 1914–15 season. Some criticism was made of league cricket clubs which kept playing during the war, but it was also argued this form of cricket relieved the tensions of the war and provided munitions workers with recreation.[21] In November 1914 *Athletic News* reported that it had not been possible to form a cricketers' battalion as so many cricketers 'of every class' had already volunteered. In 1916 Ludford Docker, a Midlands businessman with directorships in companies producing HP sauce and varnish and who was president of Warwickshire CCC from 1915 until 1931, thanked God that no cricketer had been a conscientious objector,[22] though in December 1918 a writer in *The Field* commented that, among county cricketers of military age, no amateurs but some professionals had shirked military service.[23] During and after the war apologists for cricket argued that the sportsmanship of cricket meant that cricketers made effective soldiers. In 1915, for instance, a Bolton industrialist and president of Farnworth CC, a league club, spoke of 'characters formed on the cricket field' being 'exemplified on the battle field'.[24] In 1919 *The St Helens Newspaper* claimed that cricket had made a great contribution to the war through 'the quality of the men it provided', men with capability and characters 'ready to respond to the call of country'.[25]

Much was said during the war about the value of sportsmanship in general and not in respect of any particular sport, but as cricket was assumed to have been more deeply impregnated with sportsmanship than other sports, such discourse added to the general esteem of cricket. The use of sporting imagery to draw parallels between Britain and Germany in the war, such as the comments by Sir Francis Vane that it 'was not cricket the Germans were playing in Belgium, France and Alsace' and Sir Arthur Hazlerigg, a former captain of Leicestershire, that 'we have to teach Germany to play the game ... as only British sportsmen can. Where do we learn this feeling so clearly as in the arena of games?',[26] reflected how deeply it had become assumed that sportsmanship, and consequently cricket, were essentially English qualities. The drawing together of military prowess, the public school and the sportsmanship of cricket, of which Newbolt's poem *Vitae Lampada* is perhaps the best-known example, seems likely to have contributed to the sense of service and self-sacrifice which led so many from the public schools to become junior officers, despite knowing that casualty figures among such officers on the Western Front were so high. Some felt after the war that the intense athleticism of the public schools, in which cricket figured so prominently, had contributed to the carnage of the war and needed to be curtailed, but for many others the sacrifices made in the war had been the apotheosis of English sporting qualities cultivated at the public schools.[27]

Cricket was so widely regarded as an expression of England between the wars because the game had such close connections with those privileged groups who made up what could be called the Establishment, though this phrase was not coined until after the Second World War. The MCC, the nearest that cricket had to a centralised authority, had strong links with the aristocracy and the upper classes. The majority of those who served on the MCC committee had inherited landed wealth or had made their mark in politics, the armed forces, the law or business. The same groups controlled county cricket. The moral values and social assumptions of many who formed the Establishment had been fashioned to a large measure at the public schools. Long before 1914 cricket had become a key element in the cult of athleticism at public schools. After the war criticism of the stress placed upon games at public schools grew, but cricket remained a central part of public school life. At nearly all public schools boys had to play cricket on most summer afternoons. Newspapers such as *The Times* and *The Daily Telegraph* reported on public school matches, though the extent of their coverage of such cricket decreased by the late 1930s. For the apologists of public schools, sports, but especially cricket because of its tradition of sportsmanship, was seen as having a vital role in the inculcation of public school values. W.R. Inge, dean of St Paul's from 1911 until 1934, who had taught at Eton, claimed that 'This spirit of fair play which in the public schools ... is absorbed as the most inviolable of traditions' and that 'to play cricket' had become 'a synonym for honourable and straightforward team-play in any relation of life'.[28] For a writer such as the sports journalist Bernard Darwin criticism of the public schools meant that 'whether by way of praise or blame, it is really to a great extent the English character that we are criticising ... the essential English character'.[29]

CRICKET AND ENGLISH PASTORALISM

Explanations for the reverence accorded to cricket reveal much about the cultural assumptions surrounding Englishness. Exaltations of cricket were often embedded in discourses of English pastoralism. Cricket was described as part of a rural idyll. Village cricket, and especially cricket played in rural villages, was portrayed as the purest and truest form of cricket. The playwright J.M. Barrie urged his listeners not to forget that 'the great glory of cricket does not lie in Test Matches, nor county championships ... but rather on village greens, the cradle of cricket'.[30] Writing in *The Cricketer* in 1932 under the pseudonym of Country Vicar, the Reverend R.L. Hodgson argued that it was not the 'great crowds on the famous grounds', but 'the countless village clubs throughout the length and breadth of the land [which] prove the general love of cricket'.[31] Such idealisation of village cricket in particular was related to the aesthetic appeal of cricket, and especially the visual attractions of the English countryside in summer. In a letter printed in the first number of *Women's Cricket*, the journal of the Women's Cricket Association, Lucy Baldwin, wife of the Conservative leader, wrote that

> Cricket to me is summer, and summer cricket. For my cricket was born on a hill in Sussex, below the blue of the sea flecked with its white sails as our horizon. Above, cotton-wool clouds in a blue, blue sky and the song of the lark.
> The crack of the bat against ball amid the humming and buzzing of summer sounds is still to me a note of pure joy.[32]

Neville Cardus, the cricket correspondent and a music critic for *The Manchester Guardian,* wrote extensively upon the aesthetic appeal of cricket and claimed that 'There could be no summer in this land without cricket' and that cricket 'as I know and love it, is part of that holiday time which is the Englishman's heritage – a playtime in a homely countryside'.[33] For Hodgson

> Music and Cricket are akin. Music is the 'concord of sweet sounds' – *i.e.,* harmony. And cricket is the harmony of eye, brain, hand and foot,

with beautiful, flowing strokes, and rhythmical movement of a circling arm; and there are even delicious sounds when the bat meets ball, fairly and squarely, and sends it humming, to the ropes. I await the first click of a cricket-bat as I listen for the first song of the nightingale: they are both promise of golden summer.[34]

The attraction of village cricket for Samuel Looker was that it furnished 'a setting of rare beauty ... in its best moments there is lyric poetry'.[35]

This adulation of village cricket indicates the strength of the pastoralism within English culture. In 1930 Paul Cohen-Portheim, a German observer of England, author of *England, The Unknown Isle,* first published in 1930 and re-issued three more times in the 1930s, wrote that

> Love of the country is the most fundamental thing about the English and can alone make their character and their history intelligible ...
>
> English sport, English art, English Society are all rooted in that peaceful green-tufted countryside with its gently undulating hills and lofty copses, its flocks and herds and pale scudding clouds ... and nature is human, hospitable and amiable.[36]

In their studies of English culture and perceptions of the countryside, Georgina Boyes and Alun Howkins have shown that in the late nineteenth and early twentieth centuries the rural came to be esteemed as aesthetically and morally superior to the urban. The countryside was taken to represent a traditional, purer England characterised by a social cohesion stemming from different groups accepting common moral values. Those from both the political right and left viewed the town as morally and physically degenerate, as the site of a sordid, money-grubbing commercialism, vulgarity and social conflict. Pastoral poetry, attempts to revive English folk song and dance, interest in gardening, the building of garden suburbs, the desire to preserve buildings from pre-industrial England can all be interpreted as evidence of an unease within English culture about the urban and an idealisation of the rustic.[37] Assumptions about the morality of cricket, and particularly the stress upon village cricket as the truest form of cricket, reflected and helped to strengthen the pastoral strand within English culture. The county championship, the major competition of first-class cricket, reinforced assumptions that cricket's moral worth stemmed from its rural nature. Almost all county cricket was played in towns, but the organisation of a championship upon the historic shires which had been units of administration before the industrialisation and urbanisation of England, intensified the rustic aura of cricket. The pastoral dimension of cricket was very much associated with how the countryside in the south of

England was imagined. Cricket poetry and visual presentations of village cricket were usually those of a village green fringed with trees and with the inn and parish church as part of the backcloth and gently rolling hills in the distance. J.C. Squire, the writer and editor who stood at the general election of 1918 as a Labour candidate for the Cambridge University constituency, wrote that 'cricket had a rural root, and predominantly rural it has remained ... few men ... would not rather play on a field surrounded by ancient elms and rabbit-haunted bracken than on a better field with flat black lands or gasworks around'.[38]

CRICKET AND THE REVERENCE OF TRADITION

The glorification of cricket shows the cultural value which the wealthier classes placed upon tradition. Cricket was represented as the oldest of England's team ball games. Rough football may have been played more widely at an earlier date than cricket, but cricket was the first English team ball sport to become played and organised in a more or less modern form. Written rules survive from the 1740s. By the early nineteenth century practically all cricket was being played in accordance with the laws of the Marylebone Cricket Club. Inter-county matches were played before 1800.[39] W.G. Grace, sometimes described as the most famous man in Victorian England, can be called England's first sport super-star, or at least the first super-star of England's team ball games. Even before 1800 matches between teams from different parts of the country had been played. By the early nineteenth century, cricket was played in all English counties. Between the wars, cricket discourses emphasised the antiquity and history of cricket. *The Cricketer*, a cricket magazine first published in 1921 and which appeared each week throughout the cricket season along with annuals published in spring and winter, had historical articles in almost every issue. Few of these could be described as academic history. They concentrated upon famous players and matches of the past, particularly test matches but also those played by Oxford and Cambridge and public school teams. Whilst such articles may have been an easy method of filling space in the magazine, it is unlikely that they would have been included so often had readers showed no interest in the history and traditions of cricket. Annual handbooks of the Club Cricket Conference which included a directory of several hundred clubs drawn predominantly from the Home Counties made a point of stating the formation date for each club, which again indicates the importance attached to the history and traditions of cricket. The annual editions of *Wisden*, a review of first-class, minor county and public school cricket played each season, contained lengthy sections of cricket records. By 1939, all but one of the first-class counties were publishing annual handbooks which contained sections of cricket records. The highly statistical nature of cricket meant that it was easy to produce cricket records covering a very long period, but no other English team sport produced such a wealth of historical statistics. The celebration of the anniversaries of county and recreational cricket clubs stressed further the traditions and history of cricket.

The traditions of cricket were seen to carry and reinforce moral obligations. In 1924 Lord Harris described cricketers as 'a great brotherhood, whose responsibility was to maintain the honourable traditions of the game' and Lord Hawke advised Yorkshire players that they were representing 'a county with great traditions. There must be no declining in the spirit of sportsmanship.'[40] In a collection of his speeches to which Baldwin, the Conservative leader, gave the title *Our Inheritance*, itself an indication of the importance of tradition, he included a passage about the Eton versus Harrow match – 'Lord's changes but Lord's remains ... how unchanging is each phase of the everchanging game!'.[41] As Baldwin was so often taken to be the voice of Middle England, such a comment seems likely to have struck a chord with many English people. In 1934, a writer in *The Sunday Chronicle* praised the 'moral effect upon boys ... of taking part in a game from which all petty disputes, tricks and animosities, have, by tradition, been eliminated'.[42] The traditions of cricket dovetailed with the English pastoral idyll. In 1933, an editorial in *The Times,* when discussing the match between Eton and Winchester, mentioned 'The long vistas and the murmurous elms, the swallows skimming over the outfield in the evening, the mellow brick and the grey stone, the Castle or the Cathedral benevolently remote – these things are the natural setting of the stately game, which is so much younger than Eton and Winchester, and yet holds the spirit of England even older than they'.[43]

In *The Invention of Tradition* E.J. Hobsbawm and T.O. Ranger showed that, in England before 1914, cultural and political institutions such as the monarchy and the aristocracy acquired new roles but that it was widely imagined that these were a continuation of traditions which could be traced over centuries. In England between the wars the respect and deference paid to institutions such as parliamentary government, the monarchy, common law, the Royal Navy and the universities of Oxford and Cambridge owed much to their supposed antiquity and a belief that they were perpetuating traditions originating in the middle ages or earlier. Antiquity in itself was seen to confer cultural significance and moral authority. Much of the importance attached to cricket by elite groups in England can be interpreted

11

as evidence that tradition was still an important strand in their culture, and it can be argued that this historicist outlook helped to justify the exercise of authority by those social groups who controlled established political institutions. Political metaphors figured prominently in cricket discourses and indicate how pride in English political institutions meant that parallels drawn between cricket and politics had a powerful role in causing cricket to be seen as a form of English morality. Cardus wrote that 'the laws of cricket tell of the English love of compromise between a particular freedom and a general orderliness, or legality'.[44] Writing in *The Cricketer* in 1932 Hodgson claimed that 'Cricket stands for law and order ... The umpire gives you out: out you must go. The man in the white coat is a symbol of constitutional government.'[45] In 1933 an editorial in *The Times* pointed out that 'the British constitution ... places the *onus probandi* on the disputant who ranks any other game before, or even in the same class with, cricket'.[46] The poet E.V. Lucas called the pavilion at Lord's 'the Houses of Parliament of cricket'.[47] The supposed antiquity of English political institutions and practices harmonised with the veneration of the traditional and helped to reinforce the respect accorded to cricket on account of its long history. For Baldwin 'ordered freedom' was 'our oldest tradition'[48] while for Sir Ernest Barker, principal of University College London and professor of political science at Cambridge, the co-operation between central and local government in England had originated with the Anglo-Saxons.[49]

CRICKET AND THE EMPIRE

The nature of cricket as an imperial sport was vital to the assumptions that cricket was a distillation of English moral worth. Cricket was very much a sport of the British Empire. Test matches were played only against teams from the Empire. The cricket played in Argentina, Denmark, Holland and the United States was largely ignored in England between the wars. Cricket played between teams from Britain and other parts of the Empire was seen as a highly effective means of strengthening imperial loyalties. E.H.D. Sewell, who is thought to have been the author of *A Searchlight on English Cricket*, published in 1926, was educated at Bedford School, but played cricket as a professional with Essex in the early 1900s and as an amateur previously and later, wrote of 'Paterfamilias, taking his holiday and doing his level best for the Empire by taking his children to watch cricket instead of letting them loaf on the links or swagger about tennis courts, where umpires' decisions don't matter'.[50] In the same book Gandhi was described as 'the arch humbug'.[51] An editorial in *Athletic News* claimed in 1926 that

'Profound is the chain of Empire through the agency of sport. The playing fields have done more to cement the bonds of Imperialism than many a diplomatic conference.'[52] Members of the Royal Family and leading politicians welcomed touring teams to England or attended dinners organised for them. Writing in *The Fortnightly Review* Sir Home Gordon, an Old Etonian baronet and cricket writer and cricket administrator, argued that tours to Australia carried 'an Imperial even more than a sporting significance … English cricketers to Australia are Ministers Plenipotentiary for linking the ties of Empire and counteracting the machinations of self-seeking politicians'.[53] The involvement of the Colonial Secretary J.H. Thomas, who took little interest in cricket,[54] in the negotiations surrounding the body-line controversy, shows the importance attached to test cricket by the political world. Those from the colonies and dominions also argued that cricket strengthened imperial ties. Ranjitsinhji, an Indian prince who had played cricket as an amateur for Cambridge University, Sussex and England before 1914 spoke in 1930 of cricket being 'certainly among the most powerful of the links which keep our Empire together'.[55] At the 150th anniversary celebrations of the MCC in 1937, A. Robertson, chairman of the Australian test selectors, spoke about how cricket linked the dominions with 'the Motherland'.[56]

It is not difficult to demonstrate that British imperialist expansion had been driven by economic motives, but between the wars imperialist rhetoric celebrated the Empire as a moral trust. In his book *National Character and the Factors in its Formation*, Ernest Barker wrote 'of our duty to hold our Empire, not as a possession to bring us profit or power, but as a trust-property which was intended to be administered freely for the sake of the beneficiaries to whom it ultimately belonged.'[57] Baldwin spoke of the Empire standing 'firm as a great force for good'[58] and of 'spreading throughout such parts of the world as we control … of all those ideas of law, order, and justice which we believe to be peculiar to our race. It is to help people who belong to a backward civilisation, wisely to raise them in the scale of civilisation.'[59] J.E.C. Welldon, who had resigned the headship of Harrow to become Bishop of Calcutta, wrote in 1935 that justice was the quality above all others which 'the subject, uncivilised races of mankind have gradually, but not I think, ungenerously, or inaccurately, come to associate with British administration all over the world'.[60] Even if it is argued that statements about the morality of empire did not represent the true opinions of those who uttered them, the making of such statements suggests a widespread assumption that the British Empire was a moral crusade. As cricket was so pre-eminently a sport of the Empire and was often seen as helping to strengthen imperial feeling, the moral regard for the

Empire added to the perceptions of cricket as an expression of English moral worth.

CRICKET AND PROPRIETY

The reverence for cricket demonstrated an English concern, or perhaps preoccupation, with form, etiquette, propriety, a sense that it was necessary for things to be performed in accordance with established procedures. Much was written about the correct manner of playing and conducting cricket. The sections of coaching manuals dealing with batting usually stressed that there was a correct manner of executing each stroke and in particular the need to play with a straight bat. Advice in coaching manuals was based upon long experience of what had been realised was the most effective manner of playing cricket, but it also reflected a conviction that there was a correct form of playing. Batsmen such as Hobbs and Hammond were praised widely because of the correctness of their stroke play. In the 1930s the adoption in first-class cricket by batsmen of the 'two-eyed stance' was widely condemned for not being in accordance with the correct manner of batting. For some the adoption of bodyline bowling by England on the 1932–33 tour of Australia was seen as almost a form of retribution visited upon Australian batsmen who used the two-eyed stance. Use of the expression 'playing with a straight bat' in everyday speech to signify behaving with probity shows how cricket had become entwined with notions about the correctness of manners and form which extended beyond the realm of cricket. Linked with the notion that cricket should be played with correctness was a belief that the style of batting was equally important. Those from the wealthier classes implored batsmen to play in an aggressive style. Cautious batsmen who accumulated large scores slowly were condemned for their boring and unduly defensive style. When the Yorkshire and England professional batsman Herbert Sutcliffe published his autobiography in 1935, he made a special point of producing statistics to refute the accusation that Yorkshire scored runs slowly. Risk-taking batting was accorded a moral dimension. Adventurous play was seen as an expression of sportsmanship, whereas slow defensive play was condemned as selfishness. Beliefs about the sportsmanship of cricket were very much part of the notion that there was a correct manner of playing it.

Emphasis upon the correct dress for cricket was a vital strand of this wider concern over form and the importance of conforming to accepted standards of conduct. The laws of cricket did not state that players had to wear whites, though some leagues required bowlers to wear white shirts or sweaters. At the humblest levels of cricket, many did not play in white trousers, but the fact that recreational cricketers in Bolton made what passed for white flannels out of white overalls shows the importance attached to wearing whites. In 1925 an editorial in *The Times* appealed for cricketers to pass on disused white flannels so that they could be distributed among village cricketers.[61] A writer in *The Cricketer Annual* for 1926–27 emphasised that most who played for village teams in Sussex wore whites but that they did not play shots in the approved straight-bat style.[62] Caps, colours and ties were an important aspect of cricket etiquette. In county cricket the awarding of a county cap indicated that a player had become accepted as a regular first team player, but many recreational clubs had their own ties and caps. For those from the wealthier classes who played cricket regularly, a cricket blazer was an essential item of cricket attire. Club colours were considered a matter of such importance that the annual directory of the Club Cricket Conference specified the colours of practically all member clubs. The Women's Cricket Association laid down clear guidance about how women who played cricket under its auspices were to be dressed. Observance of the tea interval at even the lowest levels of cricket shows how deeply cricket had become pervaded by the sense of proper form and of the need to observe established rituals.

CRICKET AS A MIRROR OF SOCIAL RELATIONS

Cricket was not merely a sport of the privileged classes between the wars. Those from all classes played and watched cricket, but much of cricket was riddled with privilege and social distinction. County sides were usually captained by amateurs. Amateurs and professionals had different changing rooms and entrances to the field of play. Socially exclusive clubs were found in many areas. But at the same time, cricket was portrayed as a mirror of social cohesion, reflecting the assumption of many from the privileged classes that social relations in England were characterised by harmony and co-operation. Baldwin, for instance, spoke of 'class hatred ... none of that is indigenous to English soil'.[63] Those with established wealth took cricket to be a symbol of England because they imagined that the social relations found in cricket were a reflection of how they imagined society in general. It was argued that in county cricket professionals wished to maintain the tradition of being captained by amateurs. In 1925 Rockley Wilson, educated at Rugby and Cambridge and who had played as an amateur for England and Yorkshire, claimed that 'An amateur is always respected and trusted by the professionals under him' and that 'England professionals would prefer to play under an amateur'.[64] Bob Wyatt, the amateur captain of England, believed that 'the predominance of the right spirit in first-class – as well as in school and club – cricket is, I think, evidenced by the truly friendly relations that exist between amateur and professional players, and the undoubted fact that the latter, taken in the lump, are as fine a lot of fellows as anyone could wish to meet'.[65] Much of the cultural significance focused upon village cricket stemmed from a belief that it was an expression of social cohesion. Those from all classes were thought to play for village teams. J.L. Bryan, educated at Rugby and who played as an amateur for Cambridge and Kent, wrote in *The Daily Mirror* that 'In village cricket, the game is the meeting point of all the different people, and the different classes of the community. The squire is the captain, the butcher the vice-captain. The landlord of the inn is the secretary, the blacksmith the fast bowler.'[66] Arthur Gilligan, captain of England and Sussex, argued that village cricket encouraged comradeship between the classes and promoted understanding of 'our fellow men'.[67] J.C. Squire claimed that in village cricket 'the distinctions in life are temporarily forgotten; for the time being we live in an ideal republic where Jack is not only as good as his master, but may be a little better, and all the normal conditions of life, differences of hereditary and of brains, can be forgotten'.[68]

Analysis of the language used to describe cricket between the wars shows that the dominant cricket discourse was one which emphasised that cricket expressed the essential character of England and of Englishness as a moral quality. Such cricket discourses were not monopolised by those with social and economic power, but they do help to elucidate the cultural assumptions which shaped the moral views of such groups. As cricket was esteemed such a powerful metaphor for England, the discourses in which such images of cricket were embedded indicate how the intermingling of Christian precepts, pastoralism, respect for tradition and established political institutions, concern with good form and the observance of established modes of conduct, and the supposed ethical nature of imperialism made a decisive contribution to how those with established wealth in particular imagined themselves and their moral stature. To use the terminology of Bakhtin, cricket discourses which emphasised cricket as a form of English morality were monologic; they were the discourses of those who exercised political and social power and determined how cricket should have been perceived and controlled. Not all, of course, accepted that cricket was an expression of English moral worth. Some must have been indifferent to cricket whilst others could have felt that cricket was permeated with humbug, but such opinions did not figure prominently in printed discourse. Cricket did not stimulate much of an oppositional or, to

16

borrow from Bakhtin's terminology once more, dialogic discourse which in itself can be interpreted as an indication of how widely accepted assumptions of cricket forming a vital facet of the English character and morality had become. The moral nature of cricket may have been more supposed than real, more myth than actuality, but the general drift of cricket discourse suggests that cricket was a myth by which the English lived and imagined themselves.

NOTES

1. I. Brown, *The Heart of England* (London: Batsford, 1935), p. 106.
2. *The Times*, 7 May 1925.
3. C. Hollis, *Oxford in the Twenties: Recollections of Five Friends* (London: Heinemann, 1976), p. 58.
4. R. Kircher, *Fair Play: The Games of Merrie England* (London: Collins, 1928), pp. 57, 61.
5. *The Cricketer Annual, 1924–25* (London: Cricketer Syndicate, n.d.), p. 49.
6. *Buff* (*Bolton Evening News* sports edition), 17 Aug. 1929.
7. S.J. Looker, ed., *Cricket: A Little Book for Lovers of the Game* (London: Simpkin, Marshall, Hamilton, Kent, 1925), p. XV.
8. *Athletic News*, 4 Aug. 1919.
9. *St Helens Newspaper*, 4 Nov. 1927, 6 Dec. 1929.
10. *The Times*, 31 July 1920.
11. *Buff*, 21 Dec. 1935.
12. *Sunday Chronicle*, 10 June 1934.
13. R.E.S. Wyatt, *The Ins and Outs of Cricket* (London: Bell, 1936), p. 255.
14. *The Times*, 9 May 1921; *Athletic News*, 4 Aug. 1919.
15. S.J. Looker, *Cricket: A Little Book*, p. XV.
16. R.C. Robertson-Glasgow, *46 Not Out* (London: Constable, 1985 re-issue of the 1948 edition), p. 103. The permission of Random House for the use of this quotation is acknowledged.
17. J. Bale, 'Cricket Landscapes and English Eternalism', paper presented at the 25th meeting of the Eastern Historical Geography Association, Codrington College, Barbados (Feb. 1994).
18. K.A.P. Sandiford, *Cricket and the Victorians* (Aldershot: Scolar, 1994), chapter 3 discusses the connections between Christianity and cricket in the Victorian period.
19. T. Mason, *Association Football and English Society, 1863–1915* (Brighton: Harvester, 1980), chapter 1.
20. G. Howat, 'Local History, Ancient and Modern: Cricket and the Victorian Church', *Journal of the Cricket Society*, 9, 4 (Spring 1980), pp. 60–3.
21. For a discussion of cricket and support for the war, see J. Williams, 'Cricket and the Great War', *Stand To!*, 51 (Jan. 1998).
22. *Athletic News*, 30 Nov. 1914, 8 May 1916.
23. *Field*, 17 Dec. 1918.
24. *Buff*, 18 Dec. 1915.
25. *St Helens Newspaper*, 25 April 1919.
26. *Athletic News*, 10 Aug. 1914.
27. For a discussion of the connections between the games cult at the public schools and

support for the war see J.A. Mangan, *Athleticism in the Victorian and Edwardian Public School* (Cambridge: Cambridge UP, 1981), chapter 6.

28. W.R. Inge, *England* (London: Benn, 1926), pp 55–6.
29. B. Darwin, *The English Public School* (London: Longmans, Green, 1929), p. 28.
30. *M'Connachie and J.M.B.: Speeches by J.M. Barrie* (London: Davies, 1938), p. 114.
31. *Cricketer*, 18 June 1932, p. 200.
32. *Women's Cricket*, 1, 1 (1930), p. 3.
33. N. Cardus, *Cricket* (London: Longmans, Green, 1930), pp. 1–2.
34. *Cricketer*, 11 June 1932, 168.
35. S.J. Looker, *Cricket: A Little Book*, p. XI.
36. P. Cohen-Portheim, *England, The Unknown Isle* [translated by A. Harris] (London: Duckworth, 1930), pp. 12–13.
37. G. Boyes, *The Imagined Village: Culture, Ideology and the English Folk Revival* (Manchester: Manchester UP); A. Howkins, 'The Discovery of Rural England' in R. Colls and P. Dodd, eds., *Englishness: Politics and Culture 1880–1920* (Beckenham: Croom Helm, 1986).
38. *The Cricketer Spring Annual* (London: Cricketer Syndicate, n.d.), p. 30. At the 1924 general election Squire stood as a Liberal candidate.
39. E. Midwinter, *The Illustrated History of County Cricket* (London: Kingswood, 1992), p. 15.
40. *The Times*, 28 Nov., 24 Jan. 1924.
41. S. Baldwin, *Our Inheritance: Speeches and Addresses* (London: Hodder and Stoughton), p. 303.
42. *Sunday Chronicle*, 10 June 1934.
43. *The Times*, 29 June 1933.
44. N. Cardus, *Cricket*, pp. 5–6.
45. *Cricketer*, 18 June 1932, p. 200.
46. *The Times*, 14 July 1933.
47. *Cricket All His Life: The Cricket Writings of E.V. Lucas* (London: Pavilion, 1989), p. 33.
48. S. Baldwin, *Our Inheritance*, p. 12.
49. E. Barker, *National Character and the Factors in its Formation* (London: Methuen, 1927), p. 174.
50. A County Cricketer, *A Searchlight on English Cricket* (London: Robert Holden, 1926), pp. 73–4.
51. Ibid., p. 84.
52. *Athletic News*, 6 Sept. 1926.
53. H. Gordon, 'Cricket Problems Today', *Fortnightly Review*, 109 (Jan.–June, 1921), p. 725.
54. R. Sissons and B. Stoddart, *Cricket and Empire: The 1932–33 Bodyline Tour of Australia* (London: Allen and Unwin, 1984), p. 77.
55. The full text of this speech is reprinted in *The Cricketer Annual, 1939–40* (London: Cricketer Syndicate, n.d.), p. 49.
56. *The Times*, 25 May 1937.
57. E. Barker, *National Character*, pp. 161–2.
58. S. Baldwin, *Our Inheritance*, p. 71.
59. S. Baldwin, *On England and Other Addresses* (London: Philip Allan, 1926), pp. 185–6.
60. J.E.C. Welldon, *Forty Years On: Lights and Shadows (A Bishop's Reflections on Life)*, p. 140.
61. *Times*, 24 April 1925.

62. *The Cricketer Annual, 1926–27* (London: Cricketer Syndicate, n.d.), p. 87.
63. S. Baldwin, *Our Inheritance,* p. 30.
64. *Daily Express*, 24 Jan. 1925.
65. R.E.S. Wyatt, *Ins and Outs of Cricket,* p. 257.
66. *Daily Mirror*, 24 May 1935.
67. A.E.R. Gilligan, *Sussex Cricket* (London: Chapman and Hall, 1933), p. 202.
68. *The Cricketer Spring Annual, 1930* (London: Cricketer Syndicate, n.d.), p. 30.

2

The Structure and Control of Cricket

In the 1920s and 1930s the degree of organisation within cricket was far less than that of association football or rugby union which had pyramidal structures providing a unified governing body for all levels of their sports. Much authority within cricket rested upon tradition and custom rather than written agreements. Cricket discourses usually identified three forms of cricket played in England between the wars – first-class cricket, league cricket and club cricket in which clubs played only friendly matches. Each had its distinctive forms of organisation, or in some respects, lack of organisation. Formal links between them were weak even in 1939. As cricket was so often taken to be a symbol for what was most admirable about England, the structure and forms of power within cricket reveal much about English assumptions concerning the nature and exercise of authority.

THE MCC AND FIRST-CLASS CRICKET

Between the wars the Marylebone Cricket Club decided which matches were to be considered first-class. In most seasons about 300 first-class matches were played. The great majority of these were county championship matches, but all test matches, the matches played by touring sides against the counties, the matches of the first elevens of the universities of Oxford and Cambridge, around six matches played by the MCC, Gentlemen versus Players games, festival matches and occasionally matches played by such prestigious amateur clubs as the Free Foresters were accorded first-class status.

Cricket discourses often described the Marylebone Cricket Club, or Lord's, its ground in London, as the headquarters of cricket. Though the MCC was the strongest power within first-class cricket, its authority was not absolute. The Imperial Cricket Conference, founded in 1909 and which consisted of representatives from the MCC, the Australian Board of

Control and the South African Cricket Association, laid down the rules for the conduct of test cricket. The Board of Control had been established in 1898 to control test matches played in England. The president of the MCC was its chairman and five members of the MCC committee also sat on the Board, but in theory they could have been outvoted by the representatives of the counties finishing in the top ten positions of the County Championship. The Board of Control chose those who selected teams for test matches played by England in England but the MCC selected the teams for overseas tours on which test matches were played. Except for the test matches, all matches played on those overseas tours were played by sides called the MCC.

The MCC had the final say over how county cricket was played and organised. From 1904 the county championship had been controlled by the Advisory County Cricket Committee. The President of the MCC or his nominee was the chairman of the Advisory Committee, which also included at least one representative of the MCC plus one representative of each county playing in the county championship and three representatives from the Minor Counties Cricket Association. In 1922 the Advisory Committee agreed unanimously that a permanent sub-committee would consider 'details and reporting thereon and preparing agenda for the ACCC meetings'. This sub-committee consisted of one representative from each of the five counties at the top of the county championship and one each from the three counties at the bottom of the championship with the president of the MCC as its chairman.[1] All decisions of the Advisory Committee had to be confirmed by the MCC. Practically all cricket at whatever level was played in accordance with the laws of the game drawn up by the MCC.

Founded by a group of landed aristocrats in 1787, the MCC remained a private cricket club. Only men could become members. In addition to the half dozen or so first-class matches which the MCC played each season, it played matches each week which were not first-class against club and public school teams. In 1923, for instance, it played 36 two-day and 102 one-day non-first-class matches. Between 1920 and 1934, the number of MCC members was around 5,500. In 1935, changes in the procedure for admitting new members caused the number to rise to 6,566. By 1938 the club had 6,966 members. A subscription to the MCC cost three guineas. Membership of the MCC was sought eagerly. In 1935 12,000 names were on the lists of candidates for membership. Of the 3,066 whose names had been entered in the candidates' books between 1901 and 1905, 614 still wished in 1935 to become members. The committee of the MCC chose by ballot those whose names had been reached in the candidates' books. The number of new members who could be elected each year was 120 before

1933, 200 between 1933 and 1935 and 300 after 1935, although the committee was authorised to elect an additional 800 members in 1935. The committee was empowered to elect up to 80 new members out of their turn each year 'on account of their cricketing qualifications and their express desire to play for the club'.[2] A sample of 100 who held membership between 1920 and 1926 included five peers, five knights, three baronets, three generals and ten colonels, though some of those with military titles were also peers or knights. A sample of those who were members between 1934 and 1941 included six peers, three sons of peers, three baronets and one knight. Those with military titles included six generals, 13 colonels, one rear admiral, one commander, one wing commander, eleven majors and eleven captains, but it is possible that some of these may have joined the forces only after the start of the Second World War. This data suggests that at least a fair proportion of MCC members belonged to the upper and wealthier classes throughout the inter-war period. Newspapers do not record demands from within the MCC for its membership to be recruited from a wider spectrum of society between the wars.

The MCC had strong personal links with the political and social establishment. Presidents held office for one year and chose their successors. Only six inter-war presidents were not aristocrats, and they included a Conservative MP who became the governor of Bengal, a chairman of the Midland Bank, a brigadier, the proprietor of *The Times* who was the son of a peer, and a baronet who became Lord Mayor of London and was a leading freemason. The presidency was more than a figurehead position. Most presidents attended meetings of the MCC committee and took the chair at the meetings of the Advisory County Cricket Committee. Even where presidents did not become especially involved with club affairs, their willingness to accept the presidency emphasised the social prestige of the MCC.

The treasurers exercised more direct power within the MCC, though this could have derived as much from their personalities and social standing as from the office of treasurer. From 1916 until 1932, Lord Harris, a former Conservative minister and England captain, was treasurer and often regarded as the dominant figure within the MCC. His successor, Lord Hawke, held office until 1938. The next treasurer was the ninth Viscount Cobham. The secretaries had to implement the decisions of the committee but had a great impact upon day-to-day affairs of the club and usually attended the meetings of the Advisory County Cricket Committee. The social standing of the three inter-war secretaries was not on the same plane as that of the treasurers, though their backgrounds were privileged. Sir Francis Lacey, secretary from 1898 until 1926, had been educated at

Sherborne and Cambridge and was a barrister. His wife's mother was the daughter of a ninth earl. William Findlay, secretary from 1926 until 1936 had attended Eton and Oxford, and could be described as a professional cricket administrator. In 1907 he had become the secretary of Surrey CCC and in 1919 was appointed assistant secretary of the MCC. His successor, Colonel R.S. Rait Kerr, was a professional soldier educated at Rugby.[3]

Responsibility for running the MCC was vested in its committee elected by the members at the annual general meeting. The 16 members of the committee each served for four years. Elections to the committee were not contested.[4] Usually candidates were proposed and seconded by members of the committee. Between the wars 67 served on the committee. The social background of the committee was broadly the same in 1939 as in 1919. Forty-seven had played at least one first-class cricket match and six had captained England. All came from families with sufficient wealth to have sent them to public schools. Twenty-three had attended Eton, thirteen Harrow, three Winchester, three Charterhouse, and three Dulwich. Eleven inherited peerages, at least eight were the sons or sons-in-law of peers and nine were created peers. All of the 20 who had been MPs or had stood as parliamentary candidates or who were active in local government were Conservatives and included Prime Minister Stanley Baldwin, a Home Secretary, a Governor-General of Australia, a Chief Justice of Bengal, a Governor of Bengal and one who had been Attorney-General and Lord Chancellor. Arthur Gilligan had been a member of the British Fascists when he captained the England and MCC tour to Australia in 1924–25.[5] Six owned between 6,000 and 19,600 acres each. Sixteen acquired the rank of at least colonel. Probably many held shares in a variety of undertakings, but the numbers who were connected with the management of industrial concerns exceeded those who were or had been involved with banking, insurance or the City. Each of these groups was easily outnumbered by those who had been regular army officers. The industrialists included a President of the Federation of British Industries, two directors of cotton firms, two brewers, a cement box manufacturer, a senior director of African mining concerns, and two iron and steel masters. Some, such as R.H. Mallett, a bank manager, of the Minor Counties and Durham CCC and Dr (later Sir) Russell Bencraft of Hampshire CCC were very much involved with cricket administration.[6]

Probate awards show a great disparity in the sums they left, though some could have disposed of much of their wealth before they died. Of 40 members of the inter-war committee who died between 1920 and 1976, only one left less than £1,000 and six less than £10,000. Sixteen left over £100,000 but only Lords Ellesmere, Desborough and Leconfield had probate awards above £1,000,000. The brewer and vinegar manufacturer Sir Lindsay Everard left over half a million.[7] Although inflation during and after the Second World War complicates comparisons in the value of probate awards, the great majority who served on the committee can be described as men of wealth.

Relations between the Advisory Committee and the MCC were rarely other than harmonious. Few challenges were made to the MCC's authority. In 1928 the Lancashire representative on the Advisory Committee found no seconder for his proposal that control of overseas tours be transferred to the Board of Control. A combination of factors accounted for the counties accepting the MCC's authority. The MCC rarely rejected the recommendations of the Advisory Committee. In 1920 the MCC vetoed a proposal that attending a public school would constitute a residential qualification to play for the county in which the school was situated. A year later the MCC refused to sanction a new system of points scoring in the county championship recommended by the Advisory Committee because there had been strong opposition to it and because no satisfactory system of points scoring could be established until all counties played each other.[8] In 1924 the MCC would not accept a recommendation for covered wickets unless it were restricted to one season.[9] Occasionally the Advisory Committee rejected proposals from powerful figures within the MCC. In 1921, for instance, it did not accept Lord Harris' proposal that a register of all county cricketers be prepared.[10]

A further cause underlying acceptance of the MCC's authority over county cricket was that the MCC exercised its powers with discretion and tact. When describing the relationship between the MCC and the counties, Lacey wrote that 'The MCC still remains the Parliament of Cricket, holding its position by general consent, and the county clubs in framing their rules have invited it to accept the responsibility of a Court of Appeal'.[11] The cricket journalist Colonel Philip Trevor claimed that the MCC had never tried to dictate to the counties.[12] *Athletic News* declared in 1923 that

> For ages the MCC have put a code of honour before a set of rules, regulations and provisions. There has been honour on the field and in the committee chamber ... Whenever there have been incidents which could not be approved of there has, by common consent, been a policy of hush. Cricketers have never believed in washing dirty flannels in public places. Away at Lord's, hidden in recesses called 'Private', there is a wash-house with a squeezing machine. The dirt flows down the drains ... Even reproof has been gently administered at Lord's.

It added that the MCC had always been 'more paternal and benevolent than punitive and rigorous' because of its aim 'to keep cricket a game'.[13] The background to these remarks shows how the MCC tried to minimise friction between itself and the county clubs. It had been rumoured that Durham CCC would recommend to the Minor Counties Association that the MCC should insist upon a strict adherence of the rules governing the residential qualifications of county cricketers and that Worcestershire should be penalised for knowingly playing L.G. Crawley, an amateur not qualified to play for the county. There were whispers of Worcestershire being excluded from the county championship. The MCC took no action against Worcestershire. The Advisory Committee accepted a proposal from Lancashire that it be left to the discretion of the MCC to impose penalties for breaches of the rules of county cricket, though shortly afterwards the MCC refused to accept this recommendation. The statement issued to the press after the meeting of the Advisory Committee declared that the incident was closed and that there had been no truth in rumours that the MCC had circularised counties suggesting that they penalise Worcestershire. The Worcestershire representatives apologised for having played an unqualified player.[14] The wide measure of independence permitted to county clubs also helps to account for the acceptance of the MCC's role within county cricket. To compete in the county championship a county had to arrange home and away fixtures against only seven other counties up to 1921 and eleven from 1922.[15] Fixtures were arranged at a meeting of county secretaries. Only from 1929 until 1932 did counties each have to play the same number of championship matches, which meant that in most inter-war seasons not all counties played the same number of matches.

THE COUNTY CLUBS

The main reason for the acceptance of the MCC's hegemony over first-class cricket is that those who ran the county clubs had similar backgrounds to those who ran the MCC and shared the same assumptions about how cricket should be organised. The county clubs were private clubs whose officials and executive committees were elected by their members (the numbers of county members are discussed in Chapter 3). Members at county clubs belonged to the wealthier sections of society. Very few were working-class. Extensive trawls through the sporting press and local newspapers have not produced evidence of officials at county clubs calling for working men to become members. Requests for new members were usually directed towards 'gentlemen', it often being claimed that membership of a county club was a social obligation for a gentleman. Subscriptions to most county clubs cost two guineas, but it was common for an entry fee of a double subscription to be paid in the first year of membership. Yorkshire probably had the cheapest subscription of all county clubs. A subscription for a full member at Yorkshire cost one guinea, but one shilling and sixpence were added to this to cover the cost of the entertainment tax which had to be paid on subscriptions. For most of the inter-war period, a subscription of two guineas would have been around half the adult male average weekly wage and a heavy expense for most working men. Though payment of a subscription guaranteed free admission to matches, becoming a member was not a cheap way of watching cricket. The usual cost of admission to a day's play for non-members was one shilling, though members enjoyed better amenities and more comfort.

A list of those who became members of Lancashire in 1922 has survived. The occupations of the first 100 on this list were all middle class, though it is difficult to say precisely to what level within the middle class they belonged. Six were professional men. Seventeen were buyers, salesmen or merchants. Three of the six manufacturers were cotton manufacturers but the size of their firms is not known. Five were students. In 1919 occupations of the first 50 names in an alphabetical listing of Yorkshire members from the Sheffield area included 18 company directors or managers, seven professional men, though only a professor was involved with education, three army officers and two stockbrokers. Local directories recorded no occupations for ten of this sample, though their neighbours all belonged to the haute bourgeoisie. It is difficult to establish the precise social standing of those whose occupations included drapers, ironmongers, travellers and tailors. A sample of 50 members in 1940, when the number of members from Sheffield had more than doubled, included nine directors and managers, 13 professional men of whom three were teachers, and two stockbrokers. A draughtsman was the closest to a working-class occupation, though the immediate neighbours of those for whom no occupation was stated tended to be from what could be called the lower middle class or skilled ranks of the working class.[16] It would seem that the expansion of the membership at Yorkshire between the wars had caused it to be drawn from a slightly wider section of local society, though the proportion from the higher bourgeoisie remained considerable.

Members of county clubs elected the executive committees which ran the county clubs and to which officials such as treasurers and secretaries were responsible. Of a sample of 276 elected committee members from six counties, biographical details have been found for 176 but often the biographical data is only the name of a school attended or the use of a military title. Nine were peers, the sons of peers or became peers. Four were baronets and three were or became knights. Seventy-six had attended public school with most, 17, having been at Eton, eight at Rugby and seven at Harrow. Thirty-one used military titles but over half were 'Major' or 'Captain'. Seventy-four were listed as company directors in *The Directory of Directors*. Many held more than one directorship and nearly half were directors of banking, insurance or stockbroking concerns. Even those from the sample who served on the committees of Lancashire and Yorkshire included few who held directorships in textiles or engineering, although it is possible that those who belonged to family firms were not always included in *The Directory of Directors*. Some held directorships in financial and industrial firms. Directors outnumbered professional men, though some solicitors were also company directors and several of those who had attended a public school were also company directors and used military titles. As it is easier to uncover biographical material about the more socially eminent, it is possible that the sample exaggerates the social and economic status of committee members in general, but a fair proportion of committee members seem to have been from the haute bourgeoisie. No major changes occurred in the social composition of county committees between the wars except that the aristocratic element declined slightly. At many counties vice-presidents were allowed to attend and vote at committee meetings. Vice-presidents were often from the upper class. In 1930 those for Surrey were the Earl of Midleton, Sir Jeremiah Colman, a millionaire baronet whose fortune was based upon mustard manufacturing, and Lord Ebbisham. In 1920, 11 of the 25 vice-presidents and four of the committee members of Kent were peers or sons of peers. In 1938 three of 17 vice-presidents and two of the 24 committee members were peers. Lord Hawke, who died in 1938, was the only peer to serve on the Yorkshire committee between the wars.[17] No evidence of demands for spectators to be consulted about the running of county cricket has been found.

LEAGUE CRICKET

In the North and Midlands of England the great majority of clubs which played cricket on a regular basis did so in league competitions. Some towns had socially exclusive clubs which played only friendly matches but in other areas even clubs for the local social elite played in leagues. Leagues were found in the South, though in this part of England clubs with the best facilities and those with players from the better-off classes did not play in leagues. By 1939 none of more than 1,100 clubs from the Home Counties affiliated to the Club Cricket Conference belonged to a league. Less than half of the teams mentioned by *The Sussex Express* in 1922 and 1939 and none of the socially prestigious clubs from along the Sussex coast played in leagues. In Herefordshire, *The Hereford Times* listed 39 clubs which played each week in 1922. Ten of these appeared to have played in 'the cricket championship', which may not have been a formal league but merely how this newspaper ranked the performances of a few local clubs. In 1930 the newspaper listed 67 clubs which were playing regularly though a few were from outside the county of Herefordshire. There were no reports of the cricket championship, but five clubs were playing in the Hereford Cricket League.

There is no simple explanation why league cricket was so much stronger in the North and Midlands than in the South. The example of the Football League, formed in 1888 and whose original clubs were all from Lancashire and the Midlands, may have prompted the formation of cricket leagues. Certainly by 1914 cricket leagues had become common at all levels of cricket throughout the North and Midlands and created an assumption that it was natural for cricket to be organised in leagues. Apologists for league cricket often praised its competitive ethos. In 1924 the sports journalist Ivan Sharpe wrote that league cricket was

> the keenest cricket of all … It is a far cry … from Lord's and far removed from the pattern of the headquarters of the game … Superior people say it isn't cricket. 'Slap-dash' they call it. Lord's probably doesn't think much about it. Too hurried, too tense; no poetry in it, no science … The Northerner has reached the stage when he prefers pep in his play. This League cricket goes far to meet the demand.[18]

Many must have found the nature of league cricket to their liking, whereas in the South and among some of the socially exclusive clubs in the North, leagues were seen as inimical to the moral values associated with cricket. The intense competitiveness of league cricket was viewed as a threat to the spirit of sportsmanship and of playing the game for its own sake. Socially exclusive clubs may have feared that the need for success in leagues encouraged the selection of players on the basis of ability rather than social background. The weakness of league cricket in the South perhaps reflected a greater number of clubs for the wealthier classes in the South.

There was a clear hierarchy among cricket leagues. Those at the apex of league cricket such as the Lancashire League, the Central Lancashire League, the Bolton League, the Bradford League, the Durham Senior League, the Birmingham League included clubs whose grounds could accommodate hundreds and even thousands of spectators. County matches were played occasionally on the grounds of clubs from such leagues. Their standard of play was high. Leading clubs employed professional players with experience often of county and occasionally of test match cricket. Twelve of the 14 Lancashire League clubs, for instance, had as their professionals at some time between the wars those who were or had been test cricketers. Most areas in the North and Midlands also had cricket leagues where clubs did not engage professionals but played cricket to a high standard and had well-appointed grounds. The humblest levels of league cricket were very different from the most prestigious cricket leagues. Many players did not have white flannels, though several leagues required bowlers to wear white shirts or sweaters. In the Lancashire towns of St Helens and Burnley some clubs used shale or cinder wickets and their players played in clogs. Shrubs and long grass grew in the outfields of some clubs in the Radcliffe Sunday School League.[19]

No cricket league drew its clubs from the whole of the North or Midlands. The strongest leagues usually drew clubs from a number of neighbouring towns and industrialised villages. Not surprisingly the humblest leagues were the most localised. Many northern and Midlands towns had several cricket leagues. In 1924, for instance, the Oldham, Werneth, Crompton and Royton clubs, all from or very close to Oldham, played in the Lancashire Central League, but clubs from Oldham and its immediate surroundings played in the Saddleworth League which had two divisions, the Oldham and Ashton League (two divisions), the Oldham and District League (three divisions), the Oldham Sunday School Alliance (three divisions), the Oldham Pleasant Sunday Afternoon League (two divisions), the Congregational League (two divisions) and the Oldham Primitive Methodist League (one division).

The efficient functioning of league cricket required organisation. Even the humblest leagues needed executive committees to arrange and conduct their competitions. A written constitution was necessary if a league was to operate smoothly and if disputes between clubs were to be kept to a minimum. Almost all leagues seem to have required players of each club to be registered with the league and member clubs had to surrender the right of arranging fixtures to a central body. The minute books of executive committees of leagues show that much time was spent on disputes concerning the playing of ineligible players.

No national body was established between the wars to represent the interests of league cricket, but regional organisations were created. The Yorkshire Cricket Federation, set up in 1929, was probably the first to be established. Although not intended to cater for league clubs alone, most organisations which joined were leagues. Within a short period the Bradford, Huddersfield, North Yorkshire, South Durham, Leeds and the Yorkshire Council, all prestigious leagues, had affiliated to the Federation.

The driving force behind the establishment of the Federation was Harry Knowles, secretary of the Yorkshire Council, one of the leading leagues in Yorkshire. The aims of the Federation were to watch over the interests of club cricket 'if and when proposals are made in any quarter for the alteration of the laws or implements of the game, and to take action thereon as may appear desirable'.[20] The Federation had no intention of dictating to its member clubs and organisations. Its first president, J.J. Booth of the Bradford League, declared that its policy was to be 'co-operation, not aggression' and that member organisations would not commit themselves to anything 'in direct opposition to existing cricket law and the MCC alterations'.[21] The Federation's minute book shows that it spent much time trying to have the rating assessments upon cricket grounds reduced, urging local authorities to provide more cricket pitches, protesting about football eating into the cricket season and trying to devise a system to discourage the poaching of players from clubs in other leagues. In February 1930 delegates from eight leagues in Lancashire representing 250 clubs met in Manchester to form the Lancashire Cricket Federation which was modelled on that of the Yorkshire Federation.[22]

The competitive ethos of league cricket discouraged co-operation between leagues. Oral evidence shows that all levels of league cricket were fiercely competitive. Many leagues prohibited players from playing in other leagues. Even such a humble league as the Horwich Sunday School League forbade the players of its clubs to play in any other league except for those who were invited to play for the Horwich RMI (Railwaymen's Mechanics' Institute) club, the leading club in Horwich. In part such regulations were designed to prevent clubs using talented players from other leagues in key matches. Clubs from leading leagues were often competitors for the best players and this bred a spirit of suspicion between them. Clubs with ambitious officials and supporters often tried to join more prestigious leagues. Radcliffe CC, for instance, left the Bolton League to join the Central Lancashire League in 1937. In 1938 an official of Farnworth CC described it as 'eyewash' for Radcliffe CC to send its good wishes to the Bolton League whilst it was attempting to poach the best players from the Bolton League.[23] In 1928 the Westhoughton club from Bolton complained about other clubs enticing away its best players but a few years later the Westhoughton committee decided to ask whether players with a leading club from the Bolton and District Cricket Association would be interested in joining it.[24] The difficulties of the Yorkshire Federation in framing regulations to discourage the poaching of players which would satisfy its member leagues demonstrates the animosities found in league cricket. In 1937 its special 'obligations' sub-committee decided that no club should approach a player without first notifying his club and that players could not negotiate with other clubs without the prior approval of their current clubs. Clubs were not to negotiate about joining another league without the consent of their current leagues, but leagues could not refuse to allow clubs to negotiate with other leagues provided that all obligations to the existing league had been met and that all fixtures had been honoured. This arrangement did not satisfy all leagues and in 1938 the Yorkshire Council resigned from the Federation amid accusations of 'dictatorship' from the Federation and complaints that the Federation was dominated by junior leagues.[25]

For much of the inter-war period the attitude of the MCC towards the higher levels of league cricket was one of grand indifference, though some felt that it had a low opinion of such cricket. Fred Root, the England bowler who had played county and league cricket as a professional, wrote that 'In the cabinet of first-class cricket, the Lancashire League is apt to be frowned upon as a competition likened in their minds to a circus or music-hall version of the game'.[26] There were short-lived outbursts of friction between leagues and the MCC and the county clubs. Just after the First World War, dominant figures within county cricket saw the highest levels of league cricket as a potential rival to county cricket. League clubs were attracting large numbers of spectators and county officials feared that league clubs would entice the best professionals away from county cricket. In December 1919 the Advisory Committee decided that no player could take part in representative matches or be selected for an overseas tour unless he pledged himself to help his county when so invited.[27] In 1920 the Managing Committee of Kent resolved to grant benefits only to professionals who promised that the county club could have the first call upon their services for the next seven seasons and that they would not play for any other county, club or league without the prior permission of the county. Following any breach of this regulation, a player who had already received a benefit would have to forfeit the interest which the club held on his benefit fund.[28] In 1921 Lord Hawke accused Lancashire League clubs of poaching county professionals, which caused the secretary of the Lancashire League to reply that the spectators of league clubs had a right to see the best players.[29] In 1922 after a Kent professional had signed a five-year contract with a league club Lord Harris complained that league cricket had become 'a real competitor' to county cricket,[30] but soon afterwards such complaints were made less often. Very few of the big names of county cricket who were at the peak of their powers abandoned county cricket for the leagues after the early 1920s. Soon after the formation of the Yorkshire Cricket Federation, which was very much an organisation of cricket leagues, its president, who was an official of the Bradford League, claimed that 'A great responsibility was attached to each member which would entail loyalty to the MCC and the County to which the Federation belonged.' In 1931 the Federation called upon all its affiliated clubs and leagues to write to their MPs in support of a resolution of the MCC protesting about the effects of a new land tax on cricket clubs. Lord Hawke agreed to negotiate on behalf of the Federation with the Football Association about the incursions of football into the cricket season.[31] Even in the early 1920s some prominent league clubs had recognised the informal hegemony over cricket of the MCC. In 1920 when Rochdale CC resigned from the Central Lancashire League after Cecil Parkin, its professional, had left the field as a protest against an umpire's repeated rejection of LBW appeals, the Rochdale club suggested that the dispute be settled by an appeal to the MCC.[32]

Occupations can be established for only a proportion of those who administered cricket leagues between the wars. Few if any leagues employed full-time officials. In Bolton and its surroundings, officials and members of executive committees had lower middle-class or working-class occupations. The largest cricket league in this area was the Bolton and District Cricket Association. In the 1920s its First Division was one of the leading leagues in Lancashire, its clubs hiring professionals with experience of county and even of test match cricket. The BDCA also had divisions which catered for far more humble clubs. In the winter of 1929–30, 12 of the strongest clubs from the First Division of BDCA left to form the Bolton League which immediately became the major cricket league in this part of Lancashire. In 1927 the BDCA had 88 committee members and 56 in 1933. Occupations for 45 of those from 1927 and 34 from 1933 were traced. In 1927, 22 had white-collar and 23 blue-collar occupations. In 1933, 12 had white-collar and 22 blue-collar occupations. About a third of these samples were from smaller clubs. The first chairman of the Bolton League was a bleacher. The secretary of the Walkden League whose clubs came from the south and west of Bolton but which did not play at a standard to have professionals, was a railway clerk. The Sunday School League cricket leagues of Radcliffe and Horwich formed the humblest level of league cricket in the Bolton area. In 1939 the chairman of the Radcliffe Sunday School worked for the CWS bank. Chairmen of the Horwich Sunday School League included a dance-band manager, though this may not have been his main occupation, who was also a senior member of the local Labour Party, and one who became head of the insurance section at the local locomotive engineering works. The three inter-war secretaries were all office workers. The four treasurers were a pattern maker, a textile mill office worker, a railway employee and a member of a family with a quarrying business.[33] As much of this evidence about the occupations of league officials and committee members has been collected from local directories, the proportion of blue-collar workers may have been greater than these figures suggest, and although the volume of relevant evidence is limited, no major shift seems to have occurred in the social backgrounds of those who ran cricket leagues in this part of Lancashire.

League cricket in the Bolton area was not exclusively a concern of the lower middle and working classes. Efforts were made to involve other classes. League presidents and vice-presidents were usually successful professional or businessmen or from the most socially prestigious families of local industrialists. Colonel Greg, whose family owned cotton mills at Eagley, was president of the BDCA from 1907 until 1929. Captain Lloyd, his son-in-law, had been a vice-president of the Association and became its president in 1930.[34] Greg and Lloyd were entitled to attend general committee meetings and were active in the Association's affairs. In 1924 proposals to demote six clubs from the First Division were defeated largely by Lloyd's efforts.[35] In the 1920s the BDCA usually had at least 20 vice-presidents including such local dignitaries as Colonel Hardcastle, head of a cotton bleaching concern in Bradshaw, Colonel Walker whose family owned a large tannery, and Sir William Edge, a Coalition Liberal MP for Bolton. Two vice-presidents in addition to Lloyd were town councillors. Others included a solicitor, a former professional county cricketer who owned a sports outfitting business, a hotel proprietor, an estate agent, a funeral director, a coal merchant and a Catholic priest whose brother was a doctor and holder of the OBE. In the 1930s vice-presidents continued to include large employers and directors of successful but more modest businesses. In December 1929 the Bolton League invited a list of similar figures to become its vice-presidents. Lloyd declined the presidency because he had accepted the presidency of the BDCA, while Colonel Slater of Dunscar refused to become a vice-president. Alderman Warburton, whose family owned a large bakery and who was connected with Astley Bridge CC, became its first president.[36] A list of the Walkden League's vice-presidents has not been found for the inter-war period but in 1910 they included an MP, four doctors and one BA.[37] Though not members of the industrial elite, these figures probably enjoyed a high level of local social prestige. In the 1920s Captain W.E. Nuttall of the Vale Paper Mill and W.E. Ainscow, chairman of the Beehive textile mills, donated trophies to the Horwich Sunday School League.[38]

League cricket clubs were controlled, in theory at least, by their members who elected club officials and executive committee members at annual meetings. Clubs usually divided non-playing members into vice-presidents, patrons, ordinary members, lady members and juniors, with these different categories of members paying different subscriptions. Nelson CC of the Lancashire League had subscriptions which cost 63 shillings, 42 shillings, 30 shillings, 21 shillings, 20 shillings, 15 shillings, 12 shillings and sixpence, ten shillings and sixpence, seven shillings and sixpence (ladies) and six shillings.[39] In 1919 the East Lancashire club, one of the more prestigious Lancashire League clubs, proposed to raise its annual subscription from one guinea to one and a half guineas and to 15 shillings and ninepence for country members.[40] Subscriptions at Dudley CC of the Birmingham League were two guineas for playing members and one guinea for non-playing members. Subscriptions for adult members at Durham City CC of the Durham Senior League were ten shillings for adult members in 1933.[41] At Heaton CC, one of the leading clubs in the Bolton area, playing members in 1921 paid six shillings, men members four shillings and ladies three shillings. In 1924 a patron's subscription was half a guinea.[42] Evidence about the cost of subscriptions to clubs at the humblest levels of league cricket is exasperatingly sparse, but it is probable that players were expected to pay a subscription of a few shillings.

So very few league clubs have retained addresses of members from the inter-war period that it is difficult to be confident about the social class of club members, though some inferences about this can be drawn from the cost of subscriptions. In the 1920s Dudley CC's subscription of a guinea for non-playing members may have been prohibitively expensive for many working men and there were complaints in the late 1920s about its small number of members. Only seven of the 80 new members of Durham CC whose occupations could be traced for the inter-war period by Jeffrey Hill had unequivocally working-class jobs.[43] The remainder were lower middle or middle class. Occupations which could be traced for 55 of the 297 names found in a minute book of Farnworth Social Circle, a First Division club of the BDCA and probably the most prestigious club not invited to join the Bolton League, show that club members included local businessmen, professional people and working men, but it is not clear whether this sample was representative of other clubs.[44] Subscriptions of seven or five shillings were probably aimed at working men, but evidence about how many members paid different levels of subscriptions is rare, though in 1924, 5 per cent of Nelson's members had paid subscriptions of at least two guineas, 28 per cent 15 shillings, 26 per cent ten shillings and sixpence, with just under 30 per cent being ladies who paid seven shillings and sixpence.[45] As 15 shillings was not an inconsiderable sum of money in 1924, it would seem that the Nelson membership was unlikely to have been overwhelmingly working class.

At leading league clubs, presidents were often local dignitaries and usually held office for many years, but they do not seem to have been involved with club administration, though they could make valuable contributions to club funds and provide employment for talented cricketers. In the Bolton area, members of the Deakin family, who owned the bleachworks which was the major source of employment in Egerton, were presidents of Egerton CC from 1877 until 1947. Topp, a leading textile manufacturer and colliery director in Farnworth, was president of Little Hulton CC for most of the inter-war period. In the 1920s, J. Stones, a local businessman who became the Conservative MP for Farnworth in 1931, was president of Farnworth Social Circle CC. J.O. Dixon, a JP, county councillor, and director, chief engineer and agent of the Westhoughton Coal and Cannel Company, which employed more than 1,500 in 1931, was president of Westhoughton CC for most of the 1930s. From 1899 to 1934, Colonel Greg of the Eagley Mills was president of Eagley CC[46] and seems to have been one of the few club presidents who took an active interest in club affairs.

In practice the larger league clubs were controlled by their elected officials and executive committees. Numbers serving on executive committees varied widely between clubs. In the Bolton area, for instance, Radcliffe CC usually had a committee of 30 whereas that of Westhoughton had around 12. Nelson CC for most of the inter-war period had a committee of 15. The occupations of 22 of the 30 men who served on the committee of Nelson CC between 1923 and 1935 have been identified. These show a higher proportion from the wealthier sections of local society than those of the Heaton and Westhoughton clubs in Bolton and included six manufacturers, a mill manager, a former Guards officer, but also three factory employees.[47] Available data about occupations of committee members from clubs in the Bolton area does not include any industrialists but shows a mixture of those with white-collar occupations, such as school teachers and clerks, and blue-collar jobs, often with a degree of skill though some committee members were colliers. No labourers have been discovered to have been committee members, but as most occupation data has been collected from directories, those whose occupations were not stated in directories were perhaps unskilled workers.[48] The number of officials from unskilled manual occupations, and from the working class as a whole, appears to have been disproportionately small compared with the total number of manual workers in the Bolton area. On the other hand the proportion of working-class men among these samples of club officials is sufficient to demonstrate that the running of league cricket clubs crossed class boundaries.

CLUB CRICKET

What was usually described as club cricket, the form of cricket where clubs played each week but did not participate in league or knock-out competitions, covered a vast spectrum of cricket clubs. Some clubs had grounds which were as splendid as those of the best league clubs and where county matches were played occasionally. Some, like the clubs from the Liverpool Competition, engaged professionals to play for them whilst others fielded all amateur sides but had professionals who acted as coaches. At the opposite extreme of club cricket were small clubs who played with facilities as poor as those found at the humblest levels of league cricket.

In much of the South, only the humblest level of clubs played in leagues, though there were very many humble clubs which did not belong to leagues. Practically all clubs whose players and members belonged to the wealthier classes in the South played only friendly matches. In the North and Midlands, some socially exclusive clubs with excellent facilities did not belong to leagues. The clubs of the Liverpool Competition all had excellent grounds and many of their players had wealthy backgrounds and had attended public schools. The Liverpool Competition had no written rules. Each club provided one umpire in each of its matches. Club officials denied that the Liverpool Competition was a league and claimed that they had no responsibility for the 'league' table based on their results which was published by the local press. Socially exclusive clubs from south-east Lancashire played in the Manchester Association which could scarcely be described as a league. Clubs did not have to play the same number of matches and some clubs chose never to play other clubs. Significantly these two bodies did not use the word 'league' in their titles. In some parts of the North, however, the absence of equivalents to the Liverpool Competition or the Manchester Association meant that those from the wealthier classes who wanted to play for clubs with good facilities had to play for league clubs.

A major factor for the strength of club cricket in the South was that those from wealthy backgrounds believed that friendly matches were far preferable to league games. E.A.C. Thomson of the London and Southern Counties Club Cricket Conference wrote in 1923 that there was 'sufficient spice of adventure' in friendly matches whilst leagues and knock-out competitions tended to 'crush out every ounce of the real sporting spirit of cricket' and introduced 'the contentious side which should be entirely foreign to our glorious English summer game'. For Thomson a barrier against leagues would

> tend to keep the game perfectly clean, strictly amateur, and ... see it

played in the fine old spirit which has ever characterised it since the days of those who handed on their heritage for others to follow. Competitions do not make cricket any better; rather do they make it a good deal worse by the birth of all sorts of evils, which, once entering the field of play, can seldom be ejected, so they become a permanent part of a vicious system, producing a bad cricketing atmosphere which is at once unhealthy and contentious. Furthermore, it leaves the real English spirit of amateur sport to be brushed ruthlessly aside for the more dangerous and unwholesome spirit of competitive adventure in which two league points, or a medal, or some piece of silver ware, may and does count to be of greater intrinsic value, and so becomes more cherished in the end by the players than the actual game itself.[49]

Avoiding league competitions could have been a tactic to keep clubs socially exclusive, though this was not likely to have been admitted in public. The competitive aspect of leagues, and especially where clubs could be promoted or relegated to other divisions, encouraged the selection of players on the basis of ability rather than social background, though it has been recalled that at some Lancashire League clubs those whose 'parents were well-to-do or something in the town' would be more likely to be selected than those with similar cricketing abilities but more humble backgrounds.[50] Hostility to league competitions was also connected to the belief among the wealthier classes in the South that recreational sport should be amateur. Those social groups who were most committed to opposing leagues in cricket were by and large those who supported the Rugby Football Union in its opposition to professionalism and leagues. Leagues and professionalism often went hand in hand. It is probable that those from the wealthier classes would have agreed with *The Field* which argued in 1915 that the place of the professional in club cricket was not to play for a club side but to coach younger players and help amateurs to practise.[51] Competing in leagues would have been difficult for wandering clubs based in London. These were clubs, often the Old Boys' clubs of public and grammar schools, which played regularly yet had no grounds of their own. In 1939 nearly a third of clubs from Essex affiliated to the Club Cricket Conference were Old Boys or wandering clubs.

The rhetoric which stressed the moral superiority of friendly over league cricket stemmed mainly from the wealthier classes, but many clubs from the South which played only friendly cricket were not socially exclusive. At many village clubs the majority of players were working class, but such clubs often had support from other social classes in their locality. Vicars usually took the chair at annual meetings of village clubs in rural Sussex, whilst local dignitaries acted as the patrons or presidents of such clubs.

Lord Portman, for instance, was the president of Buxted Park CC.[52] The president of Henfield CC was a captain and the vice-presidents included an admiral, one reverend, two doctors and two captains.[53] The growing numbers of clubs based upon workplaces probably meant that the number of teams for those from the lower middle and working classes increased. Workplace teams often had working-class players and affiliations to the Club Cricket Conference show that many of these in the South played only friendly matches.

Clubs playing only friendly matches had a wide measure of autonomy. No formal links existed between the MCC and club cricket. Clubs did not have to be registered with regional or national bodies though the degree of organisation within club cricket increased on a regional and modest scale between the wars. In the Home Counties the Club Cricket Conference emerged as something approaching a representative organisation for club cricket. In 1915 what became the London and Southern Counties Club Cricket Conference had been formed by E.A.C. Thomson as an emergency fixture bureau arranging matches at short notice and providing cricketers, especially servicemen, with opportunities to play. In October 1926 its title was changed to that of the Club Cricket Conference. The LSCCCC Handbook for 1923 pointed out that in some parts of southern England 'The game is not quite so healthy or progressive as it was' which justified the need for 'the self-protecting body of the Conference'.[54] The numbers of clubs affiliated to the Conference grew quickly. Originally it had 35 member clubs. By 1928 just under 500 clubs had become affiliated to it, of whom 232 had joined since 1922. In 1933, 820 clubs had affiliated to it and nearly 1,300 in 1939. In 1939 1,150 of its affiliated clubs were from the counties of Essex, Kent, Middlesex and Surrey.[55] By no means all clubs in the south-east became affiliated to the CCC, though the number of its affiliated clubs helped it to become accepted as the organ of club cricket in southern England. Matters of concern to club cricket in the south-east could be aired at its annual meetings. In 1929 it began a campaign against the increased rateable values placed upon cricket grounds and in 1934 it protested about the encroachments of amateur soccer upon the cricket season.[56] Clubs which played in leagues or knock-out competitions or who played professionals could not join the CCC.

Relations between the MCC and the Conference were generally harmonious. The MCC invited the Conference to express its opinion upon proposed changes to the laws of cricket. In 1929 the MCC had suggested that the experimental changes to the laws of having bigger stumps and batsmen being out LBW to balls which they snicked onto their pads should be adopted in club cricket. These changes had been introduced into first-class cricket in order to undermine the supremacy of batsmen over bowlers, which was thought to be affecting the popularity of county cricket. The Conference decided not to support these changes because it felt that batting was already difficult in club cricket and that making batting more difficult could discourage schoolboys from taking up the game. Such changes, it argued, were certainly not needed in village cricket. In 1927 there had been 60 occasions where whole village teams had been dismissed without scoring a run.[57] The LBW snick rule was soon abandoned in first-class cricket and in 1931 the MCC decided that the use of the larger wickets should be optional outside first-class cricket.[58] In November 1934 the MCC and the Advisory Committee agreed that in county cricket during the 1935 season the LBW law would be changed so that batsmen could be given out to balls pitching outside the off stump. Shortly afterwards the CCC decided that no alteration to the LBW law was necessary or desirable, especially as the proposed change would make umpiring more difficult.[59] In January 1936 the MCC Committee announced that it considered the new LBW law to have been successful in first-class cricket and, in order for it to given a wider trial, asked for it be used in all levels of cricket. Within a week the council of the Conférence asked all its affiliated clubs to adopt the experimental rule.[60]

The CCC never appears to have questioned the position of the MCC as the overriding authority within cricket. The MCC did not treat the CCC in a heavy-handed manner. It did not claim that it could dictate how club cricket should be played. Clubs were invited to try the experimental changes to the laws. Both bodies shared similar views about the playing and organisation of cricket and assumed that individual clubs should be permitted a wide degree of independence. Each highly valued amateurism in cricket. The CCC's prohibition upon leagues was not relaxed but relations with league cricket seemed to have become more amicable in the 1930s. It communicated with the Yorkshire Cricket Federation about the rating assessments upon cricket grounds and the incursions of football into the cricket season. In 1933 in an article for *The Cricketer* Thomson's tone towards league cricket was more conciliatory than in the early 1920s. Instead of highlighting his fears that leagues could undermine sportsmanship, he stressed that different regions preferred different forms of cricket organisation.[61]

THE STRUCTURE OF CRICKET AND ENGLISH ATTITUDES TO AUTHORITY

Cricket discourses reveal a general acceptance of cricket's authority structure between the wars. There was no crisis of authority within cricket.

The primacy of the MCC, a private club having close personal links with the political and social establishment, did not provoke widespread demands for power within cricket to be diffused more widely or for other social groups to have a bigger share in the control of cricket. Calls for cricket to have a more systematised form of authority linking the different forms of cricket were also rare. Expressions of dissatisfaction in the press concerning aspects of first-class cricket such as calls for a professional to captain England in 1926 were not usually accompanied by proposals for the MCC to be replaced as the dominant body within cricket. Occasional calls were made for those who controlled cricket to act differently. Demands for a root and branch reform of how cricket was controlled were hardly ever heard.

In part, acceptance of the existing power structure of cricket may have been the result of resignation and fatalism. Occasionally professional cricketers complained of their lack of power within first-class cricket. Maurice Tate felt that professionals 'were not supposed to have any opinions of their own'[62] and Harold Larwood, writing in the wake of the bodyline storm, mentioned 'a big hush-hush conspiracy to brand me as a dangerous bowler', and that 'the MCC have given way to political and other influences to placate Australia'.[63] Some county clubs prohibited professionals from writing in the press and the fate of Cecil Parkin, who came to feel that he had been hounded out of county cricket because he had criticised the England captain in a ghosted newspaper article, may have caused other professionals to be circumspect about expressing criticisms of how cricket was controlled. The absence of a trade union for county professional cricketers meant that there was no channel through which professionals could have organised pressure for a greater share in the control of county cricket. It is likely that many professionals accepted the control of county cricket or felt that trying to change it would be a task of immeasurable difficulty. Certainly, conversations with four professionals who played county cricket in the 1930s revealed that they accepted the established authority structure of cricket as a fact of life. The exercise of authority in so many areas of English political and social life by those who controlled cricket may well have persuaded many professionals and others to assume that it was only natural for those who controlled cricket to do so.

Acceptance of the MCC and of the existing structure of power within cricket owed much to how the MCC exercised its authority. The MCC did not usually behave in an overbearing manner. It usually acted with tact and courtesy towards other cricket organisations. It has been shown above that relations between the MCC and the county clubs were usually harmonious. The report of the Findlay Commission, which was appointed in 1937 to consider whether county cricket needed to be reformed in order to boost its finances, did not recommend major changes in the administration of county cricket or to the relationship between the MCC and the counties. The MCC consulted the Club Cricket Conference over changes to the laws of cricket. The MCC showed no desire to become the apex of a highly systematised structure for cricket which embraced all levels and forms of cricket, but calls for such a structure were hardly ever made. The attitude of the MCC towards league cricket may have been superior and perhaps condescending, but it never became overbearing. Relations between the MCC and league cricket were very different from those between rugby union and rugby league. The MCC made no attempt to take the Women's Cricket Association under its wing.

Cultural values within England do much to explain the general acceptance of how power was exercised in cricket. Cricket indicates the importance of tradition in generating approval for existing institutions. Much of the significance accorded to cricket stemmed from assumptions that cricket resonated with those strands of English culture which placed special value upon the traditional. The antiquity of the MCC and beliefs that it had been the dominant force within cricket in the nineteenth century contributed much to the acceptance of its role within cricket between the wars. The nature of authority within cricket can be interpreted as an expression of the frame of mind which saw peculiarly English virtues in the tradition of an unwritten constitution and mistrusted a highly centralised authority. The scholar and university administrator Sir Ernest Barker thought that the national character had 'a curious genius for combining local self-government with central attachment and central control'.[64] This was also intertwined with convictions that English wisdom and practical experience were superior to logical abstractions which resulted in highly systematised political and social institutions. When discussing the apparent illogicality of the MCC asking the captains of county sides to report upon the performance of umpires, Colonel Philip Trevor wrote that

> I am told that in actual practice at cricket the system works well. What a thing to be British! The majority of our administrative systems are antiquated and illogical, but by a peculiar combination of common sense and fair play we deal out better justice under those systems than they who in other lands work systems to which Euclid himself could take no exception.[65]

First-class cricket was controlled by those who exercised power in so much of English political and social life. No doubt this caused them to believe that they were the ones who should control cricket and it probably helped to persuade other groups to assume that it was natural for this elite to be in control of cricket. At the same time cricket showed a sense among those with power that it should be exercised with tact and discretion, that there should not be an excessive desire to extend the boundaries of authority. Cricket indicates the strength of that element within English culture which encouraged a predilection for leaving things as they were, for accepting established procedures and forms of authority but for authority to be practised with circumspection and concern for others. The perspective which cricket provides upon English attitudes to power suggests the strength of an essentially conservative cast of mind, an acceptance of the status quo. In this respect attitudes to power in cricket add a further dimension to explanations of why support for political extremism was so limited in England between the wars, and why the tradition of parliamentary government received such widespread support when it was being challenged in so much of Europe.

NOTES

1. *Wisden Cricketers' Almanack, 1937* (London: John Wisden, 1937), p. 40; for a general history of the MCC, see A.R. Lewis, *Double Century: The Story of MCC and Cricket* (London: Hodder and Stoughton, 1987).
2. *Wisden Cricketers' Almanack, 1933*, part 2, p. 49; *Wisden Cricketers' Almanack, 1935,* part 2, p. 64.
3. For lists of the office-holders of the MCC, see E.W. Swanton, G. Plumptre and J. Woodcock, eds., *Barclays World of Cricket: The Game from A–Z* (London: Guild, 1986), pp. 49–55. For details of their backgrounds, see *Who's Who* (London: Black, various editions), P. Bailey, P. Thorn and P. Wynne-Thomas, eds., *Who's Who of Cricketers* (London: Guild, 1984) and B. Green, *The Wisden Book of Obituaries: Obituaries from Wisden Cricketers' Almanack 1892–1985* (London: Queen Anne, 1986).
4. H. Gordon, *Background of Cricket* (London: Barker, 1939), p. 279.
5. A. Moore, 'The "Fascist" Cricket Tour of 1924–25', *Sporting Traditions*, 7, 2 (May 1991). Moore also points out that F.C. Toone, manager of the MCC tour to Australia and the secretary of Yorkshire CCC from 1903 until 1930, was also a member of the British Fascists. The British Fascists were a separate organisation from Mosley's British Union of Fascists. The employment of Gilligan to write upon cricket by *The News Chronicle*, a Liberal newspaper, in 1931 and 1932 suggests that he had abandoned Fascist sympathies by that time or was keeping them very much to himself.
6. The biographical data was collected from *Who Was Who* (London: Black, various editions), *Who's Who of Cricketers, Wisden Book of Obituaries* and *The Directory of Directors* (London: Skinner, Thomas, various editions).
7. The details of probate awards are found in *Calendar of All Grants of Probate and Letters of Administration* (various places of publication: HMSO, published annually).
8. *The Times*, 6 Jan. 1920, 25 Jan. 1922.
9. Ibid., 29 Oct., 19 Nov. 1924.
10. Ibid., 8 Dec. 1921, 25 Jan. 1922.

11. *Wisden Cricketers' Almanack, 1931*, part 1, p. 280.
12. P. Trevor, *Cricket and Cricketers* (London: Chapman and Hall, 1921), p. 212.
13. *Athletic News*, 12 Nov. 1923.
14. Ibid., 12, 26 Nov. 1923; *The Times*, 7, 21 Nov. 1923.
15. *The Times*, 16 April 1921.
16. The manuscript volume containing the list of new members of Lancashire CCC is held by Lancashire CCC; the annual editions of *Yorkshire County Cricket Club* provide the addresses for all members of Yorkshire CCC. Occupations of Yorkshire members from the Sheffield area were collected from *White's Directory of Sheffield and Rotherham, 1919–20, 40th Edition* (London: Kelly's Directories, n.d.) and *Kelly's Directory of Sheffield and Rotherham, 1940, 60th Edition* (London: Kelly's Directories, n.d.).
17. Names of committee members were collected from the annual handbooks or annual reports of the Lancashire, Kent, Nottinghamshire, Surrey, Sussex, Worcestershire and Yorkshire clubs. Biographical details were collected from *Who Was Who, Who's Who of Cricketers, Wisden Book of Obituaries* and *Directory of Directors*.
18. *Sunday Chronicle*, 18 May 1924.
19. Interviews with Messrs T. Blackburn (retired tannery operative), B. Simpson (retired teacher), N. Wilcock (retired glass manufacturers' invoice clerk, later departmental manager) and Sir Robert Southern (retired bank official).
20. *Athletic News*, 27 May 1929.
21. Yorkshire Cricket Federation minute book, 11 July 1929, West Yorkshire Archive Service acc. 2772.
22. *Buff*, 22 Feb. 1930.
23. Ibid., 30 Jan. 1937.
24. Ibid., 27 Oct. 1928; Westhoughton CC minute book, 17 Aug. 1931, 22 Nov. 1932, 9 Jan. 1933, Westhoughton CC.
25. Yorkshire Cricket Federation minute book, 8 Oct. 1937, 25 Oct., 15 Nov. 1938.
26. F. Root, *A Cricket Pro's Lot* (London: Arnold, 1937), p. 185.
27. *Athletic News*, 15 Dec. 1919.
28. Kent CCC Managing Committee minute book, 10 Nov. 1920, Kent County Record Office Ch 75 A3/4.
29. *Buff*, 5 March 1921.
30. *Athletic News*, 20 Feb. 1922.
31. Yorkshire Cricket Federation minute book, 11 July 1929, 16 June 1931, 26 Jan., 28 June 1932.
32. *Rochdale Observer*, 31 July 1920.
33. J.A. Williams, 'Cricket and Society in Bolton between the Wars', Lancaster University unpublished PhD thesis (1992), pp. 165–7, 198–9.
34. R. Cavanagh, *Cotton Town Cricket: The Centenary Story of Lancashire's Oldest Cricket League* (n.p., n.d.), p. 127; annual issues of *The Bolton and District Cricket Association Handbook* (n.p., n.d.).
35. *Buff*, 11 Jan. 1933.
36. Bolton Cricket League minute book, 13 Dec. 1929, 10 Jan. 1930, Bolton Cricket League.
37. *Walkden and District Amateur Cricket League Handbook for 1910* (n.d., n.p.), p. 1.
38. E.J. Hester, E. Ward and L.E. Perry, *Horwich Churches Welfare League 1922–1972* (n.p., n.d.), pp. 18, 20.
39. J. Hill, 'League Cricket in the North and Midlands, 1900–1940', in R. Holt, ed., *Sport and the Working Class in Modern Britain* (Manchester: Manchester UP, 1990), pp. 131–2.

40. *Athletic News*, 24 Feb. 1919.
41. J. Hill, 'League Cricket', pp. 128–9.
42. Heaton CC minute book, 14 Dec. 1920, 22 Jan. 1924, Heaton CC.
43. J. Hill, 'League Cricket', pp. 124, 128.
44. J.A. Williams, 'Cricket and Society in Bolton', p. 93.
45. J. Hill, 'League Cricket', p. 131.
46. *Egerton Cricket Club Souvenir Brochure 1864–1989*, (n.p., n.d.); Little Hulton CC minute book, Little Hulton CC; *The Colliery Yearbook and Coal Trades Directory 1931* (London: Louis Cassier, 1931); G. Cleworth, *Cricket at Eagley: The Story of Eagley Cricket Club, 1837–1987* (n.p., n.d.), p. 15.
47. J. Hill, 'League Cricket', pp. 124–5.
48. J.A. Williams, 'Cricket and Society in Bolton', pp. 97–9, 142.
49. *London and Southern Club Cricket Conference: Annual Handbook and Directory... 1923* (Wimbledon: LSCCC, London and Southern Cricket Conference, 1923), pp. 22–3. The permission of the Club Cricket Conference to use this quotation is acknowledged.
50. The respondent who made this observation does not wish to be identified.
51. *Field*, 17 July 1915.
52. *Sussex Express*, 11 Dec. 1925, 15 Oct. 1926.
53. H.F. Squire and A.P. Squire, *Henfield Cricket Club and Its Sussex Cradle* (Hove: Combridges, 1949), pp. 171–2.
54. *London and Southern Club Cricket Conference Annual Handbook ... 1923,* p. 18.
55. *The Times*, 30 Sept. 1927, 1 Feb. 1933; *The Official Annual Handbook of the Club Cricket Conference ... 1939* (Wimbledon: CCC, 1939).
56. *Athletic News*, 13 May 1929; *Buff,* 10 Feb. 1934.
57. *The Times*, 2 Feb. 1929.
58. Ibid., 7 May 1931.
59. Ibid., 22 Nov., 19 Dec. 1934.
60. Ibid., 8, 11 Jan. 1936.
61. *The Cricketer Spring Annual, 1933* (London: Cricketer Syndicate, n.d.), p. 54.
62. M. Tate, *My Cricketing Reminiscences* (London: Stanley Paul, 1934), p. 119.
63. *Daily Mail*, 18 June 1934.
64. E. Barker, *National Character and the Factors in its Formation* (London: Methuen, 1927), p. 130.
65. P. Trevor, *Cricket and Cricketers*, p. 20.

3

Interest in Cricket

The extensive interest in cricket was a major reason why cricket was regarded as a totem of Englishness between the wars. The numbers playing cricket were higher than those playing any other team sport except association football and in some localities more played cricket than football. Far more paid to watch association football than cricket, but it is likely that the numbers of cricket spectators compared favourably with other team sports and except for test matches were higher than those who watch cricket in the 1990s. Those who played cricket were probably drawn from a wider spectrum of society than any other team sport in England. Whilst much more research needs to be undertaken into the social composition of the following for sports in the 1920s and 1930s, impressionistic evidence suggests that the social ambience of association football and rugby league was very largely working-class, whereas rugby union in most of England was a sport of the better-off. Cricket was as much a sport of the upper and middle classes as, say, croquet, real tennis or golf, but unlike them, it was also a sport with an extensive working-class following.

THE PLAYING OF CRICKET

It is not clear even to the nearest 100,000 how many played cricket regularly in England between the wars. No reliable estimate of the numbers playing cricket appears to have been made and unlike association football or rugby union, cricket had neither national nor county associations with which clubs and players had to be registered. Crude indications of the maximum number who played for teams composed primarily of adults can be obtained by considering localities where much cricket was played. Radcliffe, an urban district in Lancashire situated between the county boroughs of Bolton and Bury, had an unusually high number of teams in relation to its population. In 1931 its population was 31,000 and 28 teams from there played each week. Had the same proportion of the national population played as did in Radcliffe, nearly 420,000 would have played cricket each week throughout England in 1931. However, as the ratio of teams to population in Radcliffe was exceptionally high, the numbers playing each week throughout England must have been less than 420,000. Much cricket was played in Bolton and its surroundings, which included Radcliffe but also localities with only one or two teams, but had the game been played to the same extent throughout England, in 1931 the number playing each week in the whole country would have been around 200,000.[1] Around 300 teams, excluding those which took part in the internal competitions of firms, played each week in Birmingham in 1931, but had cricket been played on the same scale throughout England, that number would have been about 120,000. Calculations based on the predominantly rural county of Herefordshire, hardly ever described as a stronghold of cricket playing, show that 240,000 could have been playing each week nationally in 1931. In 1937 a representative of the Club Cricket Conference estimated that 5,000 cricket matches were held each Saturday in London and the South, but provided no details of how great an area he took London and the South to cover, nor did he explain how such a number had been obtained.[2] If this figure of 5,000 matches was accurate and referred to all the LCC area plus the rest of the four Home Counties, which was from where the vast majority of clubs affiliated to the CCC were drawn, then about 380,000 would have played cricket each week nationally had cricket been played to the same extent throughout England. It is probably safe to say that at the mid-point between the wars the numbers playing cricket each week would have been between 100,000 and 400,000. These calculations refer to the playing of cricket by males and ignore schools cricket. Chapter 5 discusses how many women played cricket.

In most districts the numbers of teams primarily for adults were rising during the 1920s, but this trend did not continue for all the regions in the 1930s. Between 1933 and 1939 the number of clubs affiliated to the Club Cricket Conference from Essex increased from 112 to 159 and from Surrey from 208 to 344, which would seem to support a claim made by *The Cricketer* in 1936 that the expansion of London had encouraged the playing of cricket.[3] In 1934 *The Daily Mail* reported that village cricket was 'in danger of decay' and that the average age of players in village teams in Kent, Hampshire, Surrey, Sussex and Yorkshire was rising, whilst more were playing in the towns,[4] but the number of teams mentioned by *The Sussex Express,* whose coverage of cricket remained equally detailed across the inter-war period, rose from 83 in 1930 to over 170 in 1939, and by no means all of this increase occurred in the coastal towns. In the North,

Barnsley, Bolton, Burnley, Halifax, Oldham, St Helens, Sunderland and Wigan and their surroundings all had more teams playing in 1930 than in 1922 or 1939, but only the Barnsley and Burnley areas had more teams in 1922 than in 1939.[5] The number of teams playing in each inter-war season have been counted for Bolton and its surroundings. 1931 and 1933, when 180 teams played each week, were the seasons with the highest numbers of teams. The number of teams rose from 77 in 1919 to 148 in 1923, but then fell slightly in 1924 and 1925 before steadying around 165 from 1926 to 1929. The numbers in 1930 and 1932 approached 170, and dropped from 165 in 1934 to 140 in 1938; 143 teams were playing in 1939.[6]

The greatest number of cricket clubs was in London and its surroundings and the industrial towns of the North and Midlands and their surroundings. Affiliations to the Club Cricket Conference are a rough guide to the numbers of clubs in the Home Counties. By 1939, 430 clubs from Middlesex, 344 from Surrey, 215 from Kent and 159 from Essex had affiliated with the Club Cricket Conference. Most ran more than one team, the 159 clubs from Essex having a total of 400 teams. As membership of the Conference was not open to clubs playing in leagues, these numbers underestimate the extent of cricket played in the Home Counties, though league cricket was not strong in the south-east, and some clubs playing at the humblest levels of club cricket in those areas were probably not affiliated to the Club Cricket Conference.[7] Localised data show that large numbers played in Yorkshire; 272 teams from the area covered by Bradford, Pudsey and Shipley were playing in 1930 and 288 in 1935. The county boroughs and the immediate surroundings of Barnsley, Doncaster and Halifax had more than a hundred teams playing each week in 1930. In Lancashire the county boroughs of Bolton, Burnley and Oldham and their surroundings were strongholds of cricket playing. In 1930, 168 teams were playing each week in the Bolton area, 145 in Burnley and 169 in Oldham. Other parts of Lancashire did not support so many teams. In 1930 fewer than 50 teams were playing each week in both the St Helens and the Wigan areas, whose populations were about equal to that of Burnley and its surroundings. Because their sporting newspapers did not always provide a detailed coverage of the lower levels of recreational sport, the strength of cricket playing in very large northern cities such as Liverpool and Manchester is unclear, but *The Sports Argus* shows that the number of teams other than those playing in the internal competitions of firms in Birmingham was around 200 in 1922, 300 in 1930 and over 320 in 1939.

In Lancashire localities with the highest ratios of cricket teams to population were urban districts or the smaller municipal boroughs, but the numbers of teams could vary considerably even between neighbouring localities. In 1931 Farnworth and Radcliffe, urban districts situated close to Bolton, with populations of around had broadly similar industrial structures 30,000, and both supported clubs playing at high levels of league cricket, but the total number of teams from Radcliffe was 28 and 13 in Farnworth. The ratio of cricket teams to population in many rural localities compared favourably with those of urbanised areas. In 1930 only two villages from the rural hinterland of East Sussex did not have a cricket team.[8] About 60 teams were playing in the overwhelmingly rural county of Herefordshire in 1930, which had a population of 112,000. In 1931, although cricket playing was especially strong in the surroundings of Bolton, there were only 39 teams from Bolton county borough which had a population of 177,000.

The proportion of teams playing with poor facilities was greater between the wars than today. The most humble forms of cricket playing in much of the urban North and Midlands were church and Sunday school leagues. Outfields of some clubs in the Radcliffe Sunday School League were so rough that there was a special rule that not more than four runs could be run when the ball became lost in the long grass of an outfield without having crossed the boundary.[9] It has been mentioned in Chapter 2 that some clubs in Burnley and St Helens played on shale or cinder wickets. Facilities could be equally primitive in other areas. Henfield, a Sussex Wealden village club, was described as having 'a cow ridden outfield … in the winter of 1934, cattle could be seen up to their knees in the bog on the eastern side of the ground'.[10] The ground of the Coldharbour village club in Surrey measured only 58 yards by 35 yards.[11] Cricket could not be played without bats, balls and wickets, but at some levels of cricket pads were a luxury. On a Sunday at Regents Park in London in 1922, there were matches where no players wore pads, those where some had one pad and others where all players were properly equipped.[12] At the lower levels of cricket not all players wore whites. In 1925 *The Times* declared that nearly every village team would have one player without white flannels,[13] an observation borne out by photographs of village teams in *The Sussex Express*. In the 1920s these usually showed at least two to four players in dark trousers. Oral evidence from Lancashire shows that in the 1920s some playing for Sunday school teams did not have whites, though by the late 1930s almost all playing at even the lowest levels of league cricket in Lancashire wore whites, but in industrial districts white trousers were sometimes made from white overalls.[14]

Precise statistics of the number playing association football each week are scarce, but local studies suggest that for most of the inter-war period more played football than cricket. In 1937, 35,000 clubs were affiliated to the Football Association.[15] If half of them had run two teams, nearly 580,000 would have been playing for them each week. How many football clubs were not affiliated to the Football Association or its county associations is not known. Local newspapers indicate that in parts of the industrial North a sharp drop in the number of football teams in the late 1930s meant that the numbers of cricket teams exceeded or nearly equalled those playing football. Local newspapers suggest that the numbers of cricket teams were usually at least double those playing hockey or either rugby code.

FACTORS INFLUENCING THE PLAYING OF CRICKET

Identifying the social backgrounds of those who played cricket is the first step in establishing what factors influenced the extent of cricket playing. Localised data suggest that many who played cricket were working class. Backgrounds of players in the Bolton area seem likely to have been typical of other industrialised areas. Most had blue-collar occupations, often requiring a measure of skill, but a fair number of clerks and other white-collar workers who could perhaps be called lower middle class also played. Teams of factory or colliery clubs usually consisted of blue-collar workers, office workers and often one or two managers. Newspaper photographs of teams from rural areas such as East Sussex suggest that those wearing dark trousers would have been working class. Annual subscriptions of three shillings at Uckfield CC and three shillings and sixpence at Chailey CC, two Sussex village clubs, could probably have been afforded by working men.[16]

There were many clubs whose members belonged to the wealthier classes. Practically all public schools had Old Boys' clubs, whilst other clubs had players drawn predominantly from the public schools. Many who played for the Liverpool Competition clubs on Merseyside, for instance, had attended public schools. The greatest number of clubs for those from the upper and middle classes were in the south-east, reflecting perhaps the distribution of wealth in England. Until the mid-1930s the annual handbooks of the Club Cricket Conference stated the subscriptions charged by more than half its affiliated clubs. In 1933 at least 25 of the 112 clubs from Essex affiliated with the Club Cricket Conference and 42 of the 208 from Surrey had subscriptions of at least 30 shillings which probably meant that their members belonged to the wealthier classes. Throughout England all towns seem to have had at least one club which was regarded locally as being primarily for the local social and economic elite. In the Bolton area, Bolton CC and Worsley CC were perceived as 'gentlemen's clubs'. In the 1930s players of Bolton CC had usually attended minor public schools or grammar schools and were employed in family businesses or the

49

professions, though the club did have three or four players with blue-collar occupations who had been invited into the club to boost its playing strength.[17]

Apologists for cricket often contended that the teams of rural villages reflected the full range of local society. Reports upon village cricket in Kent, Surrey and Sussex written in 1931 by Arthur Gilligan, the former captain of Sussex and England, for *The News Chronicle* show that some village sides did include those with occupations from different levels of the middle and working classes, though it is possible that these teams were reported on because they contained those from a wide variety of backgrounds. Occupations of some of those playing in seven matches included a colonel, an accountant, an income tax collector, four schoolmasters, including one teaching at a public school, three bank clerks, a dentist, an electrical engineer, an author, an estate agent, a borough surveyor, three farmers, two clerics, two publicans and two auctioneers. The working-class occupations included four painters, six gardeners, three labourers, four factory workers, two bricklayers, two carpenters, a wheelwright, a chauffeur and an airman.[18]

The impact of economic factors upon the extent of cricket playing varied between regions. The increase in the numbers of clubs affiliated to the Club Cricket Conference and in those from rural East Sussex may have been related to rising levels of prosperity, especially among the wealthier classes and usually associated with much of the south-east between the wars. In the north of England real wages for most groups of workers except those from the cotton and coal industries rose modestly in the 1920s and 1930s, though unemployment caused great hardship. High levels of unemployment were experienced in much of the industrial North between 1930 and 1934, but in the Bolton area the number of teams playing in 1931 and 1933 made them among the highest of all inter-war seasons. The number of teams playing regularly in later 1930s, when real wages were a little higher and unemployment lower, dropped slightly. Oral evidence from the Bolton area shows that recreational cricketers who became unemployed did not usually stop playing, though unemployment may have deterred some from taking up the game. Collections for meritorious performances, possibly illicit payments for playing and perhaps an offer of employment at works with teams may have been economic inducements for talented cricketers to continue playing. Tending the grounds of their clubs was one way in which unemployed cricketers passed their time in the Bolton area.[19] In 1936 the MCC allowed Lord's to be used for the final of a cricket competition for teams of the unemployed.[20] Presumably this was a competition for the unemployed in the London area. Newspaper references to teams for the unemployed in other areas are scarce, though a team of miners from Kearsley near Bolton who were not working because of the coal strike formed themselves into a team which won the medal competition of Farnworth Social Circle CC in 1926.[21]

Playing at the lower levels of cricket was not expensive. Even small clubs provided bats, balls, pads and possibly gloves. Subscriptions at the more humble levels of cricket cost little. The growing number of cricket clubs based on workplaces increased the opportunities of working men to play. Playing cricket for works clubs was usually very cheap. Workplaces with large numbers of employees, such as collieries or engineering works, often had recreation clubs to which all or nearly all employees paid weekly subscriptions of only a few pence deducted from their wages and which management often subsidised. The standard of cricket facilities provided by works recreation clubs was often very high. Between 1922 and 1939 the number of works teams playing in the Bolton area rose from five to 31, from two to 21 in Burnley, from three to 24 in Halifax and from 21 to 38 in Sunderland. In 1922, 20 teams played in the Birmingham Works Cricket League. By 1939, 56 teams were playing in its eight divisions and 54 in the six divisions of the Birmingham Business Houses Cricket Association. Similar increases in the number of works teams did not occur in all industrial areas. In 1922 and 1939 only one works club played each week in Oldham and its surroundings.[22] In some coalfields colliery sport facilities were provided out of the Miners' Welfare Fund which was financed by a levy on coal production. In the 1930s the Mansfield area of the Nottinghamshire coalfield had a cricket league solely for colliery teams. In 1925, 15 of the first hundred mentioned in an alphabetical listing of clubs affiliated to the London and Southern Counties Club Cricket Conference, which were almost all from the Home Counties, were workplace clubs. By 1939, 95 of the 430 affiliated clubs from Middlesex but only 22 of the 157 clubs from Essex were workplace clubs. Many of these works clubs from Middlesex were of firms whose employees nearly all had white-collar jobs. The number of workplace clubs mentioned by *The Sussex Express* rose from seven in 1922 to 18 in 1939. Some very large firms had their own internal interdepartmental cricket competitions. In the early 1930s at least 14 teams played in the cricket competition of the BSA engineering concern in Birmingham, whilst ten teams played in the interdepartmental cricket league of Pilkington Brothers in St Helens. In some areas clubs which appeared to be open clubs had such close ties with some clubs that they were in effect workplace clubs. Mass-Observation commented in the late 1930s that the connections between Eagley CC in Lancashire and the Eagley Mills were so intimate that promising cricketers were offered employment at the mill.[23] Chapter 7 discusses the strength of church cricket teams at the lower levels of recreational cricket in the north of England and to a lesser extent the Midlands. In much of the North the playing of cricket for church clubs was encouraged by assumptions that churches were the social institutions onto which cricket clubs should be grafted, but at the same time the church presence within recreational cricket tended to restrict the playing of cricket to those who felt comfortable in church-related organisations. The expansion of works cricket may have stimulated the playing of cricket by those who did not wish to play for church teams.

The extent of cricket playing owed much to the strength of cricket in local and national culture. Those areas where cricket was played widely between the wars were usually localities where the game had become a significant element in local culture before 1914, although almost everywhere the numbers of cricket teams for most of the inter-war period were higher than in 1914. Counties with the highest numbers of cricket teams were usually those counties which did well in the county championship, but assumptions that county cricket strengthened the desire to play cricket have to be treated with caution. Counties with sides which usually did well in the county championship and where large numbers of teams played recreational cricket were generally the more densely populated counties and the numbers of their teams playing recreational cricket were no greater in relation to population than those found in more thinly populated counties such as Herefordshire. On the other hand, the success of Yorkshire in the county championship seems to have consolidated assumptions that being a Yorkshireman enjoined an interest in cricket and a desire to play it. In Lancashire and Yorkshire the greatest concentrations of cricket playing were centred in those towns and their surroundings where the highest levels of league cricket were played. As early as 1903 *The Nelson Leader* claimed that league cricket had 'infused an extraordinary amount of interest' in cricket in north-east Lancashire. 'In many towns', it argued,

> cricket clubs exist primarily for the amusement of the better classes. Consequently interest is confined to a limited circle, whereas in the case of the League system, where wins count points, and where wins count championships, every one, more or less, is anxious that their town's team should occupy the premier position. This has another effect, viz., making the youths ambitious to occupy a place in the team, and thus the noble pastime is participated in by thousands Saturday after Saturday in our Sunday School leagues.[24]

Most men who played cricket had played first as boys. Interviews have established that boys played knockabout games of cricket but the need for some kind of a bat may have meant that this was played less often than football. Cricket as an organised school sport expanded between the wars. Those who attended public or grammar schools almost certainly played cricket. Cricket playing increased modestly at elementary schools, which the overwhelming majority of working-class boys attended, but its growth varied between localities. In 1926 the LSC Club Cricket Conference declared that only 10 per cent of elementary schoolboys had the chance to play cricket, though this comment may have been restricted to the London area.[25] The publicity given to a scheme started in Oxford in 1921 whereby the university allowed elementary schoolboys to play on college grounds suggests that many elementary schoolboys had no opportunity to play cricket. By 1936 more than a thousand boys were participating in this scheme and college grounds had been used 5,584 times. In 1926, 50 clubs belonging to the Club Cricket Conference began to allow local schoolboys to use their grounds.[26] In Liverpool 63 school teams took part in inter-school competitions organised by the Sports Committee of the Liverpool and District Teachers' Association in 1920. By 1937 the number of teams exceeded 180.[27] In 1919, 51 school teams played in leagues organised by the Manchester Schools' Cricket Association. By 1939 their number had grown to 149.[28] In 1930, 61 schools were playing in the East Sussex Elementary County Cup.[29] No national schools' cricket organisation was established before the Second World War, but in several counties school cricket associations were formed which organised matches between teams representing the elementary schools of different towns. The Lancashire Elementary Schools Cricket Association was set up in 1922 with nine affiliated LEA associations. In 1939 it had 27 affiliated associations. The first match between the associations of Lancashire and Yorkshire was played in 1930.[30] The London Schools' Cricket Association was formed in 1925,[31] although matches between sides representing elementary schools from the east and west sections of south London had been held since the 1890s. Elementary school cricket was not always strong even in localities where much cricket was played by adults. The Bolton and District Schools Association had organised an inter-school football league before 1900 but it established an inter-school knock-out cricket competition only in 1933 and inter-school leagues in 1935.[32] One restriction on the playing of cricket at schools in Bolton, which was probably common in other towns, was the shortage of playing fields. In 1944 only five out of 82 elementary schools in Bolton had playing fields.[33]

CRICKET SPECTATORS

The exact numbers that watched cricket between the wars will never be known. No records of spectator numbers were kept at those levels of cricket where spectators were not charged for watching matches, but oral evidence shows that even the humblest levels of recreational cricket attracted spectators. Matches in the Horwich and Radcliffe Sunday school leagues, the humblest forms of cricket in the neighbourhood of Bolton in Lancashire, were watched by friends and relatives of players and also by those out for an afternoon stroll who paused to watch the cricket.[34] In 1922, the first year that cricket matches were permitted on Sundays in London parks but when no charge could be made for spectators, *The Times* found matches in Regent's Park with 'a few score spectators who are not particular about the finer points of the game' and others which drew 'a real crowd'. One match had 'between six and seven hundred spectators, fifteen deep at some points'. In 1937 *The Times* reported that 5,000 watched the cricket each weekend on Mitcham Green in London.[35] 10,000 watched the final of the Southampton Parks competition in 1933.[36] In 1932, 600 watched a match of the Southborough village team from Kent.[37] Evidence about the numbers watching the highest levels of club cricket is frustratingly scarce. In 1921 during a campaign against the imposition of entertainment duty on cricket club subscriptions, the Chancellor of the Exchequer recognised that some cricket club non-playing members paid subscriptions with no intention of watching matches, which could mean that others did intend to watch.[38] In 1939 the *Worcester Evening News & Times* claimed that the number of spectators who watched the home matches of Hereford CC over a whole season was little more 300.[39] Eton versus Harrow was probably the non-first-class match which attracted the highest number of spectators at Lord's and in some seasons perhaps anywhere in England. In 1922, 17,000 paid at the turnstile to see this match and in 1930 15,700.[40]

Source material about the numbers paying to watch first-class cricket is suprisingly sparse. Most county clubs have not retained statistics of the spectators attending matches but annual balance sheets did record gate receipt income; unfortunately not all counties have a complete set of gate receipts for all inter-war seasons. Gate receipt income, moreover, provides only an approximate guide to the numbers paying to watch matches. The Findlay Commission collected details of gate receipts income and the numbers of paying spectators at all first-team home matches of the county clubs in 1934, 1935 and 1936. These show that one pound of gate receipt income did not represent the same number of spectators at all counties or even at the same counties in different seasons. Matches against the

TABLE 1

NUMBER OF PAYING SPECTATORS ATTENDING THE HOME FIRST ELEVEN MATCHES
OF ALL FIRST-CLASS COUNTIES 1934–36

Season	1934	1935	1936
County			
Derbyshire	82,279	89,585	76,077
Essex	N.A.	75,948	73,801
Glamorgan	68,972	92,038	53,111
Gloucestershire	78,440	52,842	62,230
Hampshire	77,749	57,325	79,251
Kent	113,922	97,410	74,505
Lancashire	107,999	87,650	93,094
Leicestershire	44,980	47,175	31,795
Middlesex	120,536	67,226	110,532
Northamptonshire	37,230	30,429	25,540
Nottinghamshire	65,145	72,749	73,882
Somerset	49,447	55,931	64,170
Surrey	162,923	128,914	129,940
Sussex	102,067	78,759	68,447
Warwickshire	80,762	86,853	38,670
Worcestershire	50,722	34,067	33,932
Yorkshire	177,155	175,790	153,383
Total	1,338,049	1,330,691	1,242,360

Source: Findlay Commission, Schedule VII.[41]

Australians usually attracted high attendances and counties often doubled the price of admission to them. In 1934, the year of an Australian tour and a dry summer which encouraged the watching of cricket, one pound of gate receipt income represented 23.2 spectators for Derbyshire but only six for Nottinghamshire. One pound of gate receipt income represented fewer than ten paying spectators for seven counties in 1934 and for ten counties in 1936.

Table 1 records the numbers of playing spectators attending the first-class matches played by all counties between 1934 and 1936. Table 2 shows how many attended the home matches of Yorkshire except those played at Scarborough between the wars, and those of Kent from 1923, and all matches played at Lord's from 1922 which, in addition to test matches, the first-class matches of the MCC and of Middlesex, the University match and sometimes the Gentlemen versus Players game, included some non first-class matches.

Table 3 records fluctuations in gate receipt income for Derbyshire, Lancashire, Kent, Northamptonshire, Somerset and Surrey for most inter-

TABLE 2

NUMBER OF PAYING SPECTATORS AT THE HOME MATCHES FOR KENT AND
YORKSHIRE AND FOR LORD'S

Season	Kent	Yorkshire	Lord's
1919		112,603	
1920		199,746	
1921		284,677	
1922		226,747	270,950
1923	109,769	269,451	285,531
1924	91,323	224,656	242,443
1925	122,805	326,239	323,241
1926	137,805	237,662	404,428
1927	112,267	162,519	248,057
1928	143,246	165,451	337,603
1929	122,862	135,619	335,641
1930	112,563	148,651	372,952
1931	104,083	139,160	275,721
1932	121,682	174,032	267,439
1933	117,016	223,650	290,367
1934	114,424	181,086	334,694
1935	96,891	182,604	276,023
1936	79,979	157,364	200,163
1937	87,649	205,207	282,153
1938	111,388	207,768	324,897
1939	95,891	189,047	295,684

Source: Annual handbooks of Kent CCC and Yorkshire CCC, MCC Daily Receipts
books. The Yorkshire figures do not match exactly those for 1934, 1935 and 1936 given
in Table 1 because Table 2 excludes matches at Scarborough but includes some second-
team matches. Table 1 includes first-team matches played at Scarborough but omits
second-team matches. The numbers of spectators given in the annual handbooks of Kent
CCC for 1934, 1935 and 1936 differ slightly from those found in Schedule VII of the
Findlay Commission.

war seasons. Surrey and Lancashire were usually among those with most
spectators, whilst Derbyshire, Northamptonshire and Somerset were
usually among those with less than the average for county clubs. As has
been mentioned, gate receipts are only a crude guide to the number of
paying spectators, but they do give a rough indication of fluctuations in
spectator numbers between seasons. They suggest that more paid to watch
county cricket in the 1920s than in the 1930s and that except for 1938, a
year of an Australian tour, attendances were lower for most counties in the
late 1990s than in the earlier. There was an enormous gulf between the
number of spectators attending the matches of the best and the worst
supported counties. Between 1934 and 1936 Surrey and Yorkshire had at
least five times as many spectators as Northamptonshire.

TABLE 3
FLUCTUATIONS IN GATE RECEIPT INCOME FOR SELECTED COUNTIES

| Season | Income in £s | | | | | |
	Derbyshire	Lancashire	Kent	N'amptonshire	Somerset	Surrey
1919	1,545					
1920	1,643	8,306	10,336	1,823	2,591	
1921	3,546	16,252	14,538	3,474		
1922	2,260		10,711			20,796
1923	3,010	9,794	10,026		2,126	18,687
1924	1,913		9,063	1,881	5,149	18,832
1925	2,825	12,065	10,527	3,298	6,061	20,240
1926	3,514	14,328	12,633	3,641	4,119	16,902
1927	3,129	9,340	8,785	2,160	1,880	10,848
1928	3,626	10,197	11,408	2,551	2,471	16,584
1929	3,889	6,887	10,744	2,549	2,548	10,285
1930	3,326	6,696	9,969	3,544	3,744	9,397
1931	2,756	6,205	8,141	1,940	1,934	7,408
1932	3,019	6,151	8,993	1,800	2,871	11,891
1933	3,874	6,245	9,096	2,479	2,396	10,225
1934	3,552	5,040	9,295	2,371	3,826	13,347
1935	2,944	4,115	7,968	1,662	3,470	9,080
1936	3,090	3,887	6,466	1,383	3,886	7,504
1937	3,152	4,693	5,916	1,579	3,669	9,302
1938	3,262	8,813	8,538	2,079	4,846	11,225
1939	2,982	6,075	6,130	3,601		8,068

Note: These statistics are derived from statements of gate receipt revenue provided in annual balance sheets. It is not always clear whether they include sums paid in entertainment duty or the proportion of gate income paid to touring sides.

No counties appear to have kept records of how many members attended matches. Members were admitted to matches free and usually could be accompanied by a guest who was also admitted free. Balance sheets did not include members' subscriptions in gate receipts. Table 4 shows that the numbers of members varied between clubs, though not so much as gate receipts. What is not clear is how often members and their guests attended matches. In the seasons immediately after the First World War the numbers of members attending matches regularly may not have been great. The secretary of Lancashire CCC estimated in 1919 that only 5 per cent of members watched all a county's matches.[42] In 1920 *Athletic News* claimed that many members 'support their county club simply because they consider it their duty to do so. Many of them will never visit the ground to see a match. They merely give an order to their banker to pay a certain sum annually into the club's account and perhaps think nothing more of the

TABLE 4
NUMBER OF MEMBERS OF SELECTED COUNTY CLUBS 1919–39

Year	Derby	Essex	Kent	Lancs	Surrey	Sussex	Yorks
1919	900		2,971	1,849		1,313	1,400
1920	1,000	1,493	3,648	2,744	2,860	1,785	2,100
1921	1,100	1,734	4,461	3,643		2,577	5,300
1922	1,200	870	3,239	3,611	4,500	2,286	5,600
1923	1,300	1,440	3,345	4,509	4,400	2,593	6,100
1924	1,300	1,753	3,260	4,598	4,400	2,643	7,100
1925	1,500	2,538	3,299	5,016	4,500	2,753	7,500
1926	· 1,600	2,916	3,567	6,600	4,500	3,408	8,100
1927	1,800	2,677	3,638	5,000	4,900	3,283	7,600
1928	2,100	2,726	3,771	5,097	4,700	3,496	7,100
1929	2,100	2,651	3,824	5,258	4,700	3,355	6,700
1930	2,300	2,323	3,809	5,620	4,700	3,500	6,800
1931	2,200	2,240	3,694	4,738	4,400	3,441	6,200
1932	2,000	1,943	3,451	4,032	4,200	3,161	5,800
1933	2,000	1,825	3,398	4,384	4,000	3,212	6,000
1934	2,150	2,343	3,663	4,923	4,316	3,543	6,356
1935	2,123	2,284	3,490	4,689	4,125	3,324	6,403
1936	2,220	2,308	3,450	4,649	5,465	3,518	6,592
1937	2,200	2,426	3,284	4,497	5,000	3,249	6,400
1938	2,230	2,650	3,174	5,179	5,200	3,393	6,700
1939	2,100	2,560	3,166	4,883	4,700	3,181	6,200

Source: Annual balance sheets of county clubs, Findlay Commission, Schedules I, V. Estimated numbers are based on statements of membership revenue. From 1923 the figures for Lancashire include women members.

matter.'[43] In 1922, when protesting about the burden of entertainment tax upon county cricket, Francis Lacey, the MCC secretary, explained that the pavilions of most counties could accommodate only half their members,[44] which may mean that a very high proportion of members were never expected to be present at one time. Usually the number of members at all counties increased in those seasons when the Australians were touring England, which suggests that some may have taken out membership only to watch the match against Australia. Occasionally large numbers of members did watch matches. In 1920 3,500 members attended one day's play of the Lancashire and Yorkshire match at Old Trafford and possibly around 2,000 and their guests were present on the first day of the Surrey and Kent match.[45] In 1938 nearly 24,000 members and their guests attended the test match against Australia at Leeds, and 13,000 that at The Oval.[46] In 1934 the total number of members for all first-class counties was just under 51,000. If on average each member had attended five days' play in 1934, and there is no evidence to suggest that this was the average number of days on which members did attend, this would equal about 20 per cent of the number of paying spectators.

The highest attendances at first-class cricket matches in England between the wars were usually at test matches. The largest number present, including members and those who paid for admission, at an inter-war test match in England was just under 115,000 at the Lord's test match against Australia in 1930. The average number present on each of the four days' play would have been nearly 29,000, though in 1938 as many as 99,614 paid to watch a test match against Australia which lasted only three days, giving an average daily attendance of over 33,000. However, the gate receipts for this match may have included ticket sales for the day on which there was no play. The highest attendance, which included members, their guests and paying spectators, at a county match was 78,617 for the Lancashire and Yorkshire match at Old Trafford in 1926.[47] It was unusual for the total number of paying spectators at a three day county match to exceed 20,000. Yorkshire was always among the best-supported clubs. Between 1920 and 1939 Yorkshire played 221 first-class matches at grounds in Yorkshire other than Scarborough. Only 48 were attended by more than 20,000 paying spectators. Thirty-five of these were in the 1920s and 13 in the 1930s. 54,154 paid to watch Yorkshire's home match against Lancashire in 1925, which was Yorkshire's only home match to attract over 50,000 paying spectators.[48] In the 1920s Durham, one of the minor counties, was able to attract large attendances to its matches against the Australian tourists. In 1926, 8,000 attended the first day of the Australian match and 4,000 the second, attendances which would have been respectable for some first-class counties.[49]

Data from Lancashire indicate the popularity of league cricket in one of its strongholds and suggest that on most Saturdays in this county more would have paid to watch league matches than the home matches of the Lancashire county team. The 14 clubs of the Lancashire League were concentrated within a 20-mile radius of Blackburn. In 1921, 350,794 paid to watch Lancashire League matches and 'about 300,000' in 1922. In 1933 they exceeded 297,000. Between 1924 and 1939, attendances exceeded 200,000 in 12 seasons and never dropped below 172,000.[50] Spectator numbers in the Lancashire League were far higher than those of counties such as Essex and Derbyshire and exceeded those of Lancashire in 1921 and 1922 and from 1929 until 1939. How many members of Lancashire League clubs attended matches is not clear, though for each season between 1921 and 1939 the total number was higher than those of any county club. Their lowest figure was 7,913 in 1931 and the highest 11,660 in 1922. In

1921 and 1922 and from 1934 until 1939 the number of members was above 10,000.[51] The club alone had probably more than 75,000 paying spectators at its home matches in 1929, over 65,000 in 1930 and over 50,000 in 1922, 1932, 1934 and 1935.[52] In 1934 and 1935 paying spectators at the home matches of Nelson were higher than those at the home first-team matches of Leicestershire and Northamptonshire. The highest number of spectators for a Lancashire League match was probably 14,000, at the Worsley Cup tie between Nelson and Colne in 1934.[53]

Other leagues attracted spectator numbers which rivalled those of well-supported counties. Many in Lancashire considered the Central Lancashire League to be the equal of the Lancashire League. In 1921, 8,838 paying spectators and over 400 members attended Rochdale's Central Lancashire League match against Littleborough, which was more than had watched a Lancashire League match to that date.[54] The Daily Mirror claimed that that average match attendances for the Central Lancashire League had been 2,000 in 1937 which, if correct, would have made aggregate match attendances over 330,000,[55] about 80,000 more than the total of paying spectators at Lancashire League matches and at least three times higher than the number of paying spectators at the Lancashire County club. In 1921 about 100,000 paid to watch the matches of the First Division of the Bolton and District Cricket Association, and 1923 and 1927 were the only seasons when fewer than 60,000 paid to watch the matches of this league. In the 1930s spectator numbers for the Bolton League which had been formed when 12 leading clubs seceded from the First Division of the BDCA after the 1929 season, exceeded 50,000 from 1930 to 1934 but fell to 34,000 in 1936, although this was higher than the number who paid to watch all the home matches of Leicestershire in the same season, and nearly 10,000 more than Northamptonshire's paying spectators.[56] In 1919 the number of paying spectators at matches of the Bradford League in Yorkshire was 265,770, more than double the number of paying spectators at Yorkshire CCC's home matches, and 225,000 in 1921.[57] The Daily Mirror believed that 450,000 had watched the 600 matches played by the 55 Yorkshire Council league teams in 1937.[58] This figure may be an exaggeration, but even half of it would be higher than the number of paying spectators at the home matches of Yorkshire CCC in 1937. In the 1920s crowds of 4,000 watched the matches of Old Hill CC of the Birmingham League.[59]

The number of paying spectators attending first-class cricket did not compare favourably with league football or other forms of mass entertainment. In the late 1930s the Reports of the Commissioners of Customs and Excise indicated the volume of receipts from the entertainment tax collected from various forms of entertainment. For the year ending March 1938, admittedly a year when attendances at county cricket were well below the inter-war average, receipts from cricket matches, which were collected from league as well as county clubs, were £20,000, whereas those from cinemas came to £5,400,000 and from theatres and music halls £1,060,000. The receipts for football, which would have included cup-ties, non-league football and Scottish football, were £450,000 and for horse-racing £270,000[60] but as these returns provided figures for no other team ball sports it is probable that only association football attracted more spectators than cricket. Brian Tabner has collected what appear to be reliable statistics of the annual attendances for football league clubs from 1925.[61] These show that from 1925–26 until 1938–39, the attendances at the home league matches of the worst supported first division football club were always at least 60,000 higher than those at the home matches of Yorkshire CCC, one of the best supported county clubs. Between 1925–26 and 1938–39, Ashington FC with just under 35,000 spectators at all home games in 1928–29 was the football league club with the lowest number of spectators attending its home league matches in one season, a figure probably lower than that of all county clubs in 1929. It must be remembered, however, that this is the figure for the worst supported of the 88 football league clubs. Yorkshire's highest number of paying spectators between 1926 and 1939 was 237,000 in 1926. In the 1925–26 season, seven of the 11 football league clubs from Yorkshire each had a higher number of spectators. In 1936 Northamptonshire was the county with the lowest number of paying spectators – 25,540. In the 1935–36 season, over 157,000 paid to watch the Third Division South home matches of Northampton Town FC. If the average number of paying spectators at the league matches of the first-class rugby league clubs had been 2,000 between the wars, which is probably an underestimate, then the total number of paying spectators at the home matches of the rugby league clubs from Lancashire and Yorkshire would have been around half a million in each county, a figure higher than the numbers paying to watch the county cricket matches of Lancashire or Yorkshire but perhaps lower, though not vastly so, than the numbers watching county and league cricket in either county.

The numbers watching cricket between the wars were higher than those paying to watch county championship cricket in recent years. In 1986, 447,702 paid to watch the first-eleven matches, including the one-day competitions, of the county clubs, a figure far below those for the seasons with the lowest attendances between the wars.[62] In 1995, a hot-dry summer, 192,343 paid to watch county championship matches, and even when allowance is made for the smaller number of county championship matches being played in the 1990s, match attendances were lower than in the inter-war seasons.[63] The numbers paying to watch test match cricket, especially against the Australians, compare more favourably with those of the inter-war period, though in the 1920s these test matches lasted for only three days, and for four days in the 1930s. In 1993, 110,802 paid to watch the test match against Australia at Lord's.[64] The numbers paying to watch league cricket in recent decades have been far lower than between the wars. In 1988 a little over 28,000 paid to watch the matches of all the Lancashire League clubs, about a fifth of the number for the inter-war season with the lowest attendance figures. By the early 1990s so few paying spectators were watching matches in the Bolton League that most clubs no longer charged for admission to league matches.

THE SOCIAL BACKGROUND OF CRICKET SPECTATORS

Evidence about the social background of those who paid to watch cricket is not abundant. There is little doubt that the great majority of spectators were adult males, and although women and children watched cricket, it is not clear how their numbers compared with those attending other sports. Chapter 5 shows that women and boys made up between 10 and 20 per cent of the membership at most county clubs.

Large crowds must have included a fair proportion of working men, but except during their holidays it was probably difficult for many men to attend first-class cricket in midweek. Demands of work may also have meant that many middle-class men were able to watch matches only on Saturdays. In fine weather Saturday attendances were usually higher than on other days, but a county would not usually play at home on more than ten Saturdays in one season. The absence of contemporary analyses of spectators at test and county cricket matches makes it difficult to determine to what sector of the working class most spectators belonged or whether there were significant regional and temporal changes in the social composition of cricket crowds. It is likely that the higher cost of grandstand seats meant that these were usually occupied by the upper and middle classes, though some middle-class men may have been content to watch from the popular side of a ground. In 1925 over 13 per cent of spectators at Lancashire's home matches paid for admission to the more expensive part of the ground which could mean that at least this percentage of Lancashire's spectators were middle or upper class.[65] Those counties where one pound of gate receipt income represented a relatively high number of paying spectators may have been those with the highest proportion of working-class spectators, though it could also indicate the limited extent of more expensive accommodation at grounds. For the seasons 1934 to 1936 Derbyshire, Essex, Glamorgan and Middlesex were the only counties where one pound of gate receipt income represented at least sixteen spectators. For Northamptonshire it represented only 5.7 spectators, 6.7 for Nottinghamshire and 6.8 for Worcestershire, which may mean that these three counties were those with the lowest proportion of working-class spectators. For Yorkshire, the county with the highest number of paying spectators, one pound of gate receipt income represented nearly 12 paying spectators, but at Surrey, the county with the second highest number of spectators, one pound represented nine spectators. At Lancashire, the county with the third highest number of spectators, the figure is 7.2. Precise sociological data about the nature of football crowds is also scarce, but the great mass of descriptive evidence suggests that most football supporters were working class. There are occasional comments that the working-class presence at first-class cricket was less than at football. William Pollock, who wrote under the pseudonym 'Googly' for *The Sunday Express*, stated that 'The football public is a cloth-capped, fried fish lot … The cricket public is on an altogether higher plane. Cricket attracts the intelligentsia – a word which I hate, but I cannot think of another.'[66]

Detail about the social background of those who paid to watch league cricket is not abundant, but it seems probable that many were working class. The clubs which attracted most spectators were situated in industrial centres with large numbers of blue-collar workers. Playing matches on Saturday afternoons and on midweek evenings meant that they did not trespass upon work time and admission prices of sixpence or eightpence were affordable by many working men. The dress of spectators in photographs of matches indicates that they were usually working men. What is not clear is the section of the working class to which they belonged or whether this varied over time or between localities. Scraps of evidence from Bolton confirm that working men watched league cricket. During the miners' strike of 1926 miners were admitted to matches free.[67] Reports prepared for Mass-Observation on two Bolton League matches in the late 1930s contained little about the social class of the spectators. Seven hundred were present at a match between two clubs at the top of the League. They included about 50 women and 150 boys, with the rest being men of all ages but mostly over 40. Four hundred attended another match. As there were only seven cars parked at the ground, this may have meant that most of those present were working class.[68] In the Bolton area numbers of paying spectators were higher in the 1920s than the 1930s and higher in the late 1930s than the early 1930s which could mean that working-class interest in watching league cricket in this locality was declining between the wars.

The impact of economic trends was more pronounced on watching than on playing cricket. Tables 2 and 3 show that the numbers of paying spectators for well-supported clubs such as Surrey and Yorkshire were lower during the depression in the first half of the 1930s than in the 1920s, although this was not the case to such a marked extent with Derbyshire, a less well-supported county. But a wet summer, such as 1927, could always have dire consequences for gate receipts. The figures for Surrey and Yorkshire improved a little over those of the early 1930s, but did not reach the level of the best years of the 1920s. In the late 1930s there were frequent reports of county cricket facing financial disaster. It would seem that the depression of the early 1930s caused spectator numbers to fall at most clubs, whilst the economic recovery of the late 1930s may have hit attendances by widening access to alternative leisure interests.

Table 4 shows that membership numbers at most county clubs rose modestly in the 1920s which suggests that the gentle rate of economic expansion in most of this decade encouraged more to become county members. In the 1930s membership numbers seem to have been hit by economic hardship: 1930 and 1934, years of Australian tours, had relatively high numbers of members at most counties, but for all counties listed in Table 4 membership numbers in the first half of the 1930s were lower than in the late 1920s. Except for Kent and Northamptonshire, the counties listed in Table 4 recorded slight increases in subscription income in the later 1930s which could mean that the improving economic situation had stimulated membership numbers.

The average number of paying spectators in the Lancashire League between 1924 and 1929 was just below 200,000, whilst that for 1930 to 1935 was over 260,000. At first sight this seems to indicate that the more buoyant economic climate of the late 1920s did less to encourage the watching of league cricket than the depression in the first half of the 1930s, but this view requires qualification. The economies of the towns where Lancashire League clubs were situated were based on the cotton industry and though levels of unemployment were lower in the 1920s than in the 1930s, the real value of wages for cotton workers remained stationary. A further complication was the enormous spectator appeal of the West Indian test match cricketer Learie Constantine who was the professional with the Nelson club from 1929 to 1937. Almost half the gate receipts for the whole of the Lancashire League was taken at matches in which Constantine played. League cricket in the Bolton area reveals a different pattern of spectator numbers. In the 1920s the average seasonal total of paying spectators was 71,000. The seasonal average for the combined numbers of paying spectators for the Bolton League and for the BDCA between 1930 and 1934 was 59,000 and between 1935 and 1938 fell even further to 40,000.[69] These figures seem to show that economic hardship in the early 1930s may have discouraged the watching of league cricket in this area and that limited economic improvement during the late 1930s did nothing to revive it. The number of members for Lancashire League clubs was over 11,500 in 1921 and 1922, but by 1928 had fallen to 8,225: 1931 was the inter-war season with the lowest number of members, just under 8,000, but numbers recovered to over 9,000 in 1932 and 1933, and exceeded 11,000 between 1935 and 1937.[70] It is hard to draw firm conclusions about a relationship between these figures and economic trends. Unfortunately, data about the number of members at the leading league clubs in the Bolton area are not sufficient to support generalisations about the possible impact of economic trends upon membership numbers.

READING ABOUT CRICKET

Apologists for cricket have long maintained that interest in cricket is far greater than the numbers of players and spectators suggest. James Kilburn, who wrote on cricket for *The Yorkshire Post* in the 1930s, claimed that no editors or newspaper publishers 'questioned the significance of cricket among journalistic features ... Cricket was assured of favourable consideration in any competition for space.'[71] The extent of cricket coverage in *The Times* and *The Daily Telegraph* indicates that interest in cricket was widespread among those from the upper and middle classes. No examination of the social background of newspaper readers between the wars seems to have been so comprehensive as that of the first *Hulton Readership Survey* published in 1947.[72] If it is assumed that the social background of readers in the 1930s would not have been vastly different from that in 1947, nearly 70 per cent of the male readers of *The Times* and 50 per cent of *The Telegraph* would have belonged to social classes A and B, who were described as 'the well-to-do' and the middle classes. *The Times* devoted more space over a year to cricket than to any other team ball game, but in part this was because cricket was played six days a week during the summer. Generally, the number of column inches devoted to cricket on any particular day was as extensive or greater than the coverage of association and rugby football on Mondays in winter. Much of the cricket coverage consisted of full scorecards of each day's play in first-class cricket but there were also shorter reports of club and public school cricket. On a daily basis *The Daily Telegraph* gave more coverage to cricket than to other team sports, but during the cricket season, the coverage of horse-racing was approximately equal to that of cricket.

The extent of cricket reporting in the daily newspapers with the largest circulations seems to indicate that interest in cricket was widespread among working-class men. In the 1930s *The Daily Express, The Daily Herald* and *The Daily Mail* accounted for more than half the daily circulation of newspapers.[73] In 1947, 62 per cent of male *Express* readers belonged to social classes D/E, which were defined as the working classes and the poor, compared with 80 per cent of those for *The Herald* and 53 per cent for *The Mail*. During the cricket season *The Daily Express* usually devoted half of one page to cricket, which was about the same as its reporting of racing, but on Mondays during the football season, it was usual for a whole page to be given over to football. Test matches against Australia were often reported on the front page. Over a year the number of column inches devoted to cricket, though this included detailed score cards of county matches, was as great as those for any sport except horse-racing. *The Daily Mail* also gave the full score cards of county matches and devoted as many column inches over a year to cricket as to any other team ball game. During the General Strike of 1926, *The Daily Express* issued some tabloid-size news sheets. Each sheet usually consisted of only four columns and some issues had between a quarter and half a column of county cricket scores, though not full scorecards. This coverage of cricket during a national crisis and when news space was so scarce suggests that the Beaverbrook press believed that there was strong public interest in cricket and that cricket was sufficiently important for it to be reported at such a time. During the summer months *The Daily Herald*'s daily reporting of cricket covered more column inches than all other ball sports combined except during Wimbledon or the Open Golf Championship. Reports of test matches often made the front page, though they were rarely the main front page story. On many days horse-racing was given more space than cricket. By the end of the 1930s *The Daily Herald* had two pages of football reporting on Mondays, but much less on other days, and usually one page of cricket on each day during the summer. While *The Daily Herald* does suggest a widespread working-class interest in cricket, it reveals little about whether levels of interest varied between sections of the working class.

The Daily Mirror on the other hand indicates that working-class interest in cricket may not have been very extensive. In 1930 its share of total newspaper circulation was over 12 per cent and 13 per cent in 1937; in 1947, 74 per cent of its male readers were from classes D/E.[74] In 1921, a year of an Australian tour to England, coverage of sport in *The Daily Mirror* was not extensive. On most days there was only one page of sport reporting, but photographs of sport appeared on other pages. It printed photographs of cricket almost every day during the summer but usually provided a full scorecard of only one county match and merely the innings totals of other matches. In 1938, another Australian tour season, *The Daily Mirror* gave full scorecards usually only for the Australian matches and only the innings totals for county championship games. Its coverage of cricket was far less than that of horse-racing, less than that of speedway and usually about as extensive as that for greyhound-racing. *Athletic News* was perhaps England's closest equivalent to a weekly general sports newspaper, but as it was published in Manchester, its circulation may have been strongest in the North. It devoted more space to professional football than other sports, which suggests that its readership was primarily working class, and as its coverage of cricket was second only to association football, this can perhaps be interpreted as further evidence of a working-class interest in cricket. Its closure in 1930 does not seem to have reflected a decline in the desire to read about sport. Its collapse coincided with popular newspapers increasing their coverage of sport.

The extent of cricket coverage in *The Sporting Chronicle*, the daily horse-racing newspaper, also seems to indicate a working-class desire to read about cricket. Although betting on horses was not exclusively a working-class pastime, estimates about scale of illegal off-course prepaid betting suggest that many of those who read *The Sporting Chronicle* would have been working class. In the summer of 1926, each issue of *The Sporting Chronicle* usually consisted of six pages, with four devoted to horse-racing. Usually between half and one page was concerned with first-class cricket with one column on league cricket in Monday editions. In 1938, the size of each issue had grown to eight pages. Four were concerned with horse-racing and at least one half page with cricket. In the summers of both years the coverage of cricket usually exceeded that for other ball sports except during the Wimbledon or the Open Golf Championships. In 1938 daily cricket coverage was about equal to that for greyhound-racing.

Sample inspections of evening newspapers from the big cities also indicate that over a year the reporting of cricket often occupied more column inches than any other team sport, but of course the fact that county cricket was played six days a week meant that there was almost always cricket news to be reported in the summer. Some Saturday sports editions of evening newspapers incorporated the word 'cricket' in their titles. That of *The Bradford Evening Argus* was called *The Yorkshire Sports and Cricket Argus*, but *The Liverpool Football Echo,* which had appeared throughout the summer and contained much cricket material, ceased to appear during the summer in 1932. In many Saturday sports specials the coverage of football in the summer issues was usually more extensive than the reporting of cricket during the football season. Weekly or twice weekly local newspapers in towns with no local daily or evening newspapers also gave extensive coverage to cricket, though this varied between localities. In Lancashire *The Burnley Express* and *The Radcliffe Times*, newspapers from towns where relatively large numbers played and watched cricket, the reporting of football during the summer was more extensive than the reporting of cricket during the football season, but in the summer more column inches were devoted to cricket than to football during the winter months. The two weekly newspapers in St Helens, where playing cricket was less popular, did not devote as much space to cricket in the summer as they did to rugby league and association football in the winter. Their reporting of rugby league in particular during the summer was always greater than their reporting of cricket in winter.

There was no daily cricket or football equivalent to *The Sporting Chronicle*. There was sufficient interest to sustain *The Cricketer*, started by Pelham Warner in 1921, as a weekly publication during the cricket season. Its extensive coverage of public school and club cricket in the South in addition to first-class cricket, suggests that it appealed mainly to those from the upper and middle classes. Whilst it must be recognised that news about cricket may not have been the major reason for buying newspapers and that printing score cards may have been easy or cheap methods of filling column inches, newspapers were commercial undertakings. Their survival depended on selling copies. It seems improbable that so many editors would have given such extensive coverage to cricket had they not believed that many of their readers wished to read about cricket. The extent of cricket reporting seems to confirm that interest in cricket was greater than the numbers of cricket spectators would indicate.

More books were published between the wars about cricket than any other team ball game. Whilst little is known about which cricket books sold most copies, the number of titles alone suggests that the desire to read about cricket exceeded that of other sports, which in itself indicates the cultural significance accorded to cricket. The demand for books of cricket statistics grew modestly. At least ten cricket annuals were published, but none ever seemed likely to rival the status of *Wisden* as the major statistical work concerned with cricket. Before 1914 the Hampshire, Kent, Somerset, Surrey and Yorkshire county clubs issued annual handbooks which included the full scores of all their matches and by 1939 all first-class counties except Middlesex had similar volumes. Test match cricket was the form of cricket about which most books were written, but there were less than 50 of these and nearly all of them were about test matches against Australia. Padwick's bibliography of cricket records nearly 30 autobiographies written by cricketers between the wars, whilst Cox's bibliography of British sport[75] shows that only one soccer player and one rugby union player who were not also cricketers, wrote autobiographies or had biographies written about them between the wars, though receiving royalties for an autobiography could have caused rugby union players to be banned from the game. No biography or autobiography of a rugby league player seems to have been published in the 1920s and 1930s. Some highly popular cricketers, such as Wilfred Rhodes, Percy Chapman and Walter Hammond did not write autobiographies before the Second World War.

There is only indirect evidence about the social backgrounds of those who read books about cricket. Over 60 books were published about coaching and presumably these would have been read by those who played cricket or possibly by parents or teachers who wanted to help children to become better players. Most interest seems to have been in the contemporary cricket scene, but five general histories of cricket and histories of 11 counties were published, though *Wisden* and the county handbooks had collections of records and statistics which were a form of cricket history. Only eight novels in which cricket was the major theme were published for adults, but Padwick lists over 170 novels for children in which cricket was an important if not the major theme. Many of these were based on public schools, but the enormous popularity of *The Magnet,* the weekly magazine of boarding school fiction in which Billy Bunter was the main hero, may mean that these books were not necessarily read by those who attended public schools. It is also likely that such books may have been bought by adults for children who imagined that these were the sort of books which children ought to have read. The fact that two ghosted children's novels supposedly written by Jack Hobbs were issued in the 1920s shows a belief that the fame of one professional cricketer, which in part rested upon his reputation as the personification of cricket's spirit of fair play, could help to sell books. Cricket was a key element in these two novels which had a public school setting.

Nearly a dozen books which dealt with cricket as part of the English scene were published. Only three collections of cricket poems were published between the wars, but about 20 collections of poetry which included cricket poems were issued and many of these were concerned with cricket as an expression of English life and character. Much literary critical acclaim was lavished on the cricket books of Neville Cardus: all four, in which cricket as an assertion of Englishness was a recurring theme, were reprinted between the wars, which suggests that the readership for what were thought to be well-written books about cricket was as extensive as the readership for most categories of cricket books. If reading or buying books between the wars are thought to have been habits primarily of the middle and upper classes, and such a generalisation is obviously open to challenge, then the number of cricket books would confirm a general interest in cricket among these classes, but this does not mean that there was no working-class demand for books about cricket.

The most obvious explanation of why the number of cricket books exceeded those of other sports is that this reflected interest in cricket, but to explain why interest in cricket took this form is more difficult. Many of those who read about cricket may have received a secondary education, but this was also the case with rugby union and golf about which less was written. The praise heaped on Cardus for the quality of his prose and the occasional writings on cricket of such literary figures as J.M. Barrie, Edmund Blunden, Conan Doyle, Alec Waugh and Hugh de Selincourt probably helped to create a belief that cricket writing was superior to that on other sports and may have added to its attractions among those who considered themselves educated. The status accorded to cricket as an expression of English character and moral worth may have encouraged reading about cricket. *Cricket* by Neville Cardus was first published in 1930 as part of the Longmans Green English Heritage Series edited by Sir John Squire. The other titles in this series included *The English Constitution, Shakespeare, The Face of England, The English Inn, London, The English Public School, English Music, The English Country Town, The English Parish Church, English Humour, The English Adventurers, English Folk Song and Dance* and *Fox-hunting*. Assumptions about cricket being an essential aspect of the rustic scene and the strength of the tradition of English pastoral poetry possibly contributed to the writing of cricket verse. For those with affectionate memories of their public schools, the central role of cricket in public school life may have created a desire to read about the game.

Reading about cricket may have been a substitute for watching first-class cricket. Test matches were staged at only six grounds between the wars and for many travelling to these venues would have been difficult. Only eight county championship matches can have been held at any one time. No county can normally have played at home on more than ten Saturdays in a season and many spectators may have had difficulty in attending county matches on more than one or two days each year. To some extent the moral status accorded to cricket may have caused book publishers to issue cricket books, but as publishing was a commercial undertaking, it seems unlikely that so many would have been published had there not been a reasonably strong supposition that the demand to read about cricket was sufficiently strong to guarantee a profit. The extent of cricket literature, while hard to explain, was without parallel in other sports and was, in itself, a major reason why cricket was regarded as more than a game.

NOTES

1. For the number of teams playing in Bolton county borough and its surroundings, see J.A. Williams, 'Cricket and Society in Bolton between the Wars', Lancaster University unpublished PhD thesis (1992), p. 257.
2. *Cricketer*, 14 Aug. 1937, p. 497.
3. Ibid., 30 May 1936, p. 145.
4. *Daily Mail*, 5 May 1934.
5. For the numbers of teams playing cricket each week in Barnsley, Bolton, Burnley, Halifax, Oldham, St Helens, Sunderland, Wigan and their surroundings, see J. Williams, 'Churches, Sport and Identities in the North, 1900–1939', in J. Hill and J. Williams, eds., *Sport and Identity in the North of England* (Keele: Keele UP, 1996), p. 115.
6. J.A. Williams, 'Cricket and Society in Bolton', pp. 253–6.
7. The annual handbooks of the Club Cricket Conference list all its affiliated clubs.
8. *Sussex Express*, 9 May 1930.
9. Interview with Sir Robert Southern (retired bank official).
10. H.F. Squire and A.P. Squire, *Henfield Cricket Club and Its Sussex Cradle* (Hove: Combridges, 1949), p. 201.
11. *News Chronicle*, 20 July 1931.
12. *The Times*, 21 Aug. 1922.
13. Ibid., 24 April 1925.
14. Interview with Mr. T. Needham (retired factory operative, later groundsman).
15. N. Fishwick, *English Football and Society, 1910–1950* (Manchester: Manchester UP, 1989), p. 1.
16. *Sussex Express*, 20 Oct. 1922, 11 Dec. 1925.
17. J.A. Williams, 'Cricket and Society in Bolton', p. 210.
18. *News Chronicle*, 8, 22 June, 13, 20 July, 10, 24, 31 Aug. 1931.
19. J.A. Hester, E. Ward and L.E. Parry, *Horwich Churches Welfare League 1922–1972* (n.p., n.d.), p. 11.
20. *The Times*, 14 Sept. 1936.
21. *Farnworth Weekly Journal*, 10 Sept. 1926.
22. J. Williams, 'Churches, Sport and Identities', pp. 123–5.
23. Mass-Observation Worktown Survey, Box 2, File A – Sports: General, Mass-Observation Archive, Sussex University.
24. *Nelson Leader*, 10 July 1903.
25. *Sussex Express*, 9 April 1926.
26. *The Times*, 6 May 1936, 26 July 1926.
27. *City of Liverpool Education Committee Report on Medical Inspections of School Children for the Year 1920* (Liverpool: City of Liverpool Corporation, 1921), p. 75, *City of Liverpool Education Committee Report on Medical Inspections ... 1936,*

p. 112.

28. H.F.B. Thomas, *Schoolboy Cricket in Manchester (From 1919 to 1947): A Short History of the Manchester Schools' Cricket Association* (Salford: Manchester Schools' Cricket Association, n.d.), pp. 1, 6.

29. *Sussex Express*, 1 Aug. 1930.

30. *Lancashire Schools' Cricket Association Handbook, 1936* (n.p., n.d.), p. 9; *Lancashire Schools' Cricket Association Handbook, 1939* (n.p., n.d.), pp. 5–6.

31. *London Schools' Cricket Association Jubilee Souvenir, 1925–75* (London, 1975), listed in R.W. Cox, *Sport in Britain: A Bibliography of Historical Publications 1800–1988* (Manchester: Manchester UP), p. 117.

32. C.A. Bentley, 'Provision for Physical Education within Elementary Education in Bolton between 1870 and 1940', Manchester University MEd thesis (1986) pp. 102–3; interview with H. Scholes (retired teacher); *Buff,* 10 Aug. 1935.

33. C.A. Bentley, 'Provision for Physical Education', appendix.

34. J.A. Williams, 'Cricket and Society in Bolton', pp. 229–30.

35. *The Times*, 21 Aug. 1922, 5 May 1937.

36. N. Gannaway, *A History of Cricket in Hampshire* (Marsh Barton: Hampshire Books, 1990), p. 54.

37. *News Chronicle*, 10 Aug. 1932.

38. *The Times*, 8 Nov. 1921.

39. *Worcester Evening News & Times*, 24 June 1939.

40. MCC Daily Receipts books, MCC Library.

41. I am grateful to Mr Peter Wynne-Thomas for allowing me to consult the schedules of the Findlay Commission held at the library of Nottinghamshire CCC.

42. *Athletic News*, 17 March 1919.

43. Ibid., 23 Feb. 1920.

44. *The Times*, 16 Feb. 1922.

45. *Athletic News*, 2, 16 Aug. 1920.

46. *Wisden Cricketers' Almanack, 1949* (London: Sporting Handbooks, 1949), p. 186.

47. Ibid.

48. The numbers of paying spectators for each of Yorkshire's home matches except those played at Scarborough are stated in the annual issues of *Yorkshire County Cricket Club.*

49. J. Bannister and D. Graveney, *Durham CCC: Past, Present and Future* (London: Queen Anne, 1993), pp. 83, 90.

50. The annual handbooks of the Lancashire League provide statistics of the total numbers of paying spectators at matches of the Lancashire League clubs or of the total gate receipts paid by spectators.

51. J. Williams, 'The Economics of League Cricket: Lancashire League Clubs and Their Finances since the First World War', *British Society of Sports History Bulletin,* 9 (1990).

52. *Nelson Leader*, 12 Jan. 1923, 3 Jan. 1930, 16 Jan. 1931, 20 Jan. 1933, 18 Jan. 1935, 17 Jan. 1936.

53. *The Cricketer Annual, 1935* (London: Cricketer Publications, n.d.), p. 89.

54. I am grateful to Mr Alan Edwards, who is compiling a history of Rochdale CC, for supplying me with this data.

55. *Daily Mirror*, 30 June 1938.

56. J.A. Williams, 'Cricket and Society in Bolton', pp. 258–62.

57. *Athletic News*, 1 Dec. 1919, 10 April 1922.

58. *Daily Mirror*, 30 June 1938.

59. A.E. Davis, *First in the Field: A History of the Birmingham and District Cricket*

League (Studley: Brewin, 1988), p. 152.

60. *29th Report of the Commissioners of Customs and Excise for the Year Ended March 31, 1938* (London: HMSO, 1938–39), p. 102.
61. B. Tabner, *Through the Turnstiles* (Harefield: Yore, 1992).
62. I am grateful to the Test and County Cricket Board for supplying me with these statistics.
63. *Guardian*, 15 Dec. 1995.
64. *Wisden Cricketers' Almanack, 1994* (Guildford: John Wisden, 1994), p. 351.
65. Lancashire CCC Annual Report 1925.
66. W. Pollock, *The Cream of Cricket* (London: Methuen, 1934), p. 70.
67. *Farnworth Weekly Journal*, 23 July 1926.
68. Mass-Observation Worktown Survey, Box 2, File D, Cricket.
69. For details of how these figures have been obtained see J.A. Williams, 'Cricket and Society in Bolton', pp. 224–30, 258–63.
70. J. Williams, 'The Economics of League Cricket'.
71. J.M. Kilburn, *Thanks to Cricket* (London: Stanley Paul, 1972), pp. 25–6.
72. J.W. Hobson and H. Henry, *The Hulton Readership Survey 1947* (London: Hulton, 1947).
73. *Report of the Royal Commission on the Press, 1947–1949, Appendix III* (London: HMSO Cmd. 7700 1948–49), p. 190.
74. Ibid.; *Hulton Readership Survey 1947*, pp. 26, 47.
75. E.W. Padwick, *A Bibliography of Cricket* (London: Library Association, 1984), S. Eley and P. Griffiths, *Padwick's Bibliography of Cricket, Volume II* (London: Library Association, 1991); R.W. Cox, *Sport in Britain*.

4

Cricket and Sportsmanship

Belief that cricket was pervaded by a spirit of sportsmanship which extended to other areas of social activity was crucial to the moral significance accorded to the game between the wars. Use of the expressions 'it's not cricket' and 'play the game' as condemnatory of anything reprehensible in everyday life shows how cricket had become a metaphor for honesty, selflessness and upright conduct. Frank Foster who had captained Warwickshire before the First World War wrote in 1930 that 'the word cricket means Sportsmanship'.[1] In his old age Lord Harris described cricket as 'more free from anything sordid, anything dishonourable, than any game in the world. To play it keenly, honourably, generously, self-sacrificingly is a moral lesson in itself.'[2] In 1933 a writer in *The New Statesman* described cricket as 'a world in which a man would rather lose his right hand than be guilty of doing something that wasn't cricket'.[3] Consideration of why such emphasis was placed upon cricket as an expression of sportsmanship and the degree to which cricket was characterised by a spirit of sportsmanship reveal much about the cultural assumptions which governed how the English imagined themselves.

CRICKET AND SPORTSMANSHIP

The terms 'sportsmanship', 'playing the game' and 'fair play' were used interchangeably in cricket discourses, especially among those from the wealthier classes, and were described as a quintessentially English quality. In 1925, for instance, an editorial in *The Times* claimed that 'cricket has this sovereign virtue – that it induces in both players and spectators a keen desire to play the game, and the two together, versed almost from the cradle in its principles and practice, constitute the most typically English spectacle on English soil'.[4] In his book *Character and Sportsmanship* Sir Theodore Cook, editor of *The Field*, wrote of 'the most deep-seated instincts of the English race – the instincts of sportsmanship and fair play' and of 'that spirit of fair play and sportsmanship which is the inheritance of the English village from its remote ancestors'. To Cook the spirit of English sportsmanship had helped the English survive the threat of Prussian militarism and the general strike, which he saw as having been inspired by Moscow.[5] In 1926 an editorial in *The Field* described cricket as the 'best of our English games which is the one intangible and immortal factor in the English character which no foreigner will ever understand or vanquish'.[6] It was only a short step from this to assume that the sportsmanship of cricket meant that the English were morally superior to other races and nations.

'Sportsmanship' was regarded as covering a wide variety of qualities, all suffused with notions of morality and honour. In 1925 the handbook of the London and Southern Counties Cricket Conference defined 'A Cricketer and a Sportsman' as one who

1. Plays the Game for the game's sake.
2. Plays for his side, and not for himself.
3. Is a good winner and a good loser (i.e. is modest in victory and generous in defeat).
4. Accepts all decisions in a proper spirit.
5. Is chivalrous towards an opponent
6. Is unselfish and always ready to help others to become proficient.[7]

To this list many would have added that trying to win was an essential part of 'playing the game'. In January 1925, just after England had lost a test match against Australia in Melbourne and the England rugby union side had been defeated by New Zealand, an editorial in *The Times* argued that 'wanting to win is of the essence of the game ... The real and only justification for wanting to win is that it leads to trying to win. It is the trying that counts, whatever the result ... A total blindness to the possibility of ultimate and final failure is a mark of the something unconquerable in man ... What really matters is that there should still be the strength and the will to try again, and to keep on trying.'[8] Yet to remain an expression of sportsmanship, playing to win had to be kept within reasonable bounds and did not involve deliberate cheating or keeping within the laws of cricket while manipulating them to gain an unfair advantage over an opponent. In *The Cricketer Annual* for 1922–23 Bishop Welldon wrote that 'to play the game' was 'to do, or to do only, the upright thing' and that to 'insist upon the letter and not the spirit of the rules in a game or to distort the letter of the rules for personal advantage' was 'not "cricket"'.[9]

Cricket discourses emphasised that playing in an unselfish manner was the core of 'playing the game'. Indeed association of sportsmanship with unselfishness was a major reason for regarding playing the game as an expression of morality. In 1924 Lord Harris spoke of cricketers as 'the ministers of a high moral and educational medium. It is the distinguishing feature of cricket that the self must be sacrificed, selfishness must be exorcised if a cricketer is to succeed ... each feat of skill may bring him delight, but delight because he has helped his side.'[10] In 1932, 'A Country Vicar' wrote in *The Cricketer* that cricket could be 'justly described as the finest of games ... Eleven men, each bearing his part ... not for himself, but for the team of which he is a member: Surely the highest ideal!'[11] The unselfishness of 'playing the game' included accepting the decisions of umpires and captains without question. In 1920 an editorial in *The Times* stated that 'to play the game, to play for one's side, to do nothing mean or unfair, to greet ill fortune with smiling face, to obey the laws and never to dispute the umpire – these are the accepted maxims of cricket'.[12] Welldon equated 'playing the game' with 'self-sacrifice' and wrote that it was difficult to exaggerate the moral value which 'lies in the habit of implicitly obeying the captain and of unreservedly accepting the judgment of the umpire, even when it is, or is thought, to be clearly wrong'.[13] In 1935 'The Captain' wrote in *The Liverpool Weekly Post* that

> The true cricketer must play cricket. The grocer's boy, who on the village green, reluctantly left the crease after querying the umpire's decision, was assuredly not a cricketer. With stout heart he should have marched silently to the pavilion cherishing the thought that he would do better next time. Nor indeed, was he a cricketer who voiced his true feelings about the umpire in the pavilion, for the great lesson of tolerance is inbred in the game. The ten Commandments are amplified by another. 'Thou shalt play cricket', which means that silence is golden, and that more proverbs must be honoured ... The player who can hit hundreds is surely only a cricketer if he is unassuming. This is part of our life, and a tradition not to be broken, for cricket would be intolerable without a gospel of pleasant restraint.[14]

The emphasis upon the unselfishness of 'playing the game' was seen to be consistent with Christian teaching.

Batting in an adventurous style which involved risks was seen to be more sporting and less selfish than playing in a more cautious manner, that tried to eliminate risk and allowed batsmen to compile reasonable scores regularly but at a slow rate. In the 1920s much criticism was levelled at Lancashire's tactic in the county championship of compiling large scores very slowly to ensure that matches would not be lost. Some of this criticism came from within Lancashire. An editorial in *The Manchester Guardian* asked in 1924: 'Are championship laurels ever worth the wearing if the price of this is over-cautious batting?'[15] In 1927 after a Lancashire batsman had scored only 27 runs in 230 minutes, Olympian of *The Buff*, the sports edition of *The Bolton Evening News*, wrote: 'What a joy it would be to see Lancashire forget for a time that there are such things as points and championships, and set themselves to play the sort of cricket which one expects from men who love the game and all that it stands for.'[16] In the 1920s and first half of the 1930s there was debate about whether the LBW law should be changed. Many professional batsmen in particular were criticised for employing the unsporting tactic of using their pads to defend the stumps on wickets where off-spinners were turning the ball prodigiously. Sir Francis Lacey, who had been the secretary of the MCC and was the president of Hampshire in 1929, wanted the Hampshire club to support calls for a reform of the LBW law in order to discourage pad play because he wished 'the laws of cricket to be a perfectly ethical code as well as a legal code'.[17]

Discourses of those from the privileged classes conflated 'playing the game' with the public school tradition of amateurism. In 1921, for instance, H.S. Altham, an Oxford cricket blue, public schoolmaster and later a prominent cricket administrator, in an article entitled 'Public School Cricket', wrote that 'the most important of all the widest interests of the game we may fairly demand of the public schools, its nurseries, is the sporting spirit in the best sense of the words, the combination of rigour without which cricket develops into either a dilatory exercise or an acrimonious wrangle'.[18] Pelham Warner felt that 'games have always played an important part in the life of the public schools and universities, and it this public school spirit which made us come out top in the Great War'.[19] This entangling of sportsmanship with the public school spirit can be interpreted as an argument to justify the exercise of authority in cricket by those from economically privileged backgrounds. The assumption that the public schools were so effective in encouraging the unselfishness of 'playing the game' was taken by those from such schools as evidence that they were equipped to exercise authority in a moral and unselfish manner.

Despite this conflation of sportsmanship with the public schools, the association of cricket with sportsmanship was not restricted to the economically and socially privileged. Interviews with those from working-class backgrounds who played recreational cricket in the 1930s, although only a tiny sample of all who played such cricket at the time, often indicate an acceptance of the view that cricket was played in a spirit of sportsmanship and that playing cricket encouraged moral qualities. It is not difficult to find statements by professional cricketers which subscribed to the notion of cricket playing and moral uprightness, and even though they may have made such statements merely because they assumed it was expected of them, this in itself indicates how widespread the association of cricket playing and moral worth had become. In 1924 Jack Hobbs, in his autobiography, claimed that 'the man who plays cricket cannot be selfish, and cannot be cowardly'.[20] Although this was a ghosted autobiography, public estimation of Hobbs suggests that this represented what he thought. Maurice Leyland, a professional batsman for Yorkshire and England, wrote 'If a boy or a man plays cricket as it should be played, you can term him a sportsman, and there is nothing much wrong with a sportsman.' Bill Bowes, another Yorkshire and England professional, advised schoolboy cricketers to 'Aim high, both as a cricketer and a man. Ascertain your ideal and practise until you attain it. You will be able to say, "you played the game", and whether you win or lose I know nothing finer than this.'[21]

SPORTSMANSHIP AND FIRST-CLASS CRICKET

There is much to suggest that most first-class cricket was played in accordance with the ideals of sportsmanship and fair play. Newspaper reports of cheating and player misbehaviour in county and test match cricket are rare, though it is possible that cricket journalists who subscribed to the view that cricket was an expression of morality chose not to report incidents of unsporting behaviour. E.W. Swanton has pointed out that in the 1920s, cricket journalists, and those of other sports, had 'a strong sense of the traditions behind the games concerned'.[22] Percy Fender, the Surrey captain, recalled a county match in which Surrey had taken the field with only two players, but his biographer could find no reference to this in any newspaper.[23] In 1937 the cricket correspondent of *The Times* complained about 'unseemly' conduct in a match between Surrey and Middlesex,[24] but provided no further details. No instance has been found of players coming to blows in a first-class match. Probably the only occasion when a player was dismissed from the field of play in a first-class match was in 1922 when Lionel Tennyson, the Hampshire captain, ordered from the field one of his side who had taken an inordinate amount of time to set his field after being barracked by spectators. The player kicked down the stumps and according to Tennyson had used objectionable language.[25]

There were occasional complaints about decisions of umpires not being accepted with good grace. The statement by Lord Hawke in 1921 that 'it is a grave matter when first class cricketers linger at the wicket or publicly show dissatisfaction at an irrevocable decision' suggests that there were some instances of such conduct, but does not indicate their frequency.[26] For a brief period in 1924 there was talk that Middlesex might refuse to play further matches against Yorkshire after Abe Waddington, a Yorkshire professional fast bowler, had shown his disapproval of the umpires' decisions in Yorkshire's game with Middlesex at Sheffield. A few weeks later the MCC complained about players gesticulating when appeals were turned down.[27] Charles Elliott, who played in 275 matches as a professional with Derbyshire from 1932 until 1953, can recall only one instance of a Derbyshire batsman disputing an umpire's decision on the field, and the general tenor of his remarks suggests that this would have been the case at other counties.[28] Ellis Robinson, who played for Yorkshire as a professional from 1934 to 1949, remembers that Brian Sellers, a fiercely competitive captain, insisted that there should be 'no peeping' or players looking at the position of their feet when given out LBW which could have been interpreted as showing disagreement with the umpire's decision.[29] At their annual meeting in 1927 the captains of the first-class counties recorded 'much regret' that an amateur, educated at Harrow, had criticised on the field of play an umpire's decision in the match between Derbyshire and Yorkshire.[30] At no other captains' meeting was any criticism of an amateur recorded.

Some cheating or deliberate flouting of the laws did occur. Lifting the seam of a ball was not unknown and in 1928 the annual meeting of county captains decided to remind umpires that this practice was against the laws of cricket.[31] In 1927 when the MCC changed the laws of cricket to allow a smaller ball to be used in order to assist bowlers, Frank Sugg, the cricket journalist, wrote that the smaller ball had been used unofficially and unfairly by some for many years.[32] In 1929 there was an accusation that a bail had been dislodged unfairly in a match between Yorkshire and Nottinghamshire.[33] Whether batsmen 'walked' when they knew that they had been caught, but before the umpire had made a decision, is unclear. During a match between Essex and Gloucestershire J.W.H.T. Douglas, the Essex captain, stormed into the Gloucestershire professionals' dressing room to upbraid Wally Hammond for not 'walking'.[34] This reaction by Douglas and Hammond's resentment at Douglas' accusation could mean that batsmen usually did 'walk'. Charles Elliott thinks that most, but certainly not all batsmen, did 'walk'. Where a batsman knew that he was out but had been given not out by the umpire, it was not usual to 'walk' as this would be construed as being offensive to the umpire,[35] a view shared by Jack Hobbs who was regarded as the personification of cricket's sporting spirit.[36] Winston Place, who played for Lancashire in the second half of the 1930s, recalled that in his experience there were no attempts to pressurise umpires by making an excessive number of appeals, but Charles Elliott remembers that some bowlers made very loud appeals. Both have commented that there was no 'sledging' in county cricket in the late 1930s, but Ellis Robinson has said that there was sometimes 'leg-pulling' of batsmen which could have been designed to disturb their concentration. In the 1960s Learie Constantine recalled that on the West Indian tour of England in 1928 Derbyshire players had tried to put him off his game by appealing each time the ball struck his pads, regardless of whether the ball would otherwise have hit the stumps.[37]

One difficulty in estimating how far cricket was played in a spirit of sportsmanship is that what some found acceptable others considered to be sharp practice. In 1922 the MCC criticised the university sides of Oxford and Cambridge for allowing substitutes to bat in matches because it believed that the laws of cricket should be observed at all times.[38] Occasionally in matches where rain had restricted playing time, captains of county sides declared their first innings closed after only a run or two had been scored in order to have the possibility of a definite result. Such 'freak' declarations were made in 1931 in the matches between Yorkshire and Nottinghamshire, Glamorgan and Surrey and Yorkshire and Gloucestershire. Representatives of Lancashire complained that 'freak' declarations infringed the spirit of the County Championship and Lord Hawke accused the county captains who arranged such declarations of flouting decisions of the Advisory Committee.[39] The practice persisted, none the less. *The Field* complained about it in 1932 and in 1939 *The Times* criticised 'bogus' declarations as being against the spirit of the game.[40] In 1929, Leslie Ames, the MCC wicket-keeper was injured in a match against Victoria. Jack Ryder, the captain of Victoria, offered to allow George Duckworth, the other wicket-keeper with the MCC party but who was not playing in the match, to keep wicket, which would have been contrary to the laws of cricket. Percy Chapman, the MCC and England captain, described this as 'against the laws of cricket but a great sporting action'.[41] Disregarding the regulations governing county cricket can be seen as a form of cheating. Rules concerning the residential qualifications of county cricketers were often breached. Although Lord Harris was particularly keen to see that residential qualifications were observed, there were a number of instances in the early 1920s where counties selected players who had no residential qualification for them. *Athletic News* hinted that several counties were playing those without the requisite residential qualifications and later named seven players who had probably not been qualified when they first played for Somerset.[42] The consternation caused within the Advisory Committee in 1923 when it was learned that Worcestershire had been playing an unqualified player in the full knowledge that he was not qualified, is mentioned in Chapter 2.

There was great debate during and after the MCC tour of Australia in 1932–33 about whether bodyline bowling was unsporting. Australian players, administrators and journalists had little doubt that bodyline bowling violated traditions of fair play, an opinion shared by Pelham Warner, manager of the MCC party and by Gubby Allen, an England amateur fast bowler who refused to bowl bodyline; but initially few in England took this view. Letters to *The Times* during the winter of 1932–33 tended to argue that it was merely a continuation of leg theory bowling which had been practised for many years in county cricket and which Australian fast bowlers had used in 1921. Others pointed out that Australian batsmen were unable to cope with such bowling because of the two-eyed stance. In January 1933 an editorial in *The Times* declared: 'It is inconceivable that a cricketer of Jardine's standing, chosen by the MCC to captain an English side, would ever dream of allowing or ordering the bowlers under his command to practise any system of attack that, in the time-honoured phrase, is not cricket.' It went on to claim that there was 'nothing dishonourable or unsportsmanlike or foreign to the spirit of the game' about England's bowling.[43] Lord Hawke described Jardine as a 'splendid captain' and F.S. Jackson, who had captained Harrow, Cambridge, and England and been a former chairman of the Conservative Party and a Governor-General of Australia, argued that England would not have done anything injurious to cricket.[44] When the Australian Board of Control and the MCC exchanged cables about the acceptability of bodyline bowling, the MCC seems to have bridled at the accusation that such tactics were unsporting.

After the return home of the MCC party, opinion towards bodyline bowling changed, perhaps because of a fear that the continued use of such tactics could have led to the abandonment of test matches between England and Australia which would have been a financial disaster for English cricket. In November 1933 a ruling by the MCC condemned bowling which involved a 'direct attack' upon batsmen as unfair and in the same month a meeting of the Advisory Committee, the Board of Control and county captains decided that the laws of cricket did not need to be changed but agreed that direct attack bowling was against the spirit of cricket. The county captains agreed not to employ direct attack bowling, but in the opinion of seven leading umpires, three counties and four bowlers used bodyline tactics during the 1934 season.[45] The two main bodyline bowlers for England on the tour of Australia had been the Nottinghamshire fast bowlers Harold Larwood and Bill Voce, and the bodyline bowling by Nottinghamshire bowlers in 1934 led some counties to threaten that they would not play Nottinghamshire in future. The decision of the Nottinghamshire committee not to reappoint Arthur Carr as the club captain for the 1935 season was interpreted as an indication that Nottinghamshire would cease to employ bodyline bowling. After 1934 bodyline bowling appears to have more or less disappeared from first-class cricket in England before the Second World War.

The rhetoric surrounding amateurism often stressed that amateur captains were essential if cricket was to retain its spirit of sportsmanship, which implied that amateurs were more committed to the ethic of sportsmanship than professionals. It is not easy to determine whether amateurs did play in a more sportsmanlike manner than professionals. Statements by professionals showing that they subscribed to the notions of sportsmanship are common, but a public admission of cheating would have been foolhardy. Complaints about slow batting were most often made about professionals and, while it must be recognised that a batsman's chances of being selected regularly may have been boosted by developing a reliable but cautious style of batting, many professionals who batted slowly may have been instructed to do so by their amateur captains. There is evidence of sharp practice by some amateurs. It has been claimed that the ill-feeling between the captains of Surrey and Essex in the 1920s was so intense that the Surrey groundsman would be told which wicket was to be used only after the toss had been made.[46] The amateurs J.W.H.T. Douglas and J.C. White, who both captained England, are known to have lifted the seam.[47] There were rumours that the Middlesex and England amateur Nigel Haig used a half-penny to manipulate the ball. If bodyline came to be regarded as unsporting, the decision to employ it against Australia on the 1932–33 tour was very much that of the amateur captain Jardine, but the Surrey amateur Percy Fender is thought to have pointed out to him how such bowling could neutralise the threat of Bradman's batting. In England in 1934 the amateur Ken Farnes was one fast bowler who used bodyline tactics.[48] Charles Elliott has mentioned that some men have more sporting natures than others, but he has also recalled that the power of Derbyshire captains to bring to an end the career of a professional, meant that all professionals realised it was in their interest to play in the style captains wanted. A Derbyshire professional who disputed the decision of an umpire on the field was immediately told by his captain he would never play for Derbyshire again if he repeated such behaviour.[49]

SPORTSMANSHIP OUTSIDE FIRST-CLASS CRICKET

It is impossible to gauge how far the various levels of non first-class cricket in different parts of the country were played in a spirit of sportsmanship. Reports in local newspapers of misconduct in club cricket in the south of

England are very unusual, though it is possible that, as with county cricket, journalists may have felt obliged not to report unseemly incidents. Socially exclusive clubs often had their own umpires, rather than umpires not connected with either club in a match, which was meant to emphasise that no players would be guilty of sharp practice. It is possible that the limited extent of league and knockout competitions in the South may have meant that club cricket in this part of England was not aggressively competitive. Indeed the decision of the Club Cricket Conference to deny membership to clubs which played in leagues was related to a belief that leagues resulted in matches being played in an unduly competitive manner inimical to the spirit of cricket. E.A.C. Thomson of the London and Southern Counties Cricket Conference argued in 1923 that the competitiveness of leagues would 'crush out every ounce of the real sporting spirit of cricket and introduce the contentious side which should be entirely foreign to our glorious English summer game ... The erection of a high wall ... against competitive cricket will tend to keep the game perfectly clean.'[50] On the other hand, Fred Root, the England professional bowler who also played league cricket, wrote that it was 'a fallacy to think that the "sporting" spirit of friendly cricket is entirely absent' from league cricket. He felt that 'Not often is sharp practice apparent in league cricket, but in many cases of so-called sportsmanship in friendly matches the "sporty" action is opposed both to common sense and the rules of the game'.[51]

The Bolton area of Lancashire, a stronghold of league cricket, shows how difficult it is to decide whether league cricket was less sporting than cricket played only on a friendly basis. *The Buff* reported in great detail the highest levels of local cricket. Two episodes in 1921 – one where the umpires in a match between Atherton Collieries CC and Egerton reported a wicket-keeper for using 'bad language', leaving the field and encouraging other players to follow him after the rejection of an appeal for a catch on the legside, and the other in a second team match where a player had threatened to hit an umpire with a bat[52] – are the only instances of player misconduct at the highest levels of local league cricket mentioned by this newspaper between the wars, but it may have chosen to overlook some forms of cheating. Minute books of the Bolton League have been traced only for November 1929 to January 1932 and for 1937 to 1938. These record no reports of player misconduct, but do include complaints from umpires about club officials criticising their decisions. There were occasional complaints in the local press that players sometimes played for collections rather than for the good of their sides, a practice which Learie Constantine felt occurred in the Central Lancashire League.[53] The incident from the highest levels of league cricket which attracted most attention in the regional press occurred in the Central Lancashire League match between Rochdale and Littleborough in 1920. Cecil Parkin, the Rochdale professional, left the field in protest against an umpire refusing LBW decisions. Following the League inquiry into the matter, the Rochdale club resigned from the League.[54]

Flouting league regulations can be regarded as a form of cheating. In the Bolton League no club was supposed to engage more than one professional player, but it was an open secret that many 'amateurs' were paid. Oral evidence has shown that only two of the Farnworth side which won the Bolton League in 1937 were not paid.[55] In the 1920s there were suspicions that some groundsmen at leading clubs around Bolton were in reality being paid to play cricket. The regulations of almost all cricket leagues stipulated that only those who had been registered with a club could play for it, but it seems probable that at the lower levels of league cricket unregistered players often played under false names. One of the more blatant, or careless, instances of this occurred in a cup-tie of the Walkden Amateur Cricket League in 1931. The Atherton Independent Methodist club had played an unregistered player called Gettings under the name of Pennington, but had entered his name in the score book as Gettings. When this was detected, the league committee awarded the cup-tie to the opposing side.[56] The minute book of the Horwich Sunday School League, probably the humblest level of league cricket in the Bolton area, shows that league officials were especially insistent that players could not play until they had been registered.

The minute book of the Walkden Amateur Cricket League sheds some light upon sportsmanship at the lower levels of league cricket in the Bolton area. In 1934 the batsmen of one side abandoned a match over their dissatisfaction with the decisions of an umpire and in the same season umpires reported one player for disputing a decision and using 'bad language'.[57] In 1935 one player was found to have struck another player who had sworn at him and called him 'soft' for appealing against the light.[58] As these are the sole instances of misconduct found in the minute book of the League's committee between 1924 and 1939, this may mean that forms of conduct considered to be unsporting in this locality were not common. Those who played in the Radcliffe Sunday School League during the late 1930s believe that batsmen would have 'walked' when umpires were uncertain whether a catch had been taken. On the other hand they also remember forms of sharp practice. In some grounds long grass in the outfield had led to the introduction of a rule that not more than four runs could be run when a ball became lost without crossing the boundary. Sometimes fielders pretended that the ball had become lost and then threw down the wicket of unwary batsmen.[59] In 1930 umpires in the Horwich Sunday School League complained of decisions being questioned, unpleasant remarks, mutterings throughout matches and the childish actions of some players. In 1934 umpires reported that players were not signalling whether balls had crossed the boundary.[60] The fact that the Horwich Sunday School League had always felt it necessary for umpires at matches to be unconnected with either club indicates at least a fear that umpires connected with one of the sides might not have been fair or that players would have tried to take advantage of umpires from their clubs. There can never be an objective measure of how often instances of cheating and sharp practice occurred in cricket or whether they became more common with the passage of time between the wars, but what can be said is that complaints of such behaviour in the Bolton area were sufficiently rare for them never to have challenged the belief that playing cricket was an expression of fair play and sportsmanship.

SPECTATORS AND SPORTSMANSHIP

Cricket discourses extended the notion of playing the game to spectators. Being fair-minded and generous to opponents was seen as sportsmanlike behaviour on the part of spectators, but behaving with decorum was also described as a form of sportsmanship among them. Interviews with those who played at different levels of cricket indicate that cricket crowds tended to be quieter than those of today and that the great majority of spectators were silent during a bowler's run-up and delivery. Crowds at first-class cricket in England were quieter than those in Australia. In 1927, Charlie Macartney, the Australian test match cricketer, commented that 'It has often been a cause of wonderment to me why the crowds generally in England are so quiet'.[61] Spectators in England were often fiercely partisan in their support for one side and on occasions spectators would boo at what they thought were unsporting tactics of a side. In 1932 spectators at The Oval and Old Trafford booed and voiced strong disapproval at the bowling of the Yorkshire player Bill Bowes who was delivering balls which reared up around or over the heads of batsmen.[62] This was only months before the England team adopted bodyline tactics in Australia.

Comments in *The Times* showed that there was much concern among the cricket establishment about barracking at first-class matches. *The Times* never felt it necessary to define barracking but the general tenor of its comments implies that the term covered shouting abuse at players and umpires and behaving in an unduly boisterous manner. Often barracking was discussed in relation to the behaviour of crowds in Australia. In 1921 the cricket correspondent of *The Times* wrote that barracking was 'entirely foreign to the true spirit of the game' and in 1932–33 argued that barracking by Australian spectators had been a major contribution to the ill-feeling surrounding the bodyline controversy. In the summer of 1933 an editorial in *The Times* claimed that 'barracking is not cricket' and had 'never been allowed to get out of hand in England'.[63] Charlie Macartney felt that barracking in England was 'of a very mild character compared with Australia', but added that there had been instances in England in 1921 at which Australians could have 'taken umbrage'. At Nottingham the Australian fast bowler Gregory had been barracked for short pitched bowling and for one delivery which knocked an English batsman unconscious. At Manchester there had been barracking following confusion about whether England could declare in a match which rain had reduced to two days. Macartney added that in neither case was the barracking 'intimidating'.[64] In 1921 a delayed start to a test match at The Oval led to 'an intimidating demonstration in front of the pavilion' and the England captain needed a police escort.[65] At the Old Trafford test match against South Africa in 1924 several hundred invaded the playing area when it was decided that the pitch was too wet for play.[66]

On occasions county cricketers protested about the behaviour of spectators. In 1919, Pelham Warner who was then captain of Middlesex, wrote 'It is a disgrace to the game, and the players will be compelled to refuse to go on with the match if the manners of the crowd do not improve … One thing is quite certain. The crowd cannot be allowed to dictate to the players how they are to bat.'[67] In August 1925, Jack Sharp, the Lancashire captain, refused to play in the remainder of Lancashire's fixtures at Old Trafford as a protest on behalf of his side against spectators who jeered at dropped catches and 'put players in the pillory'. One crowd, he added, was known among cricketers as 'the Wolves'. J.W.H.T. Douglas, the Essex captain, thought that there were unruly spirits who turned matches into bear gardens and that it was time to restore order.[68] Harry Lee, who played for Middlesex and became an umpire in 1935, thought that barracking was not common in England but that it could be 'a powerful weapon of offence in the north' and could very nearly ruin the career of a player who was out of form.[69] In 1926 Worcestershire decided to stop having matches at Stourbridge because spectators had hooted at the umpires and jeered a Leicestershire bowler.[70] The Sheffield crowd in the 1920s gained a reputation for being unduly partisan. In 1924 Middlesex threatened not to play Yorkshire again after the umpires had complained about the behaviour of Waddington, the Yorkshire bowler, in the match at Sheffield. *The Times* commented that 'behind this lies the much graver question of the control of ill-mannered crowds … the crowd behaved very badly indeed, making the task of the umpires almost unbearable'.[71] In 1925 Douglas and another Essex amateur had refused to play at Sheffield because of the attitude of spectators.[72] Bill Bowes, a Yorkshire player, felt that the Sheffield crowd was highly critical of faults but was unsurpassed in its appreciation of cricket's finer points. He also recalled that one umpire was so unnerved by the Sheffield crowd's reaction to his rejection of appeals that he asked Bowes not to appeal unless it was 'a plumb "un"'. After giving a batsman out, a decision which amazed Bowes, he asked: 'Will they let me alone now?'[73]

Press reports of crowd misconduct are less common in the late 1920s and 1930s, but it is not certain whether spectators were behaving differently. The need for spectator revenue may have caused counties to become less critical of spectators, but there were instances of unsporting behaviour by spectators. In 1931 a spectator kicked the umpire Frank Chester, who had lost an arm in the First World War, for deciding that the pitch was not fit for play.[74] In the later 1930s when Harry Lee and his fellow umpire had decided that the wicket at Bradford was too wet for play and so denied Yorkshire a victory, they were confronted by a 'deputation of two or three hundred angry Yorkshire spectators to see us off the premises'.[75] In 1938 *The Times* described the booing of Bradman at The Oval for not enforcing the follow on in the Australians' match against Surrey as 'an exhibition of "Yahooism" by a crowd notorious for their bad manners'.[76] But not all the press was so critical of barracking in 1938. In the test match at Nottingham, Jack Fingleton, the Australian batsman, had sat down in protest against the crowd barracking him for batting slowly in an attempt to obtain a draw for Australia. Denis O'Sullivan, a sports journalist for *The Daily Mirror,* wrote: 'Bravo the barrackers of Notts!' He claimed that he was not inciting riot or hooliganism, but would 'proudly plead guilty to inciting fans to demand their rights as true sport-lovers and as persons who pay to be entertained, not bored or disgusted or cured of insomnia'.[77]

No objective measures of how far the behaviour of spectators was characterised by a spirit of sportsmanship can be made; and there is also the possibility that some sections of the press did not wish the supposed sporting nature of cricket to be sullied by reports of unsporting spectators. Oral evidence, however, shows that the general decorum of crowds was greater than that of today. Comments on the fiercely partisan attitude of spectators at Sheffield suggest that this was not typical of spectators at most other grounds. The minutes of the Advisory Committee do not reveal that crowd behaviour ever became a matter of deep concern for those who controlled county cricket. The impression which arises from consulting a wide range of sources is that in general spectators at first-class cricket did behave in accordance with what were thought to be the standards of sportsmanship.

Accounts of spectator behaviour at other forms of cricket are even more scarce than those for test match and county cricket. In 1919 there had been so much fighting among spectators at the Eton versus Harrow match that prominent Old Boys demanded that there should be no repetition of such behaviour in 1920.[78] *The Times'* report of this match in 1919 had made no reference to spectator misbehaviour. No descriptions of spectator misconduct at the higher levels of club cricket have been found. Evidence about spectators at the higher levels of league cricket in the Bolton area suggests that their behaviour did not usually transgress the limits of what was considered to be sportsmanship. James Gledhill, who played for Farnworth CC in the late 1930s and was to have widespread experience of league cricket in many parts of Lancashire and Yorkshire after the Second World War, felt that crowds were fiercely partisan in the Bolton area and that the Westhoughton club, situated between Bolton and Wigan, had the most partisan supporters except for those encountered at Barnoldswick CC in Yorkshire. Mr Gledhill did not remember crowds in the Bolton area as unruly or unfair to opponents.[79] In 1921 the Kearsley club was ordered to put notices about crowd behaviour around its ground after one umpire had refused to officiate there again because of barracking in a second-eleven match and because a spectator had entered the pavilion to berate the umpire.[80] In 1931 umpires complained about the spectators at the Westhoughton ground and in 1937 play at a second team match was held up because of an unruly spectator.[81] Such incidents hardly seem to be evidence of widespread unruly behaviour. In the late 1930s a witness for Mass-Observation noted gentle banter among spectators at two matches in the Bolton area and in a match between the two teams at the top of the Bolton League commented upon the 'good nature' of the crowd.[82]

CRICKET, SPORTSMANSHIP AND AUTHORITY

The degree of sportsmanship within cricket cannot be gauged exactly. Sufficient instances of unsporting behaviour can be found to show that the level of sportsmanship did not always conform to the image created by cricket's apologists, but they never approached a level which queried the widespread belief that cricket was an expression of sportsmanship. There may, of course, have been deliberate turning of a blind eye to instances of unsporting behaviour and an element of self-delusion in the conviction that cricket was pervaded by a spirit of sportsmanship, but it can be argued that among the privileged classes in particular this belief was vital to their perception of English moral worth. Sportsmanship was considered a moral value. Because cricket was so often taken as a metaphor for England, and had such a close interdependency with cultural institutions which were thought to express distinctively English ethical qualities such as the churches, parliamentary government, the public schools and the Empire, any admission that cricket was not permeated with sportsmanship would have weakened assumptions of the moral value of English civilisation.

The emphasis on fair play in cricket by those from public schools in particular can be interpreted as a cultural narrative essential to their exercise of social and political power. Cricket rhetoric stressed that those from privileged backgrounds were the natural defenders of sportsmanship within the game, and because it was believed that the moral qualities associated with sportsmanship could be transferred to other areas of social activity, the cult of sportsmanship demonstrated that those who exercised power within cricket were morally equipped to be trusted with social and economic power. The links between sportsmanship and selflessness can be seen as helping to convince those from the public schools of their eligibility to exercise authority in society at large, as proof to other groups that such authority would be characterised by fairness and consideration.

The rhetoric of sportsmanship and fair play was not restricted to those from privileged backgrounds. Indeed many cricketers with working-class origins subscribed to the view that cricket was pervaded by a high level of sportsmanship and that it was important for cricket to retain this. But among those with privileged backgrounds it seems to have been believed that the acceptance of the sportsmanship in cricket by other social groups would cause them to assent to the social leadership of the privileged or to internalise values which would pose no threat to the existing structure of social authority. It can be claimed that so much of the respect accorded to Jack Hobbs was because he seemed to demonstrate that sportsmanship led to an acceptance of cricket's established structure of authority. At a dinner organised by the Lord Mayor of London to honour cricket, an event which in itself says much about the significance granted to cricket by those with economic and social power, Lord Desborough, a former Conservative MP who owned 12,000 acres and who had been President of the MCC, said that 'As long as the English race, and those in charge of it, did play the game and as long as those underneath assisted', he had 'no doubt that in cricket as in other things, England would maintain the position she has secured in the world'.[83] Such comments encapsulate why it was so necessary to believe that cricket was dominated by a spirit of sportsmanship.

NOTES

1. F.R. Foster, *Cricketing Memories* (London: London Publishing, 1930), p. 82.
2. *The Times*, 3 Feb. 1931.
3. *New Statesman*, 17 June 1933.
4. *The Times*, 7 May 1925.
5. T. Cook, *Character and Sportsmanship* (London: Williams and Norgate, 1927), pp. vii, xvi, 316.
6. *Field*, 12 Aug. 1926.
7. *Club Cricket Conference Handbook, 1925* (n.p., n.d.).
8. *The Times*, 13 Jan. 1925.
9. *The Cricketer Annual, 1922–23* (London: Cricketer Syndicate, 1922), p. 24.
10. *The Cricketer Annual, 1924–25* (London: Cricketer Syndicate, n.d.), p. 49.
11. *Cricketer*, 18 June 1932, p. 200.
12. *The Times*, 31 July 1920.
13. *The Cricketer Annual, 1922–23*, p. 24.
14. *Liverpool Weekly Post*, 18 June 1935. The permission of *The Liverpool Daily & Echo Ltd.* for the use of this quotation is acknowledged.
15. *Manchester Guardian*, 8 Dec. 1924.
16. *Buff*, 20 Aug. 1927.
17. *The Times*, 26 Jan. 1929.
18. *Cricketer*, 30 April 1921, p. 6.
19. Ibid., Dec. 1922, p. 4.
20. J.B. Hobbs, *My Cricketing Memories* (London: Heinemann, 1924), p. 12.
21. *Lancashire County Elementary Schools Cricket Association Handbook 1933* (Levenshulme: Lancashire Elementary Schools Cricket Association, n.d.).
22. E.W. Swanton, *Cricket Sort of Person* (London: Collins, 1972), p. 44.
23. R. Streeton, *P.G.H. Fender: A Biography* (London: Faber & Faber, 1981), p. 159.
24. *The Times*, 4 Sept. 1937.
25. Ibid., 1, 2 Sept. 1922.
26. Ibid., 26 Jan. 1921.
27. *Athletic News*, 4 Aug. 1924.
28. Interview with Mr C.S. Elliott (retired county cricketer).
29. Interview with Mr E.P. Robinson (retired county cricketer).
30. First-class Counties Captains Meeting, 5 Dec. 1927, Meetings at Lord's January 1927 to October 1934, MCC.
31. Annual Meeting of County Captains, 10 Dec. 1928, Meetings at Lord's Minutes January 1927 to October 1934 vol., MCC Library.
32. *Buff*, 7 May 1927.
33. *Athletic News*, 29 July 1929.
34. D. Foot, *Wally Hammond: The Reasons Why: A Biography* (London: Robson, 1996), p. 103.
35. C.S. Elliott interview.
36. M. Marshall, *Gentlemen & Players: Conversations with Cricketers* (London: Grafton, 1985), p. 7.
37. Interviews with Mr W. Place (retired county cricketer), C.S. Elliott and E.P. Robinson; *Lancashire Evening Telegraph*, 11 July 1989.
38. *The Times*, 28 June 1922.
39. Ibid., 8 Dec. 1931, 30 Jan. 1932.
40. *Field*, 2 April 1932; *Times*, 11 Aug. 1939.
41. *The Times*, 7 March 1929.

42. *Athletic News*, 28 May, 26 Nov. 1923.
43. *The Times*, 19 Jan. 1933.
44. Ibid., 26 Jan. 1933.
45. Joint meeting of the Advisory Committee and the Board of Control, 23 Nov. 1933; report of a meeting of seven umpires with the secretary and assistant secretary of the MCC, Meetings at Lord's Minutes vol. January 1927 to October 1934.
46. D. Lemmon, *Johnny Won't Hit Today: A Cricketing Biography of J.W.H.T. Douglas* (London: Allen and Unwin, 1983), p. 31.
47. A. Mailey, *10 for 66 and All That* (London: Phoenix Sports, 1958), p. 133; B. Andrews, *The Hand That Bowled Bradman: The Memories of a Professional Cricketer* (London: Macdonald, 1973), p. 44.
48. Letter of the Executive Committee of Sussex CCC to the MCC, 15 Sept. 1933, Sussex CCC Executive Committee minute book, East Sussex County Record Office.
49. C.S. Elliott interview.
50. *Club Cricket Conference Annual Handbook and Directory 1923* (n.p., n.d.), pp. 22–3.
51. F. Root, *A Cricket Pro's Lot* (London: Arnold, 1937), pp. 195–6.
52. *Buff*, 25 June 1921.
53. L. Constantine, *Cricket in the Sun* (London: Stanley Paul, n.d.), p. 91.
54. For a full discussion of the incident, see *Rochdale Observer*, 31 July 1920.
55. Interview with Mr J.A. Gledhill (retired grammar school teacher).
56. Walkden and District Amateur Cricket League minute book, 18, 26 May 1931, Salford Archives Centre U19/AM2.
57. Ibid., 10 Aug. 1934, 18 Apr. 1935; *Farnworth Weekly Journal*, 17 Aug. 1934.
58. Walkden and District ACL minute book, 18 Oct. 1935.
59. Interview with Sir Robert Southern (retired bank official).
60. *Buff*, 21 June 1930, 2 June 1934.
61. *Athletic News*, 4 July 1927.
62. *Buff*, 27 Aug. 1932.
63. *The Times*, 14 June 1933.
64. C.G. Macartney, *My Cricketing Days* (London: Heinemann, 1930), pp. 126, 237–8.
65. *Athletic News*, 15 Aug. 1921.
66. Ibid., 28 July 1924.
67. *Field*, 13 Sept. 1919.
68. *Athletic News*, 10 Aug. 1925.
69. H.W. Lee, *Forty Years of English Cricket with Excursions to India and South Africa* (London: Clerke & Cockeran, 1948), p. 37.
70. *Athletic News*, 7 June 1926.
71. *The Times*, 21 July 1924.
72. *Buff*, 18 July 1925.
73. B. Bowes, *Express Deliveries* (London: Stanley Paul, 1949), pp. 33, 169.
74. *Field*, 29 Aug. 1931.
75. H.W. Lee, *Forty Years of English Cricket*, p. 38.
76. *The Times*, 27 May 1938.
77. *Daily Mirror*, 21 June 1938.
78. *The Times*, 9 July 1920.
79. J.A. Gledhill interview.
80. *Buff*, 18 June 1921.
81. Bolton Cricket League minute book, 5 June 1931, 13 Aug. 1937.
82. Mass-Observation Worktown Survey, Box W2, File D Worktown Cricket, Mass-Observation Archive, University of Sussex.
83. *The Times*, 13 Oct. 1927.

5

Cricket and Gender

Growing attention has been focused on sport and gender identities in the 1980s and 1990s. Because of its physical nature, sport can reveal much about cultural assumptions surrounding what have been considered appropriate roles for the sexes. The emphasis in so many sports on physical strength has helped to butress beliefs that physical differences justify distinct spheres of social activity for men and women. The far greater number of men who play and watch sport, often dependent on the co-operation or exploitation of women, reflects the greater social power of men in deciding how time and money should be spent.

It can be demonstrated that sports have contributed to the emancipation of women. Jennifer Hargreaves and Eileen McCrone have shown how women playing sports in the late nineteenth and early twentieth centuries contributed to female liberation by undermining assumptions that women were physically so frail that they should be excluded from spheres of social activity monopolised by men.[1] As the form and intensity of male and female involvement with sport has varied between sports, different sports have not expressed or influenced assumptions about gender to the same degree. John Nauright and Timothy Chandler have shown, for instance, how the homosociability of rugby and its stress on physical force and toughness encouraged a distinct form of masculinity which emphasised the difference in the sexes and so helped to maintain separate social roles for them.[2] On the other hand, a sport such as tennis, which may have been played by more women than men and in which women often played against men, probably had a far different impact on gender relations. As the number of women playing cricket grew between the wars and since much male cricket depended on support from women, cricket casts an exceptionally revealing light on the cultural perceptions of gender roles in the 1920s and 1930s.

CRICKET, MASCULINITY AND MALE POWER

The number of women cricketers increased between the wars, but cricket remained predominantly a male activity and in this respect reflected and consolidated assumptions that it was natural for the two sexes to have separate areas of social involvement. Cricket discourses indicate that playing cricket was believed to promote distinctly masculine characteristics, and because it was seen as an expression of masculinity, it helped to emphasise the otherness of women. Apologists for cricket stressed that the game promoted courage, determination and endurance, qualities often described as masculine, but usually in a rhetoric which gave them an ethical dimension and emphasised that playing in accordance with the traditions of sportsmanship expressed an English form of masculinity. Those from public schools often mentioned cricket playing as a form of 'chivalry', a term with connotations of masculine courage, selflessness, devotion to others and a belief that ladies required the protection of men, and it can be argued that such male assumptions about the need of men to protect women was an ideology of male supremacy, just as its underlying assumption of female weakness could have been a motive for excluding women from certain areas of social activity. The notions of masculinity associated with cricket differed from those connected with many other sports. Cricket required strength, energy and fitness, but the fact that a few men in their forties played test match cricket, some in their fifties played county cricket and those even older were found in club cricket shows that cricket did not require very high levels of agility and fitness. The hardness of a cricket ball and the speed of fast bowling gave an element of danger in cricket, which was perhaps lacking in sports such as athletics, golf or tennis, but it did not possess the vigorous body contact of boxing or the different codes of football. Richard Holt has argued that a function of the sporting hero has been to teach men how to be men.[3] Cricket literature does not suggest that any cricket star of the inter-war years was admired for possessing the aggressively masculine toughness usually associated with boxers or some professional footballers such as the notorious Frank Barson,[4] but following Australian complaints about England's bodyline tactics in 1932–33 Douglas Jardine was praised for not flinching when West Indian fast bowlers employed similar methods against him in 1933. A theme underlying the bodyline controversy was that the Australian complaints about bodyline had been un-English.

In recent years use of the term 'blokeism' in relation to sport implies that it provides opportunities for men to express what they take to be male identities and male bonding, usually in exclusively male company. There is evidence of 'blokeism' in cricket, but this was not as excessive as in some other sports. The MCC, accepted as the leading authority within cricket, was an all-male club. The field of play had almost always been literally a male cultural space. Women playing in men's teams, though not totally unknown, was highly unusual. Women umpiring men's matches was practically unknown. Men's teams played women's teams only very occasionally and such matches often had an air of carnival about them, with all the men having to bat left-handed or with some similar handicap. Women were not admitted to the pavilions at some county grounds, which may be regarded as a form of male bonding and a desire to be away from the company of women, but it would seem that the conduct of those who frequented these pavilions was governed more by a sense of decorum than by masculine high spirits. The annual dinners and smokers' evenings of cricket clubs were often all male events, though they rarely seem to have been occasions for the sort of oafish masculinity sometimes associated with rugby club dinners or expressions of aggressively masculine 'blokeism'. The great majority of spectators at all levels of cricket were male, but the far from negligible numbers of women spectators suggests that the behaviour of male players and spectators did not offend feminine notions of propriety. The use of abusive language in the 'neighbourhood of ladies' by a Kent member in 1920 was felt to be such a serious matter that it was discussed by the Kent Committee and the member was threatened with expulsion from the club.[5] It is also likely that the need for income from female spectators at county clubs and clubs playing at the highest levels of league cricket, and the dependence of clubs playing recreational cricket on the services of women, discouraged cricket from becoming permeated with an aura of masculinity which women would have found repellent.

THE PLAYING OF CRICKET BY WOMEN

The playing of cricket by women expanded and became more organised between the wars, but the number of women who played regularly never exceeded 5,000 and was probably always fewer than those playing tennis, golf or hockey. Cricket had been played at prestigious girls' boarding schools before the First World War and although there had been one or two famous women's teams in the late nineteenth century such as the White Heather Club and the semi-professional Original English Lady Cricketers,[6] as a sport for women in the early 1920s cricket was hampered by a shortage of clubs. The growth of women's cricket in the 1920s and 1930s can be related to the legacy of the First World War, which Jennifer Hargreaves has called a 'unique and liberating experience for many women, leaving them with confidence to flout old restrictions and re-create cultural meanings'.[7]

The Women's Cricket Association (WCA) was crucial to the growth of cricket playing by women and girls. Established in 1926 by women sports enthusiasts, who included hockey and lacrosse players wishing to play a summer team game rather than the more individualistic sports of tennis or golf, it provided an organisational structure for the women's game and drew attention to women playing cricket. During 1927 ten clubs affiliated to the WCA and nearly 350 individual members were enrolled. For those far away from a club, the WCA arranged a cricket week held at Colwall near Malvern where matches between scratch elevens were played.[8] The Association recognised that the most effective method of promoting the playing of cricket among women would be through the formation of clubs. By 1929, individual membership had passed 400 and 37 clubs and 39 schools and colleges had become affiliated.[9] *Women's Cricket*, the monthly journal of the WCA, recorded in 1933 that 'All over the country, be it Leeds, Hastings, Blackpool or Gravesend, there is a real turning to the game by women, and the future seems assured' and that 'Cricket in the Midlands is developing rapidly, especially in the Nottingham district'.[10] In 1929 the first public representative match of the WCA between London and District and the Rest of England was held at Beckenham CC, and teams organised by the WCA toured the west of England and Scotland. After some years of debate the WCA established County Associations in 1933 and these seem to have fulfilled at least partially the hope that they would stimulate the formation of further clubs. The first county associations were those of Middlesex, Lancashire, Kent, Nottinghamshire and Surrey[11] and by 1937 associations had been formed in 20 counties.[12] In 1938, 105 clubs, 18 colleges and 85 schools were affiliated to the WCA. The expansion of women's cricket was reflected in the rise of representative matches organised by the WCA. From 1930 matches had been played between sides representing the South, the North and the Midlands and the first county match held under the auspices of the WCA, Lancashire and Cheshire versus Durham, was played in 1931. A two-day match between an English XI and a Scottish XI was played in 1932. In the same year the WCA organised its first matches to be held on grounds, at Worcester and Edgbaston, where men played county cricket. In 1934–35 a party of 16 who paid their own passages and expenses played three test matches in Australia and one in New Zealand. In 1937 three test matches were played against an Australian team touring England.[13]

The WCA was largely an organisation of unmarried women. All who held the posts of secretary, assistant secretary and treasurer were single (although the chairman, Mrs Patrick Heron-Maxwell, was married). In 1932 only one of the 12 members of the executive committee was married and only four of the 22 members in 1938. *Women's Cricket* often printed the score cards of matches. These gave only players' surnames, but for a tiny number of players, usually only one or two per game, the prefix 'Mrs' was added, which probably means that the overwhelming majority of players were unmarried. Most members of Bolton Ladies CC, a club affiliated to the WCA, were below the age at which middle-class women tended to marry,[14] and the general practice seems to have been that women ceased playing cricket when they married or when they had children.

The main strength of the WCA was in the south and Midlands of England. The officers of the Association lived in the Home Counties. None of the 12 committee members in 1932 lived further north than Hereford and Northamptonshire,[15] though Lancashire was one of the first WCA county associations to be formed and by the late 1930s a Yorkshire Association had been created. The ethos of the WCA shared the assumptions of men from the wealthier classes about how cricket should be played and organised. Its constitution restricted individual membership to amateurs. The first issue of *Women's Cricket* proclaimed 'How fortunate we are in having no league tables – and how pleased we should be that we can think only in terms of "real cricket".' In its fourth issue an editorial in *Women's Cricket* stated 'There will be no thought of County Championships and League Tables. We have seen too much of the influence of both on other games – and we can but "point the moral".'[16] When county matches began to be played under the auspices of the WCA, they were not organised as a county championship and *Women's Cricket* argued 'to us County Cricket is not so much County Cricket as County Association Cricket … There may come, even within a year or two, County matches, but there will be no points for a win, no league ladder to slip down and the reward will be – the inward satisfaction, that a good game played well, gives!'[17] The WCA, however, did not prohibit outright the formation of leagues. In 1936 it claimed never to have refused membership to any club or organisation.[18] The Manchester Cricket League, formed in 1939, was affiliated to the WCA.

Not all women's cricket was played under the auspices of the WCA. In the Doncaster area the Dearne Valley League which was formed with six teams in 1927 had no connection with the WCA.[19] In 1930 *Women's Cricket* emphasised that a match between Leicestershire and Nottinghamshire had nothing to do with the WCA.[20] The Yorkshire and Lancashire Women's Cricket Federations organised cricket for women in northern England, but as their archives have not been found, their development has to be patched together from newspaper reports and oral recollections. The Yorkshire

Women's Cricket Federation (YWCF) was probably formed in 1930 or 1931, though some organised cricket for women had been played in the textile towns of the West Riding in the late 1920s. Margaret Lockwood, who was to become England's wicket-keeper, recalled that around 1929 she was invited to play in the team of Meltham Mills from Huddersfield in what may have been the final of a cup competition as the players each received a canteen of cutlery.[21] In 1930 Keighley CC of the Bradford League organised the Keighley Ladies' Cricket Competition, a knock-out competition for which the mother of the captain of the Keighley men's team provided a cup.[22]

Women's Federation cricket was stronger in Yorkshire than in Lancashire. By 1932 the Yorkshire Federation had established its Inter-City and Towns League with teams from the Yorkshire towns of Keighley, Brighouse, Bradford, Holme Valley, Halifax, Sowerby Bridge and Bingley and Littleborough in Lancashire. By 1935 those from Sowerby Bridge, Bingley and Holme Valley had dropped out and a Leeds team had withdrawn for financial reasons. New teams had entered from Liversedge, Huddersfield, Horbury and Dewsbury.[23] There was no Lancashire WCF League, but in 1935 there were teams playing from Milnrow, Littleborough, Crompton, Heywood, Todmorden and Burnley and some of these played in the YWCF's Inter-City League.[24] Bradford was able to sustain a Women's Evening Cricket League which had first played in 1931 and by the autumn of 1932 had 23 teams enrolled for the 1933 season.[25] This league also had a knock-out competition which included teams from outside the league. In 1932 Bankfoot CC, a men's club near Bradford, was organising a knock-out inter-works competition for women's teams. In 1934, 12 clubs belonged to the Leeds and District Women's Cricket League.[26] Before the Lancashire WCF was formed, the YWCF organised matches between Lancashire and Yorkshire; 8,000 spectators attended the first held at Bradford Park Avenue, one of Yorkshire CCC's major grounds, whilst the second, held at Littleborough in Lancashire, attracted 2,000 spectators. In 1934 a two-day inter-county match was held at Blackpool and by 1939 the LWCF and the YWCF were playing a seasonal series of five matches.[27]

Press reports suggest that the early 1930s were the high-water mark of Federation cricket. In 1934 the number of teams competing in the Keighley competition had fallen to five[28] and by 1935 the number of teams competing in the Bradford Women's Evening CL had dropped to 16. In the late 1930s less women's cricket activity was reported by *The Bradford Telegraph and Argus,* though this could have been more a reflection of newspaper policy than an indication of a decline in Federation cricket. Even at its peak the number of Federation clubs probably did not exceed a third of those connected with the WCA. Federation cricket never expanded beyond its base in the textile towns of the West Riding and eastern Lancashire. Most Federation cricket was played in leagues. Although players would not have been paid for playing Federation cricket, collections were made for outstanding performances in matches which attracted sufficient spectators. In 1930 Mrs L. Wilson when playing in the competition of Keighley CC received two collections of £4 for taking hat-tricks in two successive matches.[29]

WOMEN'S CRICKET AND THE EMANCIPATION OF WOMEN

Whether playing cricket should be viewed as a form of liberation for women depends on how far it represented and encouraged a challenge to cultural assumptions about the social roles considered suitable for women. Some who were prominent in the WCA had been active in extending the range of women's activities. Mrs Heron-Maxwell, chairman of the WCA, had advocated the enfranchisement of women, although she had never been a suffragette, and had organised the Women's Land Army in Kent, served on the National Executive of the Federation of Women's Institutes and had held the presidency of the Women's Hockey Association, while Vera Cox, the secretary of the WCA, had been the Organizing Secretary of the West Kent Land Army.[30] Eileen Broadbent, a founding member of the Yorkshire Women's Cricket Association and the founder and captain of Leeds Women's CC, was a university graduate, ran her own duplicating agency and trained as a solicitor.[31] Yet there is little to suggest that women cricketers played cricket with a deliberate intention of promoting female emancipation. Interviews have confirmed the opinion of Marjorie Pollard that women played cricket because 'we like it',[32] though one woman has added that she felt it important that women should have been able to decide for themselves whether they played.[33] The increase in cricket playing among women can be seen as an expression of women's emancipation because it indicated that women were choosing for themselves how they should use their bodies, but there was a limit to how far cricket playing promoted the liberation of women. The total number of women who played cricket regularly was always only a tiny fraction of the total female population, though they could have served as example and an encouragement to women who wished to pursue a broader range of social activities. Throughout the 1920s and 1930s the number of women cricketers must have been exceeded by those watching and supporting men's cricket. The limited degree of media attention directed to women's cricket meant that no woman cricketer achieved national fame or became as well known a sporting star as, say, the tennis players Kitty Godfree or Dorothy Round.

The WCA was established and run by women. Its constitution declared that its main purpose was 'to provide an organization for the furtherance of Women's Cricket'. Though permitted to become honorary members, men could not play for its teams or vote at its meetings. The WCA can be seen as example of what Jennifer Hargreaves has called 'separatist sports feminism', the attempts by women to achieve liberation not by seeking inclusion in hitherto male sporting domains, but by establishing alternative sporting structures and opportunities exclusively for women. Hargreaves argues that such sports separatism 'is not incompatible with the ideology of equal opportunity – it is seen as a way of balancing the advantages that men have had for so long. Separate organizations ... provide women with opportunities to administer and control their own activities.'[34] The WCA always stressed that it wished to organise and promote the playing of cricket by women in their own style and for their own enjoyment. It did not wish to challenge men's cricket. In 1932 in an editorial in *Women's Cricket* Marjorie Pollard wrote that 'the inflexible rule has been, no cricket with or against men. The reason for this is not "anti-man". It is just the realisation of sound sense, that men and women cannot and need not play team games together as opposed to each other.'[35] In her book *Cricket for Women and Girls,* Pollard claimed that

> it is sound and sane to realise from the start that men and women cannot play team games together or against each other. Individual games, yes; but team games, no! Mixed hockey was a farce and a failure, and mixed cricket, suppose either sex asked for it, would, I am sure, be as dismal a waste of time. I am not suggesting that the standard of women's games is below that of men's that they cannot play together or against each other. I think that the standards are different – just that – different.
>
> A Bugatti car does not race in the same class as an M.G. Midget. Yet who would deny the efficacy of both in their separate classes? ... So we, from the start, said we would play cricket by ourselves, for our own amusement and, if you like, for our own self-expression.[36]

The establishment and survival of the WCA may well have added to the degree of self-confidence among women sports players in their organisational capacities.

It is harder to regard Federation cricket as a form of separatist sports feminism. The YWCF was established and run by men connected with league clubs for men in the textile district of the West Riding. In 1932 all the YWCF officials were men. The managers of the Yorkshire and Lancashire Federation teams and the umpires of their matches were men. In 1932 when YWCF officials were trying to establish a similar Federation in Lancashire, they attempted to do this through the agency of male cricket clubs. In July 1932 the YWCF appointed an all male sub-committee to contact the Lancashire, Central Lancashire and Bolton Leagues, all leagues for men's clubs, about the possibility of a meeting to establish a Women's Cricket Federation in Lancashire,[37] and when the Lancashire Women's Cricket Federation was formed, it was established by male representatives from the Central Lancashire League clubs of Rochdale, Littleborough, Milnrow, Crompton and Middleton. The Bradford Women's Evening Cricket League had been formed in 1931 after 60 male cricket clubs had been circularised.[38]

The male officials of the YWCF saw women's cricket as a means of promoting men's cricket. The president of the YWCF, Mr F.H. Timperley, who was also connected with Littleborough CC of the Central Lancashire League, declared that he 'saw no other way for the future success of men's cricket than by fostering the progress of the game among women' and felt that Central Lancashire League clubs could derive 'a tremendous advantage from taking an interest in women's cricket'. Mr J.W. Carruthers felt that women's cricket had been 'of great service' to the Keighley club.[39] Several Federation sides had close connections with men's clubs whose income could have been boosted by gate receipts of women's matches, whilst other men's clubs made money from hiring their grounds to women's clubs. In the geographically restricted area where women played Federation cricket, it extended the range of social experience open to women, but male control of the Federation management structures and the belief among some men that women's cricket would benefit men's cricket suggest that the extent to which Federation cricket promoted the emancipation of women was limited. The management of Federation cricket by men indicates the strength of the cultural assumption in parts of the North that cricket should be administered by men.

Women's cricket also reflected the force of class divisions within English culture. The WCA was controlled by those from economically privileged groups and it tried to organise the women's game in accordance with the values of men's cricket clubs for those from the wealthier classes in the south of England. The great majority of its clubs were for those from the upper and middle classes. In most parts of the country working-class women and girls did not play cricket. As a school sport for girls, cricket was largely restricted to private and selective secondary schools, educational institutions which very few working-class girls attended. All the players of

Bolton Ladies CC, which belonged to the WCA, are remembered as having attended selective secondary schools. No mill girls played for this club.

Federation cricket was more working-class. Nancy Joy has pointed out that in the 1930s 'Thanks to the Federation, many a factory and business girl was enabled to enjoy a game of cricket which the organization of the WCA was at that time and place in no position to provide.'[40] Ten of the 12 teams in the YWCF's Leeds and District Women's Cricket League in 1934 were works teams and in 1935 five of the 16 teams in the Bradford Women's Evening Cricket League were connected with workplaces.[41] Catherine Airey who played Association and Federation cricket in Yorkshire has recalled that those who played for Federation teams had usually left school at 14 whereas Association players had generally been to grammar school and college, which reflected roughly a division between the working and middle classes. Neither the WCA nor the Lancashire and Yorkshire Federations, however, were totally restricted to one class. In the late 1930s some works teams had affiliated to the WCA and one of the two Federation players selected for the WCA England squad in 1937 was remembered as 'quite wealthy' and the other as 'rather lah-di-dah'.[42]

Although the WCA and Federation cricket can be seen as evidence for the existence of class divisions between women, it is not clear whether these different forms of cricket organisation deepened class divisions among them. How the two bodies regarded each other is not wholly clear. *Women's Cricket* mentioned Federation cricket only twice in the 1930s. This may have been a sign that the WCA looked down on, and disapproved of, Federation cricket, which was clearly the attitude of one prominent Yorkshire Association cricketer in the 1930s who has been interviewed. The fact that the secretary of the Lancashire Association wrote to the press to refute a claim that the WCA had been 'too high-brow' to have been approached by the LWCF suggests that some may have harboured such a thought, but after a meeting between the two bodies the LWCF was allowed to affiliate to the WCA. The background to this was that the Federation would not have been able to arrange a match against the Australian touring party in 1937 without being affiliated to the WCA.[43] On the other hand the holding of matches in 1935 between the Yorkshire WCA and the YWCF and between a north of England WCA representative side and a Federation XI,[44] and the selection of Federation players for the Yorkshire WCA and England teams, indicate that relations between the WCA and the Lancashire and Yorkshire Federations cannot have been fiercely antagonistic.

The WCA tried hard to ensure that cricket played under its auspices met with the approval of the male cricket world. At first sight this seems to be an acceptance of male superiority in cricket and perhaps suggests that

101

women's cricket was not a particularly powerful agency for the emancipation of women. Closer inspection, however, shows that the women who controlled the WCA believed that the women's game could have collapsed without the co-operation of men's cricket. Except for some schools and colleges, no women's clubs owned their grounds and although some rented municipal pitches, very many women's clubs had to use the grounds of men's clubs. Women's cricket could not afford to antagonise men's cricket. The WCA was always concerned that women should play with decorum, but this was also related to the dependence upon men's clubs for grounds. Marjorie Pollard argued that women's matches would only be staged on good quality grounds if women cricketers displayed 'dignity, circumspection, caution and submission to public opinion',[45] which in most cases would have meant male opinion.

The desire for women's cricket to be played with decorum can also be related to those strands of feminist thought which stressed that performing tasks to the highest standards was a means of emphasising the capacity of women to undertake a wider range of social activities. The following comment made in *Women's Cricket* in 1939 shows that not all women cricketers were achieving the high standards which the leadership of the WCA espoused:

> Last season it was noticeable, especially among young players who knew nothing whatsoever of the struggle it was to get cricket established, that the standard of equipment and uniform and punctuality were all on the downgrade ... Games that were timed for 2-30 often started in the region of 3 o'clock and few seemed to mind or think it mattered ... players who fail in these respects only exhibit to the world, as if on a hoarding, that they personally are inefficient, lazy, thoughtless, inconsistent and quite incapable of even minding themselves.

If this had happened earlier, Pollard pointed out, women cricketers would not have played at Trent Bridge or The Oval.[46] The WCA was often concerned with the dress code for women cricketers. This was not an example of a female obsession with fashion but rather another aspect of ensuring that women's cricket was played with a satisfactory level of decorum and a means of demonstrating that women's cricket was not a trivial matter. In 1928 the WCA had decided that its teams had to play in white and that sleeveless dresses and transparent stockings were not permitted. Its AGM of 1930 resolved that players could have the option of wearing regulation dresses or tunics which were not to be more than three inches above the ground when kneeling and that the wearing of white shoes was to be encouraged.[47] Molly Hide, the captain of the WCA England team in 1937 was especially strict about the dress of England players. In addition to observing WCA recommendations on dress, she forbade the wearing of coloured hair ribbons and insisted that pads and footwear were put on only inside the pavilion.[48]

Not all women cricketers followed the dress recommendations of the WCA. In 1931 *Women's Cricket* complained that the

> clothing problem is still with us. Last season – without exaggeration, there were black shoes, shoes with coloured saddles. There were silk frocks, pique frocks, and all sorts of frocks – with sleeves, without sleeves and some with nearly sleeves.

In August 1936 Marjorie Pollard's editorial complained of having seen 'ankle socks with bare legs, knee-length stockings with bare knees and the usual white stockings' and of some players using the WCA ruling that players in representative matches had to wear white stockings as an excuse to play in stockings which did not cover the knee.[49] By 1939 there was debate within the WCA about what type of socks or stockings should be worn. The caption to a photograph of ankle socks, knee length socks, oversocks [socks worn with stockings] printed in *Women's Cricket* in 1939 asked: 'Which is it to be?'[50] *Women's Cricket* did not print any pictures in the 1930s of women cricketers wearing trousers, but this could have been related to Marjorie Pollard's desire never to see women 'so garbed'.[51] Oral evidence has produced no examples of women playing under the auspices of the WCA and wearing trousers.

Federation cricket had a more relaxed dress code. When the Yorkshire Federation first played Lancashire, it was decided that players should wear white, but the design of the dress was left optional so that players wishing to wear trousers could so. A newspaper photograph of the team showed three in trousers and three with skirts reaching well below their knees, whilst the rest wore knee-length skirts. By 1935, however, the players of the YWCF representative side were wearing a uniform dress.[52]

Appraisals of what playing cricket among women reveals about cultural perceptions of gender roles have to consider the responses of men to women playing cricket. Some encouraged women to play cricket. Several prominent women cricketers had fathers or brothers who were cricket enthusiasts and who helped them to play. It has been shown above that the YWCF was founded by men and that men's cricket clubs were used as the vehicle for the establishment of the LWCF. Both WCA and Federation matches were often umpired by men and men coached women's clubs. Allowing women's teams to use the grounds of men's clubs and the staging of women's matches on test match grounds such as The Oval, Old Trafford, Headingley and Trent Bridge, and the county grounds of Leicester, Worcester and Northampton expressed encouragement for women's cricket.

Some men believed that cricket was not a suitable sport for women and girls, and such an outlook can be seen to stem from the cultural assumption that the two sexes should have distinct social roles, although it is likely that the expansion of cricket among women in the 1930s weakened this view. Neville Cardus wrote of the male cricketer that 'his sister cannot follow him into the true province of the game',[53] whilst Marjorie Pollard complained about male professional cricketers writing in the press that cricket was 'no game for women or girls', but dismissed their reasons for such views as 'utterly frivolous, inane and without any foundation whatever'. She added that some men had argued that women did not possess the physical strength to play cricket.[54] Some of the comments made by women to justify their playing cricket were far from a rhetoric of women's emancipation. Marion Stockton, whose husband, Sir Edwin Stockton, had been treasurer, president and chairman of Lancashire CCC, was the first president of the Lancashire Women's Cricket Association. She claimed that women cricketers were not trying to emulate men but wished to play in their own way[55] and in *The Cricketer* wrote that besides teaching girls 'that wonderful team spirit that no other game in the world can teach', cricket playing would help a girl to 'understand all the finer points of the game and … [so] not disgrace herself or make her menfolk ashamed when taken to watch a match'.[56] Some women felt that cricket was not an entirely suitable sport for girls. In 1922 a committee of the College of Preceptors considered the effects of physical education upon girls. It received 629 replies to questionnaires which it had circulated to doctors, medical students and headmistresses. These showed approval for tennis and netball as games for girls, approval of hockey though added that it was too rough and strenuous for some girls, whilst cricket was 'generally approved' but with some doubts about its 'utility' as a game for girls. Football was the game which received least approval.[57] In 1930 Onlooker, a woman, wrote in *The Daily Herald*: 'Cricket is not a woman's game in my opinion, chiefly because some of them look rather ridiculous playing cricket.'[58]

Some men belittled and ridiculed women's cricket, which can be seen to reflect assumptions that cricket playing was an area of male social power and a demonstration of male supremacy. The fact that the male president of the YWCF felt it necessary in 1932 to declare in public that 'women's cricket is no hat-trimming or pantomime exhibition'[59] suggests that some in the North may have held such a view. When reporting on the women's test match between England and Australia in 1937, Stanley Halsey wrote in *The Daily Express* that 'Certain folk went to watch the "cricketesses" in action on Saturday much in the mood they would go to see the latest vaudeville act' but he added that they were 'surprised into serious appreciation'.[60] Most newspapers gave little coverage to the women's game, and as the press was in the main controlled by men, this probably indicated a male suspicion that the playing of cricket by women was of no great consequence and did not represent a challenge to the social power of men. Reports in *The Times* on women's cricket were brief but usually supportive. In Yorkshire *The Bradford Telegraph and Argus* supported women's cricket with such enthusiasm that representatives of Lancashire clubs 'marvelled at' the reports of women's cricket in Yorkshire newspapers while a senior official of the YWCF felt it necessary to deny that the YWCF was 'a press stunt'.[61] In the 1930s Marjorie Pollard had a regular column in *The Cricketer,* and in editorial comments *The Cricketer* generally supported women playing cricket. Pollard was also hired as the women's cricket correspondent of *The Morning Post* and she felt that the press reaction to the first public match arranged by the WCA had been 'surprised and even serious', but Jennifer Hargreaves has shown that one section of the press described it as 'Northern Lovelies' versus 'Southern Sweeties'.[62] Pollard complained that in 1929 'pictures appeared in some papers, so obviously posed, with girls in trousers, caps, head-dresses, and others with bare legs, all purporting to be "Eves at the Wicket"'.[63] A tone of condescension and male smugness was sometimes found in reports of women's cricket by male journalists in other newspapers. In 1931, for instance, it was reported in *The Daily Telegraph* that

> All the bowlers bowled overarm, and the batsmen did not long indulge in grass mowing. There was the wicket keeper taking them on the legside like any veteran, and there stood the umpires, grave as could be. Even Mrs Grundy could not make trouble here. There was not a trouser on the field nor a bare leg.
>
> Lots of batsmen were given out by the umpires, but not one argued or even stamped a foot.

A comment from *The Sunday Chronicle* can also be seen as male supercil- iousness: 'Alas! There was one thing to mar the great occasion – a wind. True it was only a summer breeze, but it was sufficient to lift the short garments which these women call a skirt well above their heads.'[64] Such comments appear to confirm the contention of Hargreaves that 'even tolerant comment was often synonymous with condescension and patronizing humour – in short, the women's game was seldom treated seriously.'[65] Press reports rarely suggested that cricket playing masculinised women, but oral evidence indicates that this was what some men believed and sheds some light on male notions of femininity. One male respondent who became a headmaster recalled that 'some very butch girls' played for Bolton Ladies CC.[66]

SUPPORT FROM WOMEN FOR MALE CRICKET

Women who played cricket were far outnumbered by those who supported men's cricket. Indeed all levels of cricket playing by men were dependent on support from women. At county clubs between 10 and 20 per cent of the members were women and for most counties the number of women members was a little higher in the 1920s than the 1930s. In 1930 Lancashire had 1,387 lady members, probably the highest number in one season for any county between the wars, and 4,055 men members. In 1921 Lancashire had 911 lady members and 3,642 men members. By 1932 the figures were 778 women and 3,128 men and for the rest of the 1930s the number of women members remained between a fifth and a quarter of the number of men members. Yorkshire, the county with the highest number of men members in most inter-war seasons, had nearly 2,000 men in 1920 and only 68 women, but by 1930 the number of men had passed 6,000 and women members exceeded 600. In the late 1930s, numbers were more or less as they had been in 1930. Samples of more than 500 members of Kent CCC show that the proportion of women declined slightly between the wars. In 1920, 15.6 per cent of the sample had been women, 13.6 in 1930 and 12.2 by 1938.[67] In 1922 the Surrey club decided that not more than 450 of its members would be women or schoolgirls and this number was reached in each subsequent inter-war season. Counties with the smallest numbers of members were often among those with the highest proportion of women members. In 1934, for instance, nine of the 40 Worcestershire members with Birmingham addresses were women. The social ambience of club membership suggests that women members of county clubs would have been predominantly upper or middle class. The samples of the Kent membership show that a little over half the women members were married in 1920, 1930 and 1938, whilst analysis of members' names and addresses shows that just over half were related to men members in 1920 and 1930 and just under a half in 1938. These figures do not include widows, daughters or sisters of members with addressees different from those of their male relations. At many counties the subscriptions for women were lower than those for men, but their contribution to the total membership income of county clubs was not inconsiderable. In 1930 around 15 per cent of the membership income of Kent and of Lancashire came from women members, though for Yorkshire the figure was only about five per cent.

Women were also members of league clubs. Subscriptions of women members made an important contribution to their finances. In 1924 nearly a third of the members of Nelson CC were women and they provided almost 30 per cent of the club's subscription revenue,[68] but scraps of evidence suggest that these figures were higher than those for league clubs in the Bolton area. In 1932 when Radcliffe CC was playing in the Bolton League, 34 of its 305 members were women and in 1937, when it had joined the Central Lancashire League, 72 of its 600 members were women.[69] Many leading league clubs in Bolton were also tennis and bowls clubs and possibly some women became members of such clubs in order to play these games. In 1937, for instance, 76 of the 630 members of the Eagley Cricket, Tennis and Bowling Club were women.[70]

The number of women who paid to watch county cricket is uncertain. As annual balance sheets did not distinguish between admission revenue paid by men and women, it is not possible to calculate the proportion of gate receipts paid by women or whether this changed between the wars. The same is largely true of those levels of league cricket which attracted paying spectators. In the late 1930s Mass-Observation found that a third of spectators at the cup final of the Bolton and District Cricket Association, and 50 of the 700 spectators at a match between the two clubs at the top of the Bolton League were women and girls.[71] It has been recalled that about a third of those who watched the home matches of Eagley CC in the 1930s would have been women, but these would have included those preparing and selling teas and playing tennis.[72] A very high proportion of those attending the annual match at Lord's between the public schools of Eton and Harrow, which was very much part of the London season, are believed to have been female. If a third of the 17,000 who paid for admission to this match in 1922 had been women,[73] this might have been the highest number of women present at any cricket match in that year. Some women may have liked to watch first-class cricket because of the sexual appeal of the cricketers. In 1926 'A Woman Critic' reviewed for *The Daily Express* the physical appearances of the England test match team and wrote that 'Taken collectively, it is not a good-looking team, judging by the standards of recognised facial beauty, and that set by this year's Cambridge crew. Individually each has his points. Two at least are handsome, and all fine, clean-limbed and pleasing.' She placed the members of the team in order of their looks. Percy Chapman was regarded as the most attractive being 'Greek perfection ... Greek line plus something more, if a little out of keeping, a powerful British jaw'.[74] The publication of such an article shows that it was considered acceptable for women to be interested in the physical appearance of male cricketers.

Many leading league clubs had ladies' committees, who boosted club funds by preparing and selling refreshments and by assisting with other fund-raising activities such as dances, concerts and whist drives. In 1929, the catering requirements at each home match for Heaton CC, for instance, included 40 dozen pies, 20 dozen tea cakes, 30 dozen fancy cakes, 6 lbs of butter, 20 lbs of sugar, 15 lbs of ham, 16 quarts of milk and 5 lbs of tea. The club's tea room could accommodate 200.[75] Many leading clubs organised bazaars as special fund-raising events and the services of women were essential to their success, especially as women were expected to serve on the stalls or to provide products to be sold at bazaars and to prepare and serve refreshments. The ritual of tea was observed even by clubs playing at the humblest levels of club and league cricket. Oral evidence indicates that teas were invariably prepared by the womenfolk of players. Some wealthy women were important patrons of cricket clubs for men. In 1934, for instance, Egerton CC to the north of Bolton was able to proceed with the purchase of its ground for £1,100 because Mrs H.T. Deakin, a member of the family which owned the local dye works, offered to lend without interest the £350 required as a deposit and to provide a further pound for each pound raised by the club.[76]

Women had little formalised power in either county or club cricket. At some county clubs, such as Lancashire and Middlesex, women could not become full members and were not allowed to vote at annual meetings or to enter the pavilion. At Yorkshire, women could not become members with full voting rights but could enter pavilions, whilst the Kent club permitted women to become full voting members with access to the pavilion. Mrs Price-Hughes at Worcestershire CCC was probably the only woman who served on the committee of a county club between the wars. At the AGM of 1921 she had been thanked for her efforts with the finance and catering departments.[77] There appears to have been no public campaign for women to be granted membership of the MCC between the wars. Very few women seem to have been elected on to the committees of clubs at other levels of cricket. Not one of the 157 cricket clubs from Essex listed in the Club Cricket Conference Handbook for 1939 had a woman as its secretary or match secretary. In the Bolton area women were sometimes members of the committees of those league clubs which had tennis or bowls sections, but it would seem that they were elected on to club committees to represent these other sports. Women were not members of the committees at those clubs which played only cricket and no women were club representatives or

1. Powerful figures in the world of first-class cricket. From left to right, Sir Francis Lacey (secretary of the MCC 1888–1926), Colonel L.W.H. Troughton (general manager of Kent CCC 1923–33), S. Christopherson (president of the MCC 1939–46 and chairman of the Midland Bank 1943–45) and Lord Harris (treasurer of the MCC 1916–32, president of MCC 1895) on the Canterbury ground in 1924.

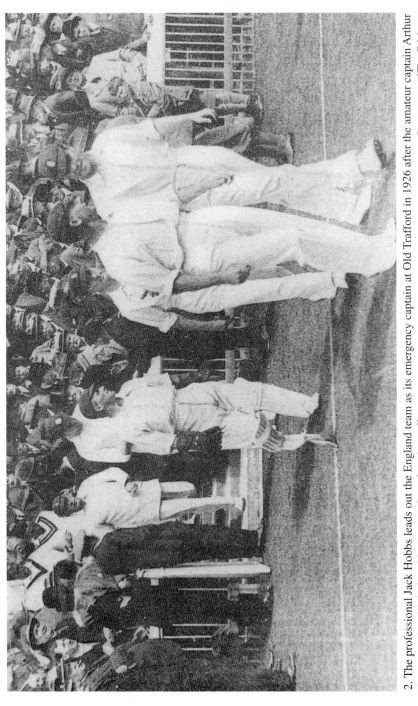

2. The professional Jack Hobbs leads out the England team as its emergency captain at Old Trafford in 1926 after the amateur captain Arthur Carr was taken ill during this test match against Australia.

By courtesy of The Cricketer

By courtesy of News Group Newspapers and the British Library

3. This cartoon from the front page of *The Daily Herald* on 24 January 1925 shows how some viewed the tradition of amateur authority in English cricket.

By permission of Lancashire County Library, Burnley Local Studies Collection

4. These two teams which played in the Burnley Sunday School League seem to confirm that cricket clubs based on churches in the North drew their players from what were thought to be the respectable sections of the working class.

By courtesy of Mr Don Ambrose

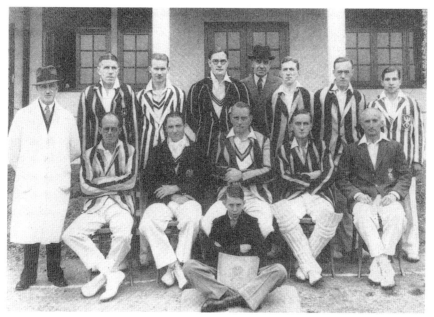

5. The extremes of cricket attire. (Above) This photograph of Hornsey CC from Middlesex shows that the blazer was an essential item of cricket dress for the better-off. (Below) Not all members of this village team from Sedlescombe (Sussex) in 1926 had whites.

6. Large crowds could be attracted to the higher levels of club and league cricket. A large crowd watching a Central Lancashire League match at Rochdale in the 1920s (above) and (below) another large crowd at a match of Mitcham CC in the early 1930s.

VICTORIOUS YORKSHIRE WOMEN CRICKETERS.

The Yorkshire women's cricket team which beat the Lancashire women's side in last night's match at Park Avenue, Bradford. "Telegraph and Argus" copyright.

Reproduced by kind permission of the Telegraph & Argus, *Bradford*

7. These two Women's Cricket Federation teams – the Yorkshire WCF team (above) and that of Littleborough CC from Lancashire – did not observe the dress code of the Women's Cricket Association.

By courtesy of Littleborough CC

By courtesy of the Bury Times Newspaper Group

8. Ladies' committees did much to boost the finances of clubs playing at the higher levels of league cricket by raising funds and preparing and selling teas. These women had helped to raise money for the new tea room of Radcliffe CC in 1925.

By courtesy of The Cricketer

9. Much publicity was given to the scheme at Oxford where elementary schoolboys were given coaching by undergraduates and allowed to practise on college grounds. This picture shows a group of boys who had participated in the scheme being taken on a visit to Lord's in 1927.

members of the management committees of any of the locality's cricket leagues. Ladies' committees of clubs playing at the highest levels of league cricket in the North and Midlands do not seem to have been part of the formal authority structure of the clubs. Their major function was the co-ordination of the preparation and sale of teas and assisting with other fund-raising activities. The almost total absence of demands from women to be admitted to positions of formalised authority within cricket suggests that women accepted that it should be controlled by men, which reflected and re-inforced cultural assumptions that social power should be exercised by men.

Despite their lack of formal authority, women were not totally powerless within the world of men's cricket. Oral testimony shows that objections from their womenfolk were a major reason why many youths and men stopped playing cricket, whilst playing and watching cricket by men often depended upon negotiation with wives about the budgeting of time. Some men who spent much time playing or watching cricket must have done so in spite of opposition from their womenfolk, but there is no way of establishing whether the scale of such behaviour varied between the wars. Interviews, however, reveal that many women encouraged their menfolk to play or watch cricket. Although such statements are generally made in the presence of their husbands, many women have said that their menfolk could have done much worse than spend so much time playing or watching cricket, and when pressed to define 'doing much worse', they usually claim that other male leisure interests were more harmful to the welfare of families. It is also likely that the emphasis in cricket discourses on sportsmanship and the moral worth of cricket helped to persuade many women that playing and watching cricket by males was an activity to be encouraged. Holding dances, whist drives and concerts and engaging women in cricket club affairs, even though this may have been in the capacity of making teas, can be interpreted as tactics to neutralise the opposition of women to their menfolk's involvement with cricket and as such are an indirect acknowledgement of women's social power. Yet when such an interpretation of women's involvement in club activities has been put to former players and their wives, none appear to have thought of it in such a light. The ability of some women to persuade their menfolk to cease playing cricket, and the dependence of clubs upon the co-operation of women in preparing teas and fund-raising events, meant that male cricket clubs had to act in accordance with what women believed to be due respect and consideration. Whatever the degree of women's opposition to their menfolk's involvement with cricket, it never appears to have been on such a scale as to have become a matter of frequent comment in the sporting press. Oral evidence suggests that some women enjoyed supporting male cricket. Preparing teas provided opportunities to socialise with other women.[78]

Probably most men assumed that it was natural for the domestic needs of cricket clubs to be performed by women. In an article in *The Cricketer* in 1923 on how to organise a village club, Laurance Woodhouse advised 'Interest the good ladies of neighbourhood ... they can certainly handle the tea intervals better than mere man, and have a pleasant way of decorating the tea tables.'[79] Many men, no doubt, would have agreed with the comment of J.T. Tyldesley, a former Lancashire and test match batsman, when he opened the new tea room of Radcliffe CC in 1925 that 'The ladies could hardly play cricket with the men but they could come to the ground and make tea for them and mix with the men over a friendly cup.'[80] The numbers of women who prepared teas for male cricketers and accepted a division of family income and time which allowed men to play or watch cricket suggest that many women as well as men accepted the culturally based assumption that the two sexes should have different spheres of social activity and that domestic tasks were the 'natural' province of women. The frequent use of the expression that 'he could have done much worse' in a context which implies that other predominantly male leisure interests could be more injurious to family welfare may indicate that many women had accepted the cultural assumption that equated femininity with a familial domestic role. Such an assumption can be seen to bolster male power by perpetuating the notion that the two sexes should have separate social roles and that economic and political life should be dominated by men, but they also harmonised with the rise of 'New Feminism' which called for greater social recognition and economic support for activities that represented distinctive areas of women's expertise, such as child-rearing and housecraft.[81] Interviews have shown that in some instances women consented to men playing or watching cricket because this could be a useful tactic in persuading men to perform other tasks.

The light which women's support for playing and watching cricket sheds on how men and women perceived the relationship between the sexes suggests that it was characterised more by sociability and co-operation than by antagonism. No doubt some women felt that they had been coerced into supporting the involvement of their menfolk with cricket and some men stopped playing because of pressure from their wives; others may have played even when their wives disliked them doing so. Yet the overall impression which emerges from interviews with the wives of cricketers is that they approved of their menfolk's involvement with cricket. In retrospect many women have realised that their support for men's cricket reflected the greater social power of men but at the time they did not seem to have resented their menfolk's involvement with cricket. The women who made teas, washed cricket clothing and assisted with the fund-raising activities of cricket clubs do not seem to have felt that they were being exploited, but rather that cricket was an activity which they enjoyed supporting. Interviews have shown that many wives felt that playing and watching cricket were superior to other sports, which tends to suggest that they may have objected to their menfolk spending an equivalent amount of time on other sports, but it also indicates that many women had come to accept that cricket was an expression of an especially English form of moral worth.

NOTES

1. J. Hargreaves, '"Playing like Gentlemen while Behaving like Ladies": Contradictory Features of the Formative Years of Women's Sport', *British Journal of Sports History*, 2, 1 (May 1985) and *Sporting Females: Critical Issues in the History and Sociology of Women's Sports* (London: Routledge, 1994), Chapters 3–5; K.E. McCrone, *Sport and the Physical Emancipation of English Women, 1870–1914* (London: Routledge, 1988). J. Riordan, 'The Social Emancipation of Women through Sport', *British Journal of Sports History*, 2, 1 (May 1985), draws upon evidence from a wide variety of countries to argue that participation in sport has helped to undermine assumptions that women were too frail for many areas of social activity previously monopolised by men. For discussion of sport and gender identities in a variety of social settings, see J.A. Mangan and R.J. Park, eds., *From 'Fair Sex' to Feminism. Sport and the Socialization of Women in the Industrial and Post-industrial Eras* (London: Cass, 1987), and J.A. Mangan and J. Walvin, eds., *Manliness and Morality: Middle-class Masculinity in Britain and America* (Manchester: Manchester UP, 1987).
2. J. Nauright and T.J.L. Chandler, eds., *Making Men: Rugby and Masculine Identity* (London: Cass, 1996).
3. R. Holt, 'Heroes of the North: Sport and the Shaping of Regional Identity', in J. Hill and J. Williams, eds., *Sport and Identity in the North of England* (Keele: Keele UP, 1996), p. 154. For a discussion of how the forms of English masculinity associated with cricket stars have changed over time, see R. Holt, 'Cricket and Englishness: The Batsman as Hero', *International Journal of the History of Sport*, 13, 1 (March 1996).
4. R. Holt, 'Heroes of the North', p. 154.
5. Kent CCC General Committee minute book, 8 July 1920, Kent County Record Office Ch 75 A2/4.
6. K.A.P. Sandiford, *Cricket and the Victorians* (Aldershot: Scolar, 1994), pp. 45–7; *The Cricketer Winter Annual, 1921–22* (London: Cricketer Publications, n.d.), p. 115; C.M. Loader, 'In the West', *Cricketer*, 8 July 1939, p. 340, traces the growth of cricket playing before 1914 among women in the West of England.
7. J. Hargreaves, *Sporting Females*, p. 113.
8. M. Pollard, *Cricket for Women and Girls* (London: Hutchinson, 1934), p. 20.
9. Ibid., p. 22.
10. *Women's Cricket*, 4, 2 (June 1933).
11. M. Pollard, *Cricket for Women*, pp. 23–6.

12. *The Times*, 25 May 1937.

13. M. Pollard, *Cricket for Women*, pp. 145–58, gives the dates and venues of representative matches organised under the auspices of the WCA between 1929 and 1933; N. Joy, *Maiden Over. A Short History of Women's Cricket and a Diary of the 1948–49 Test Tour to Australia* (London: Sporting Handbooks, 1950), pp. 148, 152–9, gives the dates and venues of England matches played in the 1930s and of the matches played by the Australian tourists in England in 1937.

14. Interview with Ms M. Hall (retired teacher).

15. *Women's Cricket*, 3, 1 (May 1932).

16. Ibid., 1, 1 (May 1930), 4, 1 (Aug. 1930).

17. Ibid., 3, 3 (July 1932).

18. *Buff*, 7 Nov. 1936.

19. P.L. Scowcroft, *Cricket in Doncaster and District: An Outline History* (Doncaster: Doncaster Library Service, 1985), p. 21.

20. *Women's Cricket*, 1, 4 (Aug. 1930).

21. Interview with Ms M. Lockwood (retired teacher, England wicket-keeper).

22. *Bradford Telegraph and Argus*, 21 Sept. 1932.

23. Ibid., 23 Aug. 1932; *Yorkshire Sports and Cricket Argus*, 15 June 1935.

24. *Yorkshire Sports and Cricket Argus*, 15 June 1935.

25. *Bradford Telegraph and Argus*, 9 Nov. 1932.

26. Ibid., 21 July 1932; *Women's Cricket*, 5, 1 (May 1934).

27. *Bradford Telegraph and Argus*, 24, 30 June, 5, 9 July 1932; *Keighley News*, 8, 14 July, 1939.

28. *Keighley News*, 8 Sept. 1934.

29. *Bradford Telegraph and Argus*, 18 July 1930.

30. N. Joy, *Maiden Over*, p. 35.

31. Interviews with M. Lockwood and Ms C. Airey (retired woollen mill warper, later restaurant proprietor).

32. M. Pollard, *Cricket for Women*, p. 13.

33. M. Hall interview.

34. J. Hargreaves, *Sporting Females*, pp. 30–1.

35. *Women's Cricket*, 3, 3 (July 1932).

36. M. Pollard, *Cricket for Women*, pp. 16–17.

37. *Bradford Telegraph and Argus*, 20 July 1932.

38. Ibid., 21 Sept. 1932.

39. Ibid., 21 Sept., 9 Nov. 1932.

40. N. Joy, *Maiden Over*, p. 44.

41. *Women's Cricket*, 5, 1 (May 1934); *Yorkshire Sports and Football Argus,* 27 April 1935.

42. The respondent who made this comment does not wish to be identified.

43. *Buff*, 7 Nov. 1936.

44. *Yorkshire Sports and Cricket Argus*, 6 July 1935.

45. *Women's Cricket*, 7, 4 (Aug. 1936).

46. Ibid., 10, 1 (May 1939).

47. Ibid., 2, 1 (May 1931).

48. M. Lockwood interview.

49. *Women's Cricket*, 2, 1 (May 1931), 7, 4 (Aug. 1936).

50. *Women's Cricket,* 10, 5 (Sept. 1939).

51. M. Pollard, *Cricket for Women*, p. 21.

52. *Bradford Telegraph and Argus*, 24, 30 June 1932; *Yorkshire Sports and Cricket Argus*, 15 June 1935.

53. N. Cardus, *Cricket* (London: Longmans, Green, 1930), p. 29.
54. M. Pollard, *Cricket for Women*, p. 17.
55. *Buff*, 4 Feb. 1933.
56. *Cricketer*, 10 Sept. 1932, p. 585.
57. *The Times*, 9 Aug. 1922.
58. *Daily Herald*, 31 May 1930.
59. *Bradford Telegraph and Argus*, 9 Nov. 1932.
60. *Daily Express*, 14 June 1937.
61. *Bradford Telegraph and Argus*, 9 July 1932.
62. J. Hargreaves, *Sporting Females*, p. 124.
63. M. Pollard, *Cricket for Women*, p. 23.
64. Quoted in *Women's Cricket*, 2, 5 (Sept. 1931).
65. J. Hargreaves, *Sporting Females*, p. 124.
66. The fact that the man who made this comment does not wish to be identified reveals much about male attitudes to women.
67. Annual reports of Essex CCC for 1920, 1924; annual handbooks of Lancashire CCC, Kent CCC and Yorkshire CCC.
68. J. Hill, 'League Cricket in the North and Midlands, 1900–1940', in R. Holt, ed., *Sport and the Working Class in Modern Britain* (Manchester: Manchester UP, 1990), p. 131.
69. Radcliffe CC ledger 1932–45, Radcliffe Public Library.
70. Financial statement of Eagley Cricket, Tennis and Bowling Club for 1937. I am grateful to Ms M. Hall for allowing me to consult this document.
71. Mass-Observation Worktown Survey, Box W2, File D Worktown: Cricket, Mass-Observation Archive, Sussex University.
72. M. Hall interview.
73. MCC Daily Receipts book, MCC Library.
74. *Daily Express*, 12 June 1926.
75. *Buff*, 14 Sept. 1929.
76. Ibid., 31 March 1934.
77. *Worcester Herald*, 14 Jan. 1922.
78. Interview with Sir Robert (retired bank official) and Lady Southern.
79. *Cricketer*, Feb. 1923, p. 24.
80. *Radcliffe Times*, 30 May 1925.
81. For a detailed discussion of New Feminism, see M. Pugh, *Women and the Women's Movement in Britain 1914–1959* (London: Macmillan, 1992), Chapter 8.

6

Cricket, Hierarchy and Class

In the 1980s and 1990s great debate has raged among historians about whether class, and particularly class identities, based on convictions that the interests of different classes were in conflict, have been the dominant form of social consciousness in Britain. Postmodernist and post-structuralist forms of social analysis and the 'linguistic turn' in historical studies have underplayed the significance of class identities and suggested that other forms of consciousness, such as nation, gender, ethnicity and religion, have been more powerful in shaping perceptions of the social order.[1] In contemporary Britain class has been pronounced dead, but by no means all historians have accepted that class should be discarded as the dominant narrative of English social history.[2] The term 'class' figured prominently in discourses surrounding social relations in England between the wars and was used readily by very many to describe their identity and status and those of others, though subscribing to the notion of a society stratified on the basis of class may not have been accompanied by beliefs that the interests of different classes were in conflict.

Cricket was associated with privilege and social distinction throughout the inter-war period. Few other cultural institutions made so clear the inequalities of economic status and social background or demonstrated to individuals their place in the social hierarchy. In recreational cricket socially exclusive cricket clubs reflected class differences, whilst in first-class cricket the distinctions drawn between amateurs and professionals emphasised the gulfs between those from different social classes. The Women's Cricket Association, the organisation under whose auspices most women played cricket, was controlled by women from economically privileged backgrounds and its ethos had much in common with that of men educated at public schools. Because so much cultural significance was attached to cricket and because it did so much to highlight social distinctions, cricket provides penetrating insights into cultural assumptions about the construction of class identities and, by helping to reveal how the social order was perceived, contributes to an understanding of the cohesion and frictions found in English society between the wars.

AMATEURS AND PROFESSIONALS IN FIRST-CLASS CRICKET

First-class cricket between the wars exuded privilege. Chapter 2 has shown that the MCC and the county clubs were dominated by those who belonged to the political and social establishment. Members of county clubs were drawn from the upper and middle classes. County teams were usually captained by amateurs who in theory could afford to play county cricket without being paid. Many working people watched county cricket but they had no formalised role in it. All counties wished to boost their gate receipts, but none established structures whereby spectators could express their opinions about the administration of club affairs, though this was also true of other spectator sports. The report of the Findlay Commission, set up in 1937 to investigate the financial problems facing county cricket, suggests that it did not consult working people with an interest in cricket.

The distinctions between those who played as amateurs and professionals highlighted differences in social background. On the whole, amateurs belonged to those social classes that controlled the MCC and the county clubs. Most had backgrounds of established wealth, though the sources of their wealth were varied and some were much wealthier than others. Many came from families with sufficient wealth to have sent them to public schools. Between the wars 92 men played in matches for the Gentlemen, the side chosen to represent the leading amateur cricketers, in matches listed in Michael Marshall's *Gentlemen & Players*. Eight had been raised and educated overseas. Seventy-one had attended public schools, though some of these could be described as minor public schools. Eight had attended Eton, six Harrow, six Winchester, five Dulwich, five Rugby, four Malvern and four Repton. A further 14 had attended such prestigious schools as Charterhouse, Cheltenham, Downside, Haileybury, Loretto, Marlborough, Tonbridge, Uppingham and Wellington. Forty-four had attended Oxford or Cambridge, usually in the 1920s and 1930s an indication of at least a middle-class background.[3] Most professional county cricketers had working-class origins, but if a grammar school education before 1939 is taken as evidence of a middle-class background, then a few professionals came from the middle class. Walter Hammond, for instance, had attended Portsmouth and Cirencester Grammar Schools, though he became an amateur in 1938, Cyril Washbrook Bridgnorth Grammar School, and George Cox the George Collier's Grammar School. Charles Barnett,

115

who played for Gloucestershire and England as a professional, had attended Wycliffe College, a public school, but very few other public school boys became professional cricketers.[4] Errol Holmes, educated at Malvern and Oxford, who played for Surrey and England as an amateur, declared that 'It was quite unthinkable that I should turn professional in those days.'[5] The incomes of some professionals, who enjoyed long careers and had the business acumen to exploit their fame, were equal to those of middle-class men. Jack Hobbs and Patsy Hendren, it has been claimed, had annual incomes of around £1,500 when the average salary of a GP was £1,094.[6]

The number of amateurs playing county cricket between the wars was always considerable, but it did decline. In 1920, 39 per cent of all appearances in county championship matches were made by amateurs, the same proportion as in 1900, and greater than the 30 per cent for 1913, the last full season before the First World War. By 1930 this figure had fallen to 20 per cent but that for 1939 – 19 per cent – was almost the same.[7] The number of appearances made by amateurs varied between counties. For most of the inter-war period Lancashire, Nottinghamshire and Yorkshire usually fielded teams with only one or two amateurs, whereas in the whole of the 1920 season only two professionals played for Somerset and four for Middlesex. Until 1928 it was the practice of Sussex to play four amateurs in each match.[8] In 1930 only nine per cent of appearances in the county championship for Lancashire were by amateurs, whilst the figure for Kent was 32 per cent, Middlesex 37 per cent and Somerset 55 per cent. By 1939 the amateur presence was distributed more evenly among counties. Lancashire, with 13 per cent, still had the lowest number of appearances by amateurs but over 20 per cent was achieved by only Kent – 31 per cent, Somerset – 29 per cent and Worcestershire – 25 per cent. Probably no team made up entirely of amateurs played a county championship match between the wars. In 1920, 17 amateurs played in a county championship between Worcestershire and Somerset. By 1939 most counties had fielded occasionally an entirely professional side, but there was probably no county championship match in which only professionals took part. Many amateurs played only a few matches each year. In 1930, 150 amateurs played in county championship matches. Twenty-four played in 20 or more matches. Eighty-five played in five or fewer matches. The decline in the number of amateurs playing county cricket was usually attributed to an economic climate which meant that many from the public schools could not afford to neglect a career in order to play cricket.

The status of amateurs within first-class cricket was superior to that of professionals. Between the wars all England teams were captained by amateurs, though in the course of the test match against Australia at Old

116

Trafford in 1926 the selectors asked Jack Hobbs to take over the captaincy of the England team when Arthur Carr, the amateur captain, fell ill. Counties appointed amateurs as their regular captains. For the 1935 season, the professional W.E. Astill was appointed captain of Leicestershire, but this may have been an interim measure while the New Zealand amateur C.S. Dempster was qualifying to play for the county. In 1927 Yorkshire had offered the captaincy to the professional Herbert Sutcliffe who had accepted, only to refuse the offer a few days later. By 1933, 13 of the 17 first-class counties had used 21 professionals as captains in matches when an amateur was not available.[9] In theory amateur captains exercised great authority over professional players. They were responsible for the discipline of county sides. Some captains seem to have selected county teams and where this was not their sole responsibility, they were usually consulted by the cricket committees of their counties. Where professionals were employed upon a match basis, captains often had a major say in deciding their earnings. Most counties had a system of merit payments for professionals who played well. At some counties the captains decided who should receive merit pay, and by deciding the batting order and bowling changes influenced the opportunities of professionals to earn merit pay. Almost all umpires in county cricket had been county professionals. County captains had to report upon the competence of umpires and adverse reports could cause an umpire to be struck from the list of umpires for first-class cricket.

At most county grounds amateurs had separate changing rooms from professionals, though sometimes the amateurs from both sides shared the same dressing room. In 1956 Harold Larwood recalled that as a professional in the 1920s and 1930s he felt that he had no option but to show deference to amateurs.[10] At many grounds professionals and amateurs entered the field of play through separate gates, and where they entered by the same gate, it was the practice for a professional batsman to allow an amateur batsman to step on to the field first. In county cricket it was common for amateurs to stay at separate establishments from the professionals when playing away matches. Professionals were expected to address amateurs as Sir or Mr, though it became acceptable to call the captain 'Skipper'. When Astill was the professional captain of Leicestershire, the other professionals addressed him as 'Skipper' and not 'Mr'.[11] In the 1930s Errol Holmes, the amateur captain of Surrey, was embarrassed and wondered whether he should report Wally Hammond, the leading English professional batsman of the time, for addressing him by his Christian name.[12] Amateurs might call professionals by their Christian names. Harry Lee remembered that Pelham Warner addressed the

Middlesex professionals by their Christian names when things were going well, but reverted to surnames when things went less well. In 1923 Lord Harris did not consider it proper that A.J. Webbe, a member of the Middlesex committee who had played cricket for Middlesex and England as an amateur, should have addressed Lee as 'Harry'. Bryan Valentine and 'Hopper' Levett, two Kent amateurs, were reprimanded for over familiarity with professionals over the use of their Christian names.[13]

In some respects distinctions between amateurs and professionals became less pronounced between the wars. The test selectors were empowered in 1921 to consult two professionals about the selection of the England team and in 1923 the Board of Control agreed that those selecting the teams for the England test trial could co-opt amateur county captains and two professionals.[14] In 1926 the professionals Jack Hobbs and Wilfred Rhodes were added to the England selectors. Such innovations were not without criticism. It was argued that professional selectors would be tempted to favour their friends and would be a disaster.[15] In 1936 Frank Woolley, the Kent and England professional, thought that professionals who were still playing ought not to be test selectors as they would prefer to be 'excused the duty of having to vote a brother professional' out of the honour of playing for England 'with its attendant financial considerations'.[16] In the early 1920s Surrey abolished the separate entrances to the field of play for amateurs and professionals and in 1926 the MCC agreed that the amateurs and professionals playing for England would use the same dressing rooms.[17] Lord Harris complained about the professionals and amateurs in the Surrey team entering the field of play at Lord's through the same gate,[18] but in 1925 Lord Hawke, usually among the firmest defenders of amateurism in first-class cricket, had declared that he had no objection to sharing the same gate or changing room with professionals.[19] During the season that he captained the Leicestershire side, Ewart Astill continued to change in the professionals' dressing room at Leicester, but at some away fixtures other counties insisted that he use the amateur dressing room.[20] Criticisms of separate changing rooms and entrances to the field usually stressed that these were forms of snobbery, but the sharing of the same changing room by the England team was welcomed by professional and amateur cricketers for cricketing reasons. Francis Mann, the amateur captain of Middlesex and a former England captain, and the professionals Patsy Hendren and Maurice Tate, believed that it would improve team spirit and have practical advantages such as making easier last minute changes to the batting order.[21] In 1934 *The Daily Mail* thought that the public had been pleased when the amateur Percy Chapman had invited Patsy Hendren, the only professional in the MCC side playing against the Australians, to take the field through the amateurs' gate.[22]

118

Those who controlled county cricket attached great importance to maintaining amateurism within county cricket. No figure of authority within cricket appears to have called for the scrapping of the amateur–professional divide or for cricket to have become an entirely professional game. Great emphasis was attached to the tradition of amateur captaincy. Some amateur captains had neither the cricketing ability nor the experience to have commanded a regular place in a county side had they been professionals. In 1921 and 1932 emergency amateur captains of Northamptonshire were 18 years old.[23] In 1919 Lancashire appointed as captain Miles Kenyon who had never played in a first-class match and was aged 33. In 1925 Major Lupton, aged 46, who had played one first-class match for Yorkshire in 1908, was made the captain of Yorkshire. The Lancashire captains, M.N. Kenyon (captain 1919–22), and W.H.L. Lister (captain 1936–39), had career batting averages of 14.79 and 18.45 and neither was a bowler. For Yorkshire, G. Wilson (captain 1922–24) had a career batting average of 12.28, A.W. Lupton (captain 1925–27) 10.43 and A.W. Worsley (captain 1928–29) 15.69. Professional batsmen with such averages could not have expected to have been selected for county sides regularly, but counties with such professional strength as Lancashire and Yorkshire could carry amateur captains who were out of their playing depth. Even counties with far weaker professional strength had amateur captains with less than moderate playing skills. The Honourable J.B. Ponsonby, the joint captain of Worcestershire in 1929 and the regular captain in 1930, had a batting average of 14.78, whilst the 16 wickets he took as a bowler each cost over 45 runs. In 1919, J.N. Beasley, the captain of Northamptonshire, had a career batting average of 6.25 and as a bowler dismissed only five batsmen. Four other captains of Northamptonshire who captained the county for a total of eight seasons scarcely bowled and had batting averages of under 16.[24]

Some county committees felt it so necessary to have an amateur captain that special financial arrangements were made to ensure that a captain could afford to play as an amateur. V.W.C. Jupp of Northamptonshire and Cyril Walters of Worcestershire were each paid £400 as county secretaries and captained their counties as amateurs.[25] Sometimes sponsors of county clubs offered employment to cricketers and allowed them the time to play cricket as amateurs. Sir Julian Cahn, a millionaire sponsor of Nottinghamshire and Leicestershire, employed the New Zealand test cricketer C.S. Dempster as the manager of a furniture store while he was obtaining a residential qualification for Leicestershire and while he was the amateur captain of the club.[26] When Errol Holmes became the captain of Surrey in 1934, he was uncertain whether his employers, an American firm in the City, would

119

allow him the time to play county cricket for a full season, but had no doubt that English firms in the City would have granted the time.[27] Some amateurs could be described as shamateurs, but it is not possible to calculate their number.

It was claimed that amateurs were essential for the welfare of cricket. They were described as the 'leaven' of first-class cricket. In 1921, just after England had lost decisively a test series in Australia, Lord Hawke claimed that 'the crucial defect of our cricket' was 'the deficiency of good amateur players' and argued that an ideal test team would contain five or six amateurs.[28] The rhetoric surrounding amateurism stressed that amateurs enhanced the spectator appeal of cricket. By not being financially dependent upon cricket, amateurs were supposed to be able to play in an adventurous, risk-taking manner with little worry about the consequences of failure, whereas professionals, and particularly the professional batsman, could not afford to 'enter into the spirit of derring-do when he knows that failure to succeed may mean his replacement by another player and consequent loss of payment'.[29] Writing for *The Field* in 1933 Neville Cardus complained of the 'old soldier, the shrewd professional who takes a hard realistic view of his job … too realistic, too utilitarian'. Cardus argued that amateurs had pioneered all the major innovations in bowling technique.[30] On the other hand, another writer for *The Field* in 1932 maintained that selection committees were beginning to favour professionals over amateurs because it was believed that successful sides attracted more spectators and that the reliability of professional batsmen was more likely to win matches.[31] Though rarely mentioned in print, a compelling reason for the amateur presence within county cricket could have been the need for economy. Playing amateurs could be cheaper than engaging professionals. In 1930, for instance, 32 per cent of appearances in the county championship for Kent were made by amateurs. Their expenses which were published in the club's annual handbook were less than 11 per cent of the total paid for amateur expenses plus the wages of professionals and the scorer in all county championship matches. The Findlay Commission found that Somerset, the county which played the highest number of amateurs but which was not among those counties with most members or paying spectators, was the only one whose income before the addition of the share of test match profits exceeded expenditure over the three seasons 1934–36.

For some the practice of appointing amateur captains scarcely needed justification. In 1920 Pelham Warner wrote that 'for obvious reasons amateurs make the better captains' and a year later *Athletic News*, a newspaper sympathetic to professional sport, wrote that 'The patrician should be the principal governor.'[32] In 1925 Cecil Parkin, the Lancashire professional bowler, had written in *The Weekly Dispatch* that for the forthcoming test match in Australia, England should have been captained not by Arthur Gilligan, the captain chosen by the MCC, but by the amateur Percy Chapman 'under the supervision of Hobbs' as 'such an unprecedented thing as a professional leading England would not be tolerated for a moment'.[33] This article caused Lord Hawke to say at the AGM of Yorkshire CCC a few days later that

> Here is a professional criticising an amateur all this distance away. If it had been a Yorkshire professional and my committee were of the same mind as myself, I do not think Parkin would ever step on another Yorkshire cricket field ... for a man who calls himself a cricketer to write an attack on the England captain and at the same time to say the best cricketer he ever played under was Hobbs is beneath contempt. I trust no professional will ever captain England.[34]

When interviewed about this speech, Hawke said 'Bless my soul! I never meant to hurt any one's feelings, especially the professionals ... As for the question whether it would be bad policy for a professional to captain England, I can only say that it has never been done before. Why, how could one possibly allow a professional to be captain over an amateur? ... No, no, no ... To have a professional captaining a team with even one amateur in it! Ha, ha, ha.'[35]

In 1926 when Captain Cornwallis, the captain of Kent, was unable to play, he appointed Seymour, a professional, to captain the county side in his absence even though two amateurs were available to play. This provoked Lord Harris into writing to Cornwallis that 'I do not consider that the very liberal discretion which the County Committee extends to the Captain goes so far as to authorise the revolutionary introduction of a professional to be Captain when an amateur is procurable ... whether an amateur has, or has not, experience of capacity as a Captain is immaterial. The Committee has never shown the remotest indication of any desire to put a professional in as Captain.'[36] It was often argued that because an amateur was not dependent upon cricket for his livelihood, he could bring greater independence of mind to captaincy than a professional. Lord Harris believed that because of this, an amateur captain would be ruthless in selecting the best players, whereas professional captains would be less independent and always have 'an excuse for the failure of a comrade'.[37] In 1927 *The Times* pointed out that captains needed 'tact, judgement, keenness, consideration, equanimity', but as this article was discussing the merits of amateur over professional captains, it implied that such characteristics were more likely to be found among amateurs. The same article explained that it would be difficult to select a professional as a captain where a team included several professionals with equal claims for such a post and that professional bowlers often lacked true appreciation of their skills.[38] It was often stated that professionals in the Gentlemen versus Players matches (the annual games played between teams representing the leading amateurs and professionals), professionals had shown themselves to be poor captains, but this overlooked the point that with more experience professionals might have become better captains. In the 1920s the obvious choice if England were to be captained by a professional would have been Jack Hobbs. The amateur Arthur Carr and the book *A Searchlight on English Cricket,* which caused a stir when it was published anonymously in 1926, both argued that Hobbs had shown himself to be an inept captain of the Players' side.[39]

Determination to maintain the amateur presence in cricket can be seen as a product of the wider culture of the wealthier classes and especially their reluctance to embrace an ethic of out-and-out commercialism. Chapter 8 discusses the fears that a more overtly commercial county championship would undermine the tradition of sportsmanship in first-class cricket. The fact that those who were shamateurs felt it necessary to appear to be amateurs indicates the strength of the belief among the wealthier classes that not all areas of social activity should be a source of maximising potential earnings. No doubt many with public school backgrounds attempted to maximise the profits of their businesses, but the moral values ascribed to cricket and the belief that large sums of money should not be made from it indicate that their cultural values were not dominated by an ethic of ruthless and boundless acquisitiveness.

The resolution to maintain an amateur presence and amateur captains within county cricket demonstrates that those with established wealth were convinced they were equipped to exercise social leadership, but it can also be linked to their anxieties about the direction of political affairs between the wars. The rhetoric defending amateur captaincy often drew upon political imagery. Harsher world trading conditions, the formation of the first Labour government and a more militant tone to much trade union activity in the 1920s, more insistent demands for self-rule in India and the establishment of the communist regime in Russia contributed to a sense of unease and threat to those classes which traditionally exercised social and political leadership in Britain. In 1921 Lord Harris claimed that 'Bolshevism is rampant, and seeks to abolish all laws and rules and this year cricket has not escaped its attack'.[40] The author of *A Searchlight on English Cricket,* wrote of 'the ever necessary convention that in our social system there must be for all time – if we are to remain an Empire – be marked distinctions between the paid and the unpaid' and added that the man who objected to amateurs and professionals having separate gates to the field of play probably 'beats his wife and treats his servants ... like dogs'. Criticism of the amateur–professional divide was 'Communistic, if not Bolshevist'.[41] The playing of county championship matches during the General Strike shows that those who controlled first-class cricket had no sympathy for what could have been regarded as a challenge to the political order. Kent's match with Oxford University was scratched, perhaps so that undergraduates could perform the work of those on strike. The use in everyday discourse of such cricketing images as 'it's not cricket', 'playing the game', 'keeping a straight bat' and the emphasis in cricket writings on the similarities between the British constitution, the Empire and the traditions of cricket show how among the establishment classes authority in cricket was intertwined with moral justifications for their exercise of authority in other areas of social activity.

The defence of amateur authority within county cricket by those with privileged backgrounds was related to their assumptions about the nature of social relations. Discourses on amateurism reveal a belief that other classes preferred authority to be exercised by those with privileged backgrounds and that relationships between the classes in cricket were characterised by harmony and goodwill rather than friction and suspicion. In 1925 Pelham Warner wrote that the English professional cricketer was 'a splendid fellow – loyal and reliable on and off the field, and full of good humour and commonsense, and his relations with his amateur colleagues are on such a high plane of mutual sympathy and understanding that I believe that nothing can disturb them'.[42] In 1936 Bob Wyatt, who had captained Warwickshire and England, wrote of 'the truly friendly relations that exist between amateur and professional players'.[43] The author of *A Searchlight on English Cricket* emphasised that 'Professionals *themselves prefer to be captained by an amateur*'.[44]

Amateur captains were seen to be indispensable if sportsmanship was to be retained in cricket. As Chapter 4 has shown, those from public schools were thought of as the 'natural' upholders of 'sportsmanship' and its associated moral qualities such as selflessness, regard for others, generosity of spirit, acceptance of authority, the observance of rules, good humour and cheerfulness. The argument that amateurism was essential to preserve sportsmanship implied, but was rarely stated, that professionalism led to cheating. Instead, contrasts were drawn with other sports. *The Times*, stated in 1922 that 'sportsmanship in professional football is today non-existent'.[45] The privileged classes saw sportsmanship, and amateurism which was considered necessary for its survival, as tending to promote social cohesion because it persuaded other classes to accept their social leadership. In *The Cricketer Annual* for 1922–23, Bishop Welldon, who had been the headmaster of Dulwich and Harrow, called for 'the Public School spirit' to be cultivated at secondary and elementary schools. He argued

> It is not, perhaps, wrong to say ... that the instinct of discipline and loyalty, the spirit of co-operation and the fine sensitive honour which is essential to true sport, have been less clearly marked in the lower than in the higher social classes; and the reason ... is the deficiency of organised games ... For organised games create a fellow-feeling among citizens of all classes; they promote good sense, good temper, and good fellowship; they exemplify the principles by which an Empire may be knit together; and they are not the least important elements in the formation of that moral character which alone has enabled the British people, while all other Empires have diminished and decayed, to maintain their own Empire in its world-wide amplitude and majesty.[46]

The scheme at Oxford in which the university colleges allowed local elementary schoolboys to receive cricket coaching on the colleges' grounds was much praised, not least because it encouraged sportsmanship among those from elementary schools. An article in *The Official Annual Handbook of the London and Southern Counties Cricket Conference* for 1925 describing the Oxford scheme, proclaimed that 'we live in a democratic age when our King and Queen and our Princes and Princesses are as much at home among a crowd of factory girls or miners as they are among their guests at a garden party at Buckingham Palace', and went on to say that through the Oxford scheme elementary schoolboys 'learn the value of discipline, they develope [*sic*] *esprit de corps* and they learn to play the game as a game, and not as a mere struggle for points'.[47] In 1935 a team of elementary schoolboys played against a team from a public school at Oxford. *The Times* found 'the spirit of sportsmanship and comradeship, so clearly evident between the two classes of boys ... beautiful to behold'.[48] After the General Strike of 1926, some argued that sportsmanship produced a spirit of social harmony which could preserve political stability. Less than a month after the strike collapsed an editorial in *The Times* maintained that giving the working-class boy the opportunity to play cricket through the provision of more playing fields would 'help in the work of moulding him, body and temperament, into a strong and happy and helpful citizen'.[49] In 1927 Sir Theodore Cook, editor of *The Field,* claimed that 'sportsmanship and fair play' were 'known and respected by nearly everyone in our community from the highest to the lowest'. He argued that the strike had occurred because the 'innate sportsmanship' of the miners 'had been falsely captured through a loyalty which had been deliberately misled. The miners' leaders would do better in Moscow for the rest of their careers.'[50]

As most professional county cricketers had working-class origins, their reactions to amateurs shed some light on how relations between the working and other classes were perceived by a section of the working class. In his autobiography published in 1924 Jack Hobbs argued that relations between amateurs and professionals were 'altogether amicable'.[51] Denis Compton, who first played for Middlesex as a professional in 1936, recalled in 1993 that 'there were no snobs among the amateurs. It didn't worry us that they came out of different gates',[52] but Hobbs and Compton, remembered as men of generous spirit and as outstanding cricketers, may have been treated more benevolently by amateurs than less talented players. Ellis Robinson, who played as professional with Yorkshire from 1934 until 1949, remembers that professionals did not object to having separate dressing rooms because this gave them more space.[53] No professional between the wars seems to have advocated in public that cricket should have become an entirely professional game, but the experiences of Cecil Parkin, the Lancashire and England professional bowler, show that criticising amateurs could be hazardous. The reminiscences of those who played in the Gentlemen and Players matches between the wars do not indicate that these matches were contested as fiercely as test matches against Australia or matches between Lancashire and Yorkshire, nor do they seem to have had the edge apparent in some matches between Yorkshire and Middlesex. Ellis Robinson was not selected for a Gentlemen–Players match but recalls that professionals looked upon these matches as test trials and not as an opportunity to defeat their social betters. Had professional resentment against amateurs been more intense, the Gentlemen versus Players match would probably have been contested more bitterly.

Autobiographies published since the Second World War of professionals who played between the wars show that not all shared the attitudes towards amateurs of Hobbs and Compton. Bill Andrews, a professional with Somerset, felt that professionals had a 'poor deal before the War' and mentioned the 'feudalistically' ringing of a bell in the professionals' dressing room to tell them that it was time to take the field. He thought that amateurs were treated more favourably than professionals. In his experience amateur bowlers bowled at tail-end batsmen, which reduced the opportunities of professionals to earn bonus pay for taking a large number of wickets, and professionals were expected to bowl at amateurs before matches to provide them with practice, but few amateurs would do the same for professionals.[54] At many counties, professionals were dropped at holiday times to make way for amateurs, which deprived professionals of match fees. Harry Lee who played for Middlesex before and after the First World War, 'loathed amateurs in Brighton games' who took the place of professionals in the Bank Holiday fixture against Sussex.[55] Bill Andrews felt that the professionals were not disappointed to see the number of amateurs decline at Somerset in the 1930s, which contradicts the recollection of N.S. Mitchell-Innes, who played for England and Somerset as an amateur in the 1930s, that 'There was never any resentment from the Somerset pros about being left out to accommodate amateurs'.[56] Andrews thought that amateurs often showed little enthusiasm for playing in difficult games.[57]

It is not possible to establish what the majority of professional cricketers thought about the tradition of amateur captains or whether their opinions changed between the wars. In 1931 Jack Hobbs wrote that a man could be appointed captain of England merely because he was an amateur and argued that an England captain should be worth his place as a player. In 1935, just after he retired from playing, Hobbs wrote that because of the socialising demands of the post and because professionals did not like bossing other professionals, it was preferable for the England team to have an amateur captain, but he did not agree with young amateurs captaining county sides which included experienced professionals.[58] In 1927 Hobbs was surprised that the professional Sutcliffe had been offered the captaincy of Yorkshire, but said that he was pleased that Sutcliffe had accepted the offer as a professional, 'for to have done so as an amateur would have given the honour and position an air of unreality'. Hobbs added that many professionals were capable of captaining county sides.[59] As Hobbs was by nature one who accepted the established customs of cricket and was far from a cricketing rebel, it seems highly unlikely that many professionals would have been less critical of amateur captaincy than he. After Lord Hawke's speech in 1925, the England professionals touring Australia protested in what *The Daily Herald* called 'a moderate and dignified manner against Lord Hawke's outrageous attack'. They claimed that his remarks were 'disparaging to professionals'.[60] No professional appears to have called in public for the appointment of amateur captains to be scrapped, and to have done so could have harmed career prospects, since many county committees began to insist on vetting before publication press articles which appeared under the name of professional cricketers.

Some professionals preferred sides to be captained by amateurs. In 1927, George Gunn, a veteran professional batsman who had played for England and was a strong personality, refused to captain Nottinghamshire in a vital championship when the amateur captain was unavailable because it was 'too important a match to be left to a professional'.[61] In 1973, Bill Andrews, who made many harsh comments about amateurs before the Second World War, stated that he had preferred being captained by an amateur captain, provided the amateur knew the game.[62] The comments made in a radio interview by Tommy Mitchell, a former miner who played as a professional with Derbyshire from 1928 until 1939 and appeared in five test matches, suggest that professionals respected amateur captains who were 'fair' to them even though they may not have been very talented cricketers.[63] It is probable that many professionals shared the fatalistic attitude towards amateurs of Winston Place, the Lancashire batsman, and of George Dawkes. Both have said that professionals accepted amateur captains and the amateur presence within county cricket as a fact of life, something to which they had always been accustomed and which did not greatly excite them.[64]

The reminiscences of professionals show that responses to amateur captains were based upon responses to them as individuals as much as representatives of a class. As captain of Essex Johnny Douglas was hard upon the slacker, but a man with strong personal likes and dislikes who was remembered with fondness by some of his professionals. After reprimanding two professionals who had been guilty of high jinks one night, they were almost reduced to tears, but as they were about to leave, he called them back, told them they were 'silly buggers' and gave them each five pounds.[65] Lord Tennyson as captain of Hampshire seems to have treated his professionals with a mixture of severity and generosity which earned their affection. At the start of one match he was reputed to have not been speaking to four of his professionals but by the end of the match had found some reason to tip each of them a pound.[66] Bill Andrews had few pleasant memories of Jack White as captain of Somerset, but recalled that Bunty Longrigg had the happy knack of knowing the right moment to buy professionals a pint.[67] Professionals could be critical of their amateur captains. In Brian Sellers' first season as the captain of Yorkshire, Herbert Sutcliffe, the senior professional, objected to his treatment of the professionals and as a protest Sutcliffe and the other professionals kept Sellers waiting in the middle with the umpires and two batsmen before they came on to the field.[68] When Sutcliffe published his autobiography in 1935, he made no reference to this incident or to the offer of the Yorkshire captaincy made to him in 1927. Alf Gover recalled that the Surrey professionals thought that Errol Holmes could be too sporting towards other sides and claimed that professionals had no respect for shamateurs.[69] Professionals seem to have respected those captains who, they believed, would stand up for the interests of players before the county committee.

Some amateur captains, such as Brian Sellers, who captained Yorkshire from 1933 until 1947, were fierce disciplinarians, but in practice the powers of amateur captains were not absolute. Very talented professionals had to be treated in a manner consistent with their expectation of how they should be treated. The 1934 season was the last of Jack Hobbs' career and Errol Holmes' first as the captain of Surrey. Holmes allowed Hobbs to choose in which matches he played.[70] Harry Lee claimed that some professionals treated amateur captains like ground staff boys.[71] James Kilburn, a cricket journalist who spent much of his career covering the matches of Yorkshire, thought that in the 1930s 'The professionals accepted the amateur in management capacity but only proof in practice on the field gave the amateur a standing in cricket interpreted by professionals.'[72] In the 1920s when the playing skills of Yorkshire captains were far below those of the professionals, *Athletic News* reported 'Now everyone knows that for all practical purposes, Wilfred Rhodes has been the captain of the Yorkshire eleven.'[73] Sir Home Gordon wrote in 1939 that some Yorkshire professionals were reputed to have regarded their captains as their cricketing inferiors. At one match in the early 1920s, a professional had signalled from the dressing room that the side was about to declare even when the captain was still batting.[74]

Professionals seem to have wanted to retain a measure of social distance between themselves and amateurs. The autobiography of Jack Hobbs published in 1924 claimed that whilst relations between amateurs and professionals were amicable, they did not see much of each other off the field of play,[75] but the phrasing of these comments does not suggest that Hobbs saw this as regrettable. Cecil Parkin wrote that 'the class distinction that exists between amateur and professional *should not be emphasised in public*', but felt that professionals preferred their own company and did not wish to mix socially with amateurs. Parkin added that much nonsense was talked about the 'snobbishness' in cricket.[76] Harold Larwood believed that professionals favoured having separate dressing rooms from amateurs, a view echoed by Alf Gover, the Surrey and England professional fast bowler, who claimed that 'In the normal way the professionals did not encourage the amateur into their dressing room ... it was their domain and they liked their privacy'.[77] Frank Woolley did not believe that it was even necessary for amateurs and professionals playing for England to stay at the same hotel.[78] It could be irksome for professionals when amateurs fraternised with them. Arthur Carr, the Nottinghamshire captain, seems to have been more than fond of a drink and would collect his professionals to go drinking with him until the small hours. John Gunn did not enjoy this but felt that he could not afford to refuse to accompany his captain.[79] The general tenor of the comments made by professionals suggests that those with broadly working-class backgrounds felt more at ease socially with those of similar backgrounds and that they were often aware of the greater privileges enjoyed by those from wealthier backgrounds, but this consciousness of social difference was not always accompanied by a strong sense of resentment or class hostility.

Many professionals accepted that county cricket should be played in accordance with the values ascribed to cricket by the wealthier classes. Counties usually appointed a senior professional. In the words of Charles Elliott, who started to play as a professional with Derbyshire in 1932, a senior professional 'had to carry out the captain's job in the dressing room' and was expected to keep players in order.[80] Only those who had established themselves as successful players were appointed senior professionals, but it seems highly probable that county committees appointed as senior professionals those who agreed with their views of how county cricket should be controlled and played. In the opinion of Arthur Gilligan, George Cox as the senior professional of Sussex instilled into other professionals 'the best traditions of an English gentleman',[81] which meant presumably that Cox ensured that the Sussex team observed the traditions of sportsmanship associated with amateurs. Early in his career, Alf Gover was severely criticised by the more experienced professionals in the Surrey team for what they felt had been a form of unsporting behaviour. Some senior professionals were even more concerned about the observance of high standards than were most amateurs. The Yorkshire senior professional Herbert Sutcliffe stressed to a young Bill Bowes that 'the thing you've got to learn is that as a professional cricketer you must be better than the amateurs. You must be better as a player. You must be better in your dress. You must be better in your manners and you've got to show why you're a professional.'[82] The attitude of county authorities, however, could have meant that professionals knew that it would be foolhardy to behave in a manner contrary to that expected by county committees. The rules of Kent concerning the granting of benefits, for instance, specified that these would be awarded only to professionals whose conduct had been exemplary.

There was a clearly demarcated hierarchy among county professionals. Harry Lee compared senior professionals to regimental sergeant majors.[83] How a senior professional behaved towards other professionals depended to some extent upon the personality of the amateur captain. Ellis Robinson has explained that as Brian Sellers was such an assertive individual, Herbert Sutcliffe did not have to exert his authority as senior professional over the other Yorkshire professionals. George Dawkes played as a 16-year-old in the Leicestershire side in the 1930s. He recalls that the Leicestershire senior professional was like a father to him but at away matches insisted that he went to bed early and would not let him into the bars at hotels.[84] Some senior professionals often believed that they could treat other professionals in an offhand manner. Even after the Second World War which is often thought to have softened social distinctions, Dick Pollard, the senior professional of Lancashire, felt that he was entitled to sit down in the dressing room after a day in the field and order another professional to fetch him a glass of water.[85]

Receiving a county cap was a crucial rite of passage in a professional career. Capped players were usually paid more than uncapped players. Becoming capped meant that a player was recognised as having the playing ability needed in a county's first eleven, though some counties were more grudging in the awarding of caps than others. Caps were awarded to amateurs as well as professionals, but uncapped professionals were expected to perform a range of menial tasks for the capped players. As an uncapped Yorkshire player Bill Bowes had to arrange to transport by taxi the kit and baggage of the capped professionals.[86] Ellis Robinson remembers that the uncapped players were the 'dogsbodies' of the Yorkshire side and that transferring the baggage of all the team from one train to another could be 'murder'.[87] At a club, professionals competed against each other for places in the first team and those not selected could lose match fees. Newcomers were not made to feel at home in the Nottinghamshire dressing room. Willis Walker, who played as a professional for Nottinghamshire from 1913 until 1937, said that it was difficult to make one's way in the side because the established players did not want to lose each others' company. When Joe Hardstaff first came into the Nottinghamshire side in 1930 and asked Fred Barratt where he should put his bag, he was told 'Over theer', near the door, 'then thou'l't be soonest out o' bleddy door'.[88] Young professionals were not treated in such a manner at all clubs. George Dawkes, Charles Elliott and Ellis Robinson do not recall that they were made to feel unwelcome when they started to play in a county first team, although not surprisingly, as Ellis Robinson commented, it helped 'if you showed that you could do a bit'. George Dawkes made a special point of emphasising that when he took the place as the Leicestershire wicket-keeper of Paddy Corrall, who was not retained by the club at the end of the season, Corrall showed no resentment and continued to be friendly to him.

Older professionals could take advantage of the naivete of younger players. When Alf Gover first played against Middlesex, Patsy Hendren, who was then a veteran of county cricket, mentioned to Gover that his eyes were no longer very sharp and asked him not to bowl short balls. Gover did bowl short pitched balls to Hendren but realised that he had been duped when Jack Hobbs pointed out that he was playing to the strength of Hendren's hook shot.[89] In 1938 Laurance Coates claimed in *The Daily Mirror* that the opposing captain of a player making his debut in county cricket had promised that the first ball woul be on the leg-side, but instead the novice was bowled out by a ball pitching outside the off stump. Coates added that 'this sort of thing will not be easily stamped out. It's gone on a long time and is part and parcel of the game.' Coates wrote that a former county player who left to play league cricket had said 'If you're in the clique running the team, you're OK. If not, then catches are dropped off your bowling, and everything possible is done to let the county committee see that you're not likely to be a success.'[90] There is little doubt that the kinds of exploitation practised upon young professionals were similar to what occurred in other predominantly male workplaces. The forms of hierarchy found among professionals may have convinced them that the world of cricket was not one of equality, and this could also have persuaded them that it was appropriate for sides to be captained by amateurs.

It would seem that professionals were very much aware of the differences in status between themselves and amateurs and that some clearly felt that they were treated unfairly at the hands of amateurs, but there was also a strong desire to keep a social distance between themselves and the amateurs. Most seem to have accepted that sides should be captained by amateurs and were committed to the belief that cricket should be played in a spirit of sportsmanship. Acceptance of amateur authority may have been a form of fatalism and to a degree reflected the forms of class privilege found in other walks of life between the wars, but awareness of the gulfs between amateurs and professionals was not accompanied by a strong sense that the interests of amateurs and professionals were in conflict. Relations between amateurs and professionals were not quite as amicable as the upper and middle class apologists for the amateur tradition supposed, but on the whole they do seem to have been harmonious. Those within the world of cricket were acutely aware of the social distinctions of cricket but in general they do not seem to have thought that cricket was permeated by class conflict. A sense of class as an expression of fierce class antagonism does not seem to have been the dominant narrative of social relations in first-class cricket.

CRICKET AND SOCIAL HARMONY

The forms of class co-operation found in cricket suggest that class antagonism was not the chief characteristic of social relations in England. Cricket discourse had long celebrated club cricket as an expression of class harmony. Village cricket in particular was believed to have had a long tradition of promoting understanding between the classes. In 1922 Pelham

Warner wrote that village cricket 'represents the essence of the game; for a village match is the truest democracy' which encouraged 'the feelings of freemasonry, camaraderie, and *esprit de corps*. I cannot imagine a man who has been bowled out by the village blacksmith not having a fellow feeling towards him afterwards. Can you imagine a cricketer becoming a Lenin?'[91] It is not difficult to find examples from rural England between the wars of village teams whose players had widely differing backgrounds, but most players seem to have been drawn from blue-collar workers, clerks and small businessmen. The patronage of village clubs by those from the elite can be interpreted as a form of inter-class harmony. In 1921 Sir Stuart Samuel entertained the Newick players who had won the Nutley league – a league for village clubs in East Sussex. The next year, the champions and representatives from five other clubs were treated to supper at the Bull Inn in Newick by T. Baden-Powell, a local landowner.[92] The Oxford scheme where the university colleges allowed elementary schoolboys to use college grounds can be seen as a form of upper and middle-class patronage of working-class cricket. Village cricket may not have been so permeated by social harmony as cricket discourse suggested, but the importance accorded to such commentaries suggests a widespread desire to believe that cricket was a form of social co-operation and harmony. The elite would not have patronised village cricket had they considered that it could provoke social friction or criticism of their social status.

The degree to which cricket encouraged forms of identity which crossed class boundaries suggests that social relations in England were not dominated by a strong sense of class conflict. The desire for England to succeed in test matches against Australia united social classes. Regaining of the Ashes in 1926 was a source of national rejoicing. In Yorkshire the county identity expressed and intensified through support for the county cricket side was especially strong. Occasional rivalries flared between league clubs in Yorkshire and the county club, but generally those who controlled league cricket seem to have felt obliged to promote the interests of Yorkshire county cricket. Flourishing league cricket and a strong county team were seen as mutually supportive. In 1932, as part of the Yorkshire Cricket Federation's campaign against the football season being extended into the cricket season, Lord Hawke, president of the county club, arranged to discuss this matter with the Football Association.[93] In 1936 Hawke agreed to become the Federation's honorary president.[94] In 1938 Brian Sellers, the Yorkshire captain, declared that the county club depended upon the leagues for its players and in 1938, when he became an England selector, the Yorkshire Federation made a point of forwarding its congratulations.[95] For some senior figures at the county club, Yorkshire cricket was more important than

England. In the 1920s Lord Hawke had argued against test matches being longer than three days because of the impact of this upon county cricket. In 1932 Hedley Verity and Bill Bowes both reported that they were not fully fit for Yorkshire's match with Lancashire because of reactions to the inoculations they had received before the tour to Australia. The response of Sellers, their captain, was 'Inoculations for Australia! [An appalled gasp here.] Yorkshire means more than England. You should know that ... Well, you can both bloody well play.'[96]

Cricket also reinforced northern identities which crossed class boundaries and were mixed with an animus against the South. Matches between Lancashire and Yorkshire were fiercely partisan affairs in which both sides played with extreme caution, but in both counties this partisanship was a cause of pride, a pride which expressed northern as well as county identities which those from other parts of the country could not comprehend fully. In 1929, Dr Cyril Norwood, the headmaster of Harrow who had been born in Lancashire, complained that Lancashire and Yorkshire 'play the most miserable game and set the most miserable example to the whole country of how games should not be played'.[97] Sir Edwin Stockton, the Lancashire chairman, who had held directorships of insurance and transport concerns and had been a Conservative MP, replied that no matches were so tense as the Roses matches and boasted that the slow play stemmed from 'Northern doggedness'.[98] The Lancashire professional batsman Winston Place has agreed that Roses matches were fiercely contested but has also expressed his admiration of Yorkshire playing 'in a grand way' and particularly of the attitude which meant that even if the last two batsmen were at the crease and needed 200 to win, they would play with every determination and belief that they could get the runs.[99]

Dave Russell has shown that a northern hostility towards the South was especially marked in matches between Yorkshire and Middlesex. The Middlesex team usually included more amateurs than the Yorkshire side which often consisted of ten professionals plus the amateur captain. The Yorkshire amateur was seen in a different light from the Middlesex amateurs. In Yorkshire, the Yorkshire amateur captains were regarded as having agreed to play county cricket out of 'an acute sense of duty and obligation' to the county, a quality which the Middlesex amateurs were thought not to possess.[100] The strong feelings engendered in such matches fed upon a conviction that the North was denied its true worth in the South. In the summer of 1924 a fierce correspondence raged in *The Cricketer* over whether there was prejudice against northern players when England teams were selected, which may have caused Lord Hawke, the president of

Yorkshire, to write in *The Cricketer Annual* for 1924–25 that 'the sooner any imaginary sense of injustice is dispelled the better'.[101] In 1929, Frank Sugg argued that extending the powers of the counties over first-class cricket and reducing that of the MCC would result in more northern cricketers being selected for England.[102] In 1931 Neville Cardus, writing in *The Field*, claimed that England selectors gave preference to London amateurs over professionals from the North, Midlands or the West, an allegation which Pelham Warner promptly denied.[103] In 1935, whilst admitting that North–South animosities had lost some of their force, a cricket correspondent of *The Yorkshire Sports and Cricket Argus* recalled that it was 'only ungraciously, and only because England couldn't very well manage without them, that Yorkshire players were tolerated in Test matches by some of their caustic critics who ... were badly bitten by jealousy of a county that couldn't be "held down" for any length of time in the championship'.[104]

In the North and Midlands leading league clubs stimulated loyalties to towns and industrialised villages which transcended class boundaries. Alan Tomlinson has shown that in Colne, a cotton town in north-east Lancashire, 'To be a "Colner" was a way of making sense of an otherwise "difficult to situate" wider world' and that in cricket, 'To be a Colner, as player or spectator, could be more important than to be a member of this or that class'.[105] The extent of support for league clubs shows how they could be a focus of a town identity. In 1935 the *Nelson Gazette,* which usually supported the Labour Party, complained about the Liberal dominance among the officials and committee of Nelson CC, which it claimed was 'a town's institution, non-political, non-sectarian and all the rest of it'.[106] In 1938 Radcliffe Council included the ground of Radcliffe CC in a public playing fields scheme and spent £1,480 on building a new pavilion for the club. The mayor of Radcliffe praised the cricket club for having 'done their best to put Radcliffe on the map and that is what we want ... We hope further success will attend the efforts of the club to enhance the importance of Radcliffe in the country.'[107] Calls for funds by league clubs could draw support from across the population of a town. In 1925 Rawtenstall CC in Lancashire held a bazaar to clear debts of £2,500. The 67 patrons of the bazaar included the mayor, four county councillors, the local MP, five JPs and a colonel. Seventy local businesses took whole or half-page advertisements in the bazaar brochure.[108] Two or more clubs within one town, however, could be a cause of social division, but this was not usually a division between those from different classes. Loyalty to a club was an expression of social cohesion within a town but could also emphasise the sense of otherness between one town and its neighbours. In the 1960s

Learie Constantine recalled that 'as a West Indian I did not feel the chronic, long-standing rivalry' between Colne and Nelson which was 'almost enmity' and described his experience of a Nelson versus Colne match as 'not cricket' but 'more like a bloody civil war'.[109] A fierce rivalry existed in the early 1920s between the clubs from the neighbouring towns of Rochdale and Littleborough. In 1920 Cecil Parkin, then the Rochdale professional, had left the field as a protest against an umpire refusing LBW appeals in a match against Littleborough, which led to his suspension and the Rochdale club leaving the Central Lancashire League for a short period. The representatives of the Rochdale believed that a meeting with the league committee to solve this dispute had achieved nothing because of the attitude of the Littleborough delegate.[110]

Chapter 2 provided details from the Bolton area of how members of the local economic and social elite patronised leading league clubs and also the more humble levels of league cricket. Such patronage of cricket by the elite suggests that although league cricket was often thought to be infused with values different from those espoused by cricket enthusiasts with public school backgrounds, it was not considered a threat to the social authority of those with established wealth. Such forms of co-operation between social classes do not mean that there was no social conflict between the different social classes in the Bolton area, but they do show that conflict between classes was not so entrenched as to prevent the existence of such forms of social co-operation as those expressed through cricket.

CRICKET, CLASS IDENTITIES AND SOCIAL COHESION

Perceptions of amateur privilege and authority within cricket suggest that the middle class in general tended to share the cultural assumptions of the upper classes about the exercise of social leadership. It has already been shown that members of county clubs were drawn from the upper classes and from across the middle class. Calls for a dilution of the amateur–professional divide from the members of county clubs were rare. Shortly after the offer of the Yorkshire captaincy to Sutcliffe in 1927, the Yorkshire members were balloted over whether they wished the county to retain an amateur captain, and if a professional captain were preferred, whether it should be Sutcliffe or the more senior Wilfred Rhodes. Nearly 3,000 of Yorkshire's 7,000 members voted in the ballot, with a majority of five to one in favour of an amateur captain,[111] which seems to indicate a wide measure of support for the tradition of amateur captaincy.

Inferences about how far cricket shows that the middle and upper classes shared the same values concerning social leadership can be drawn from newspapers, though it must be recognised that newspapers are not always an infallible guide to the opinions of their readers. It seems likely that newspapers such as *The Times* and *The Daily Telegraph* were read by the upper and middle classes. These two newspapers were rarely critical of amateur authority within county cricket. *The Daily Mail* had a larger circulation, whilst its readership probably included more working-class readers than *The Times* or *The Telegraph,* but it does seem to have been read by many from the middle class. In 1934 its sports editor wrote that 'we must break down these cricket barriers … We put him [the professional cricketer] on the highest plane as a cricketer, but on a little lower plane as a man … Every field of sports activity teems with illustrations of our muddle-headed and hypocritical attitude to amateurism';[112] but in the 1920s *The Daily Mail* had expressed neither approval nor disapproval of Hawke's speech about a professional never captaining England, or of the offer of the Yorkshire captaincy to Sutcliffe. Chapter 3 has shown that *The Daily Express* also had a mass circulation which stretched across the middle and working classes. In 1926 it argued that a professional captain might be necessary if England were to regain the Ashes, pointing out that the amateur commanders of the Spanish Armada had been defeated by English professional sea captains.[113] In 1925, however, *The Daily Express* had merely reported Lord Hawke's outburst against Parkin, but in 1927 an editorial described Sutcliffe's appointment as the Yorkshire captain as 'a victory for democracy with no nonsense or camouflage about it'.[114] In the 1930s *The Daily Express* rarely called for the appointment of amateur captains. If it assumed that most of those who bought cricket books were middle class, it seems that Hawke's speech in 1925 had provoked a degree of middle-class hostility. Sir Home Gordon's firm had just published Hawke's autobiography, but sales slumped after the speech and plans for another edition had to be scrapped.[115] Yet the general acceptance among the middle class of amateur authority in county cricket, and the acceptance of an authority structure in which many aristocrats and those from the highest ranks of the bourgeoisie held power, suggests that many from the middle class shared the cultural values of those from the upper classes. Had there been a very strong sense of animosity between these groups in other areas of social life, it is unlikely that there could have been such agreement and co-operation within cricket. In this respect, cricket helps to explain the high level of support between the wars for the Conservative Party, which still tended to be dominated by landed aristocrats and the very wealthiest sections of the bourgeoisie.

As a newspaper partly owned by the TUC *The Daily Herald* sheds some light upon attitudes to class privilege within cricket among those sections of the working class who sympathised with socialism, an outlook often seen as an expression of class antagonism. Its reporting of Lord Hawke's speech in 1925 was pervaded with the rhetoric of class antagonism. Hawke's comments were condemned on the front page as a 'gratuitous insult' and it was asked whether only amateurs had the right to express criticisms in cricket.[116] A reader's letter, also printed on the front page, described Hawke's views as 'snobocratic'.[117] *The Daily Herald* also asked whether, 'as many cricketers think, Hobbs is the man to captain England, then surely snobbish ideas about distinctions between amateur and professional should not be allowed to handicap English cricket'.[118] But in 1926 *The Daily Herald* did not join the calls for England to be captained by a professional. When the Yorkshire captaincy was offered to Sutcliffe, it printed an editorial headed 'Bravo Yorks' and declared that it was 'high time that an end was put to all the claptrap about the divine right of amateurs to leadership'.[119] In the 1930s, however, *The Daily Herald* commented less frequently on the issue of amateur captaincy.

Prominent trade unionists and Labour politicians rarely commented on the forms of class distinction found in cricket. A trade union for county cricketers was not formed until 1968, but trade unionists hardly ever called for one to be formed between the wars. Clement Attlee, educated at Haileybury, became leader of the Labour Party in 1935. He was known to take a keen interest in cricket but none of his biographies show that he considered that the social relations of county cricket needed to be reformed. In 1926 trade union leaders do not seem to have complained about county cricket continuing to be played during the General Strike. To avoid harassment by strikers, a poster stating 'Sussex CCC' was put in the window of the coach taking the Sussex team to its matches,[120] which may have meant that county cricketers believed that county cricket should have been seen to be outside the labour dispute which had resulted in the strike. It is highly likely that between the wars Labour politicians and trade unionists may have considered that other forms of inequality were far more important than those found in cricket, but given the extent of working-class interest in cricket and ways in which cricket made class privilege so very obvious, this lack of passionate interest in reforming the authority structure of county cricket suggests that working-class antagonism to other classes was probably not very intense. Cricket also shows that forms of social identity, such as those centred upon England, the region, the county or the town and which crossed class boundaries, could be felt in some situations more strongly than those based on class. The extensive coverage of county cricket in *The Daily Herald* and in other newspapers with large numbers of working-class readers suggests a widespread working-class interest in cricket, even though county cricket was riddled with class privilege. Had a sense of working-class antagonism towards other classes been felt fiercely in other areas of social and political activity, then it would seem unlikely that there could have been such a level of working-class interest in cricket. At the same time cricket could have helped working people to be aware of social and economic inequalities. The extent of working-class interest in cricket and the limited calls for a reform of county cricket's social structure help to explain why working-class support for the reformist Labour Party was so much greater than that for the more stridently class-confrontational forms of socialism. Cricket would seem to confirm the observations of a German commentator on England that 'England is a land of classes ... where it has proved possible to unite a class system with democracy ... Nor do the English working classes regard themselves as a distinct section of the population ... They certainly realise that their conditions of life are unfavourable and form associations for their amelioration or for introducing social reform. But this does not imply that they look upon members of other classes as permanent antagonists.'[121]

NOTES

1. P. Joyce, *Visions of the People: Industrial England and the Question of Class 1848–1914* (Cambridge: Cambridge UP, 1991) and *Democratic Subjects: The Self and the Social in Nineteenth-century England* (Cambridge: Cambridge UP, 1994).
2. See, for instance, N. Kirk, 'History, Language, Ideas and Post-modernism: A Materialist View', *Social History*, 19, 2 (May 1994); M. Savage and A. Miles, *The Remaking of the British Working Class 1840–1940* (London: Routledge, 1994). N. Kirk, ed., *Social Class and Marxism: Defences and Challenges* (Aldershot: Scolar, 1996), discusses whether class should be seen as the dominant form of social consciousness in nineteenth- and twentieth-century Britain.
3. M. Marshall, *Gentlemen & Players: Conversations with Cricketers* (London: Grafton, 1987), pp. 261–82; data about the education of those who played for the Gentlemen was found in P. Bailey, P. Thorn and P. Wynne-Thomas, *Who's Who of Cricketers* (London: Guild, 1984).
4. *Who's Who of Cricketers*; R. Sissons, *The Players: A Social History of the Professional Cricketer* (London: Kingswood, 1988), pp. 200–1; D. Foot, *Wally Hammond: The Reasons Why* (London: Robson, 1996), p. 61.
5. D. Lemmon, *For the Love of the Game: An Oral History of First-class Cricket* (London: Michael Joseph, 1993), p. 142.
6. R. Sissons, *The Players*, p. 125.
7. The proportions of amateur appearances are calculated from the issues of *Wisden Cricketers' Almanack*.
8. H. Gordon, *Background of Cricket* (London: Barker, 1939), p. 241.
9. *Cricketer*, 9 Sept. 1933, p. 554.
10. H. Larwood with K. Perkins, *The Larwood Story* (London: W.H. Allen, 1965), p. 39.
11. Interview with Mr G.O. Dawkes (retired professional cricketer).
12. R. Mason, *Walter Hammond: A Biography* (London: Hollis & Carter, 1962), p. 130.

13. H.W. Lee (edited by L. Thompson), *Forty Years of English Cricket with Excursions to India and South Africa* (London: Clerke & Cockeran, 1948), pp. 23–4; D. Lemmon, *The Crisis of Captaincy: Servant and Master in English Cricket* (London: Christopher Helm, 1988), p. 65.
14. *The Times*, 21 April 1921, 17 April 1923.
15. A County Cricketer, *A Searchlight on English Cricket* (London: Robert Holden 1926), pp. 207–8.
16. F. Woolley, *The King of Games* (London: Stanley Paul, 1936), p. 185.
17. *Buff*, 23 April, 29 May 1926.
18. M. Marshall, *Gentlemen & Players*, p. 22.
19. *Athletic News*, 15 June 1925.
20. G.O. Dawkes interview.
21. *Buff*, 29 May 1926.
22. *Daily Mail*, 16 May 1934.
23. *Athletic News*, 15 Aug. 1921; M. Engel and A. Radd, *The History of Northamptonshire County Cricket Club* (London: Christopher Helm, 1993), p. 17.
24. Statistics of the playing records of those who played county cricket are found in C. Martin-Jenkins, *The Wisden Book of County Cricket* (London: Queen Anne, 1981). These averages refer only to performances with county teams.
25. M. Engel and A. Radd, *History of Northamptonshire,* p. 97; D. Lemmon, *The Official History of Worcestershire County Cricket Club* (London: Christopher Helm, 1989), p. 94.
26. D. Lambert, *The History of Leicestershire County Cricket Club* (London: Christopher Helm, 1992), p. 120.
27. E.R.T. Holmes, *Flannelled Foolishness: A Cricketing Chronicle* (London: Hollis & Carter, 1957), p. 40.
28. *The Times*, 30 March 1921.
29. *Field*, 5 Sept. 1931.
30. Ibid., 15 Aug. 1931, 10 June 1933.
31. Ibid., 23 April 1932.
32. P.F. Warner, *Cricket: A New Edition* (London: Longmans, Green, 1920), p. 121; *Athletic News*, 20 June 1921.
33. *Weekly Dispatch,* 11 Jan. 1925.
34. *Daily Mail*, 21 Jan. 1925. It is often thought that Hawke had said that he had prayed to God that no professional would ever captain England, but these words do not appear in *The Daily Mail* report of his speech. *The Cricketer* mentioned that Hawke had used the words 'prayed to God.' It is probable that Hawke had issued a text of his speech to the press before the AGM, but added the words 'prayed to God' whilst he was delivering the speech.
35. *Sunday Express*, 25 Jan. 1925.
36. Lord Harris to Captain Cornwallis, Kent Managing Committee minute book, 24, 25–27 June 1926, Kent County Record Office Ch 75 A3/5.
37. J.D. Coldham, *Lord Harris* (London: Allen and Unwin, 1983), p. 148.
38. *The Times*, 19 Dec. 1927.
39. *Searchlight on English Cricket*, pp. 162–3.
40. *Cricketer*, 19 Aug. 1922, p. 19.
41. *Searchlight on English Cricket*, pp. 140, 147.
42. *Cricketer*, Feb. 1925, p. 716.
43. R.E.S. Wyatt, *The Ins and Outs of Cricket* (London: Bell, 1936), p. 257.
44. *Searchlight on English Cricket*, p. 163.
45. *The Times*, 7 Nov. 1922.

46. *Cricketer Annual 1922–23* (London: Cricketer Syndicate, n.d.), p. 24. The permission of *The Cricketer* for the use of this quotation is acknowledged.
47. *Official Annual Handbook of the London and Southern Counties Cricket Conference ... 1925* (Wimbledon: LSCCC, 1925), p. 95.
48. *The Times*, 26 June 1935.
49. Ibid., 19 June 1926.
50. T. Cook, *Character and Sportsmanship* (London: Williams and Norgate), pp. viii–ix, xvi.
51. J.B. Hobbs, *My Cricket Memories* (London: Heinemann, 1924), p. 50.
52. *Guardian*, 15 May 1993.
53. Interview with Mr E.P. Robinson (retired professional cricketer).
54. B. Andrews, *The Hand That Bowled Bradman: Memories of a Professional Cricketer* (London: Macdonald, 1973), pp. 28, 33.
55. H.W. Lee, *Forty Years*, p. 53.
56. B. Andrews, *The Hand That Bowled Bradman*, p. 53; D. Lemmon, *For the Love of the Game*, p. 150.
57. B. Andrews, *The Hand That Bowled Bradman*, p. 53.
58. J. Hobbs, *Playing for England: My Test-cricket Story* (London: Gollancz, 1931), pp. 131–2; J. Hobbs, *My Life Story* (London: Hambledon, 1981 reprint of the 1935 edition), pp. 237–8.
59. *Daily Mail*, 3 Nov. 1927.
60. *Daily Herald*, 24 Jan. 1925.
61. B. Haynes and J. Lucas, *The Trent Bridge Battery: The Story of the Sporting Gunns* (London: Collins Willow, 1985), p. 160.
62. B. Andrews, *The Hand That Bowled Bradman*, p. 165.
63. Interview of Mr I.W. Hall with Mr T.B. Mitchell (retired professional cricketer), 19 Jan. 1993. I am grateful to Ian Hall for letting me listen to his recording of this interview.
64. Interview with Mr W. Place (retired county cricketer).
65. D. Lemmon, *Johnny Won't Hit Today: A Cricketing Biography of J.W.H.T. Douglas* (London: Allen and Unwin), p. 27.
66. H. Gordon, *Background of Cricket*, p. 224.
67. B. Andrews, *The Hand That Bowled Bradman*, p. 65.
68. M. Marshall, *Gentlemen & Players*, p. 43; F. Trueman and D. Mosey, *Fred Trueman Talking Cricket with Friends Past and Present* (London: Hodder & Stoughton, 1997), p. 92.
69. A. Gover, *The Long Run* (London: Pelham, 1991), pp. 18, 30.
70. E.R.T. Holmes, *Flannelled Foolishness*, p. 45.
71. H.W. Lee, *Forty Years*, p. 65.
72. J.M. Kilburn, *Thanks to Cricket* (London: Stanley Paul, 1972), p. 40.
73. *Athletic News*, 4 June 1927.
74. H. Gordon, *Background of Cricket*, p. 133.
75. J.B. Hobbs, *Cricket Memories*, p. 50.
76. C. Parkin, *Cricket Reminiscences: Humorous and Otherwise* (London: Hodder and Stoughton, 1925), p. 124.
77. H. Larwood and K. Perkins, *Larwood Story*, p. 39; A. Gover, *Long Run*, p. 27.
78. F. Woolley, *King of Games*, p. 198.
79. B. Hayes and J. Lucas, *Trent Bridge Battery*, p. 150.
80. Interview with Mr C.S. Elliott (retired county cricketer).
81. A.E.R. Gilligan, *Sussex Cricket* (London: Chapman & Hall, 1933), p. 147.
82. M. Marshall, *Gentlemen & Players*, p. 44.

83. H.W. Lee, *Forty Years On*, p. 25.
84. G.O. Dawkes interview.
85. B. Bearshaw, *From the Stretford End. The Official History of Lancashire County Cricket Club* (London: Partridge, 1990), p. 292.
86. B. Bowes, *Express Deliveries* (London: Stanley Paul, 1949), p. 170.
87. E.P. Robinson interview.
88. B. Hayes and J. Lucas, *Trent Bridge Battery*, p. 139.
89. M. Marshall, *Gentlemen & Players*, p. 28.
90. *Daily Mirror*, 15 Aug. 1938.
91. *Cricketer*, Dec. 1922, p. 4.
92. *Sussex Express*, 13 Oct. 1922.
93. Yorkshire Cricket Federation minute book, 28 June 1932, West Yorkshire Archives Service Acc 2772.
94. R. Genders, *League Cricket in England* (London: T. Warner Laurie, 1952), p. 144.
95. Yorkshire Cricket Federation minute book, 22 March 1938.
96. *Athletic News*, 30 Jan. 1922; A. Hill, *Hedley Verity: A Portrait of a Cricketer* (London: Guild, 1986), p. 89.
97. *Buff*, 29 June 1929.
98. Ibid., 6 July 1929.
99. W. Place interview.
100. D. Russell, 'Amateurs, Professionals and the Construction of Identity', *Sports Historian*, 16 (1996), p. 74. For a further discussion of cricket and Yorkshire identity, see D. Russell, 'Sport and Identity: The Case of Yorkshire County Cricket Club, 1890–1939', *20 Century British History*, 7, 2 (1996).
101. *The Cricketer Annual, 1924–25* (London: Cricketer Publications, n.d.), p. 59.
102. *Buff*, 11 May 1929.
103. *Field*, 8, 29 Aug. 1931.
104. *Yorkshire Sport and Cricket Argus*, 22 June 1935.
105. A. Tomlinson, 'Good Times, Bad Times and the Politics of Leisure. Working-class Culture in the 1930s in a Small Working-class Community', in H. Cantelon and R. Hollands, eds., *Leisure: Theory and History* (Toronto: Garamond, 1988), p. 57.
106. *Nelson Gazette,* 9 April 1935, quoted by J. Hill, *Nelson: Politics, Economy and Community* (Edinburgh: Keele UP, 1997), p. 123.
107. *Radcliffe Times*, 7 May 1938.
108. *Rawtenstall Cricket Club Bazaar ... with a Brief History of the Cricket Club from 1868 to 1925* (n.p., n.d.).
109. *Lancashire Evening Telegraph*, 13 June 1989.
110. *Rochdale Observer*, 31 July 1920.
111. *Daily Herald*, 16 Dec. 1927.
112. *Daily Mail*, 12 May 1934.
113. *Daily Express*, 10 Aug. 1926.
114. Ibid., 3 Nov. 1927.
115. H. Gordon, *Background of Cricket*, p. 121.
116. *Daily Herald*, 22, 24 Jan. 1925.
117. Ibid., 23 Jan. 1925.
118. Ibid., 22 Jan. 1925.
119. Ibid., 3 Nov. 1927.
120. M. Tate, *My Cricketing Reminiscences* (London: Stanley Paul, 1934), p. 81.
121. K. Von Stutterheim, *Those English!* [translated by L.M. Sieveking] (London: Sidgwick & Jackson, 1937).

7

Cricket and Christianity

Discourses on cricket between the wars emphasised that it expressed Christian morality. Taking an interest in cricket, but particularly playing cricket, were represented as almost a form of religious observance. Some described cricket in language usually reserved for religious occasions and institutions. The sports journalist Bernard Darwin, for example, in 1940 wrote that a big match at Lord's would impress spectators 'particularly with the solemn rite or ceremony'.[1] In 1931 'Second Slip' in *The Cricketer* claimed that 'The Church militant has always been an upholder of the game.'[2] Cricket and the churches were considered to be mutually supportive. R.L. Hodgson, whose regular column in *The Cricketer* was headed 'A Country Vicar', wrote in 1922 that 'the cricket field is quite an appropriate place for the parson, and the parson not only an appropriate, but a welcome, figure in the foreground'.[3] In 1937 the Worcestershire and England fast bowler Fred Root, or perhaps his ghost writer, felt it necessary to claim in his autobiography that 'the sporting parson is the very centre of our village cricket'.[4] Cricket was also seen to represent a distinctively English expression of Christian morality. Dean Inge, the Anglican cleric, wrote that 'I still maintain that cricket is probably the best game yet devised by the wit of man, and, as Milton says, when Providence has a great idea, he reveals it first to his Englishmen'.[5] Because cricket was so widely assumed to reflect Christian teachings, appraisals of the social significance of organised religion in England between the wars have to consider the role of churches within cricket.

Not all accepted that cricket should have been regarded as an expression of Christian morality. In his book *Cricket,* first published in 1930, Neville Cardus complained about speakers at cricket club dinners praising cricket, as synonymous with 'straight conduct, honour bright and all the other recognised Christian virtues'. 'Moral superiority', he continued, 'is the worst form of priggishness; for that reason I hate to hear the familiar cant about cricket … By all means let cricketers lose matches graciously; they can do so without indulging in humbug.'[6] Robertson Glasgow, the cricket writer, who had played for Charterhouse and Oxford, and for Somerset as an amateur, declared that he had 'never regarded cricket as a branch of religion'.[7] Such responses to cricket were rare and their tone and context suggest that cricket was widely described as a form of Christian morality. It is possible, of course, that many of those who described cricket as an expression of Christianity may have done so because they believed that it was expected of them, but this too can be interpreted as evidence for a widespread conviction that cricket and Christian values were mutually supportive.

Assumptions about the parallels between cricket and Christianity were inherited from the Victorians. Keith Sandiford has explained how muscular Christian clerics encouraged the playing of cricket in the hope that this would lead to an acceptance of Christian moral teaching.[8] The association of cricket with institutions which were represented as expressions of English moral worth strengthened the perceptions of cricket as a form of Christianity. By the second half of the nineteenth century it was claimed that a prime aim of the public schools was to produce English Christian gentlemen, and the games cult, to which the playing of cricket was central, was seen as essential for the achievement of this aim.[9] Most public school headmasters, and many public school teachers, were ordained Anglicans. Some, such as J.E.C. Welldon, who had been the head of Dulwich and Harrow, wrote forcefully about the playing of games producing ethical qualities.[10] Beliefs in the Empire as a moral trust and the status of cricket as a sport played primarily in the Empire added to suppositions that cricket was synonymous with Christian values. Representations of cricket as part of the pastoral tradition reinforced the supposed connections between cricket and the churches. As mentioned in Chapter 1 Georgina Boyes has shown how in the late nineteenth and early twentieth centuries the rustic was seen as morally superior to the urban.[11] In celebrations of cricket as part of the rural idyll, the vicar was often seen as a vital member of the village cricket team which played on the village green against a backdrop of parish church and village inn. The numbers of clerics who played first-class cricket before the First World War and the numbers of church teams strengthened assumptions that an intimate relationship existed between cricket and organised Christianity. A third of all Oxford and Cambridge cricket blues between 1860 and 1900 became ordained,[12] although in 1900 only six clerics appeared in the county championship and four of them played for Hampshire. In many northern towns Sunday school and church cricket leagues had been organised by 1914.

Heavy gambling had been a feature of cricket in the eighteenth and early nineteenth centuries. The Australian captain Warwick Armstrong alleged that there had been betting on the 1921 test matches and Jeffrey Hill has found evidence of betting upon league cricket matches in Lancashire,[13] but the absence of public debate about gambling on cricket and the absence of odds and betting forecasts in newspapers such as *The Sporting Chronicle* suggest that betting on cricket cannot have been as extensive as that on other sports. In 1934 an attempt to organise betting on county and Lancashire League matches along the lines of football pools seems to have fizzled out.[14] It is possible that cricket was not as suited to gambling as many other sports, and since clerics were often critical of gambling, it would seem that the relative absence of gambling on cricket made it easier to see cricket as morally pure and impregnated with Christian values. At the same time, the strong amateur presence within first-class cricket and the resistance to greater commercialisation of county cricket resonated with those aspects of English culture which saw an aggressive pursuit of profit as morally tainted. Many clerics accepted capitalism, but few of them between the wars argued that a ruthless pursuit of wealth was in harmony with Christian ethics.

The strongest encouragement to assumptions that cricket represented Christian morality was the belief that the tradition of sportsmanship within cricket reflected Christian ethics. Statements from a wide variety of sources about the Christian merit of cricket, and particularly its tradition of sportsmanship, are not hard to find. An editorial in *The Times* in 1920 claimed that 'All cricketers, who are, because they play the game, all good men'.[15] Statements similar to the following drawn from Bolton and its surroundings could easily be provided for other localities. At a sale of work for the Whittlebrook Methodist CC from Walkden a speaker argued that 'The man who played cricket in the true sense of the word was obviously a man capable of the deepest sense of religious thought' and went on to mention the 'splendid co-operation between the noble and ancient game of cricket and the best thoughts one could apply in helping one another'.[16] In 1925 Donny Davies, who played cricket as an amateur for Lancashire and for the England amateur soccer team and who was to become a sports journalist with *The Manchester Guardian,* spoke at a Congregationalist brotherhood meeting about cricket always being associated with honourable conduct. For him the great value of cricket was that it trained character and encouraged collective effort.[17] At the annual prize-giving of the Radcliffe Sunday School League in 1934 it was stated that cricket 'fostered the spirit of sacrifice'.[18] It was not unusual for professional cricketers to speak about the compatibility of cricket and Christian morality. Bill Bowes, the Yorkshire fast bowler whose use of short-pitched fast bowling caused him to be accused of using unsporting tactics, mentioned at a sportsman's service held at a Methodist chapel in 1935 that the 'teaching of sport' ran 'parallel with certain Christian ideals' and that cricket was 'a game every Christian should be interested in 'because it demanded self-discipline, self-control and team spirit'.[19] Justifying amateurism on the grounds that amateur captains were essential for the maintenance of sportsmanship drew together the suspicion of commercial-isation, the moral force of sportsmanship and Christian ethics.

CLERICS AND CRICKET BETWEEN THE WARS

The degree of clerical involvement with cricket between the wars was less than the celebration of cricket as an expression of Christian values would lead one to expect. Twelve clerics played in the county championship between the wars, but only F.H. Gillingham for Essex in 1919 and J.H Parsons for Warwickshire from 1929 until 1932 played in more than half a county's championship matches in one season. Except for W.I. Rice, a Benedictine monk who was headmaster of Douai from 1915 until 1952, all those who played in the county championship were Anglicans. All played as amateurs, though Parsons, who was ordained in 1929 at the age of 38, had played as a professional for Warwickshire from 1910 to 1914 and from 1924 to 1928 and as an amateur from 1919 to 1923. During the First World War and in the early 1920s he had been an officer in the Indian Army. Some clerics were highly talented cricketers. E.T. Killick opened the batting twice for England in 1929. Parsons was often described as the best batsman of his day not to have played for England.[20] The number of clerics who played first-class cricket between the wars was not very high but was probably at least comparable with that of the highest levels of other team sports. It is doubtful whether any clerics played in the football league or in the rugby league during this period. No clerics played county championship cricket in 1927 or from 1935 to 1937.

Clerics were also involved with the administration of county clubs. The Reverend Henry Ellison was the honorary secretary of Derbyshire in the 1930s and usually represented the county at meetings of the Advisory Committee.[21] The Reverend G.W. Gillingham managed the club and ground matches for Worcestershire CCC and in 1923 organised a bazaar which raised £2,300 for the club. In 1929 he became the club's honorary secretary which enabled Cyril Walters, the salaried secretary and a test match batsman, to play for the county.[22] A few clerics served on the executive committees of county clubs. In addition to Gillingham, an archdeacon and another reverend were members of the Worcestershire committee in 1930, but Kent, Northamptonshire, Somerset, Surrey, Sussex, Worcestershire and

Yorkshire never had more than one cleric on their committees in years selected for a sample of committee membership. The numbers of clerics on the executive committees of counties were about equal to those using the title Doctor and far fewer than those with military titles, though some of these could have held commissions only during the First World War. The number of clerics who were members of county clubs varied widely between counties. Nine of the first hundred names in an alphabetical listing of county members for Somerset in 1939 were clerics; there were three for Kent in 1920 and four in 1938. In 1920, two of the first hundred names for Surrey were clerics but there were none in 1939, whilst none of a similar sample from the Sheffield area were members of Yorkshire in 1921 and only two in 1940.

The exact number of clerics who played recreational cricket regularly between the wars cannot be established. Clergy elevens were formed in some Anglican dioceses. The holding of an annual match at Lord's between the clergy of the London and Southwark dioceses indicates the prestige attached to clerical cricket. Canterbury, Chichester, Rochester and Southampton were other dioceses with clergy teams. There were also Nottinghamshire and Worcestershire clergy teams. The panegyrics of recreational cricket seem to have exaggerated the number of clerics who played for village clubs. An article in *The Cricketer* in 1923 argued that vicars usually made the best captains of village teams because their experience of cricket at school or university had given them insight into tactics and strategy, but later in the same year another article maintained that only parsons who were competent cricketers should play, because poor performances could cause respect for a parson to decline, whereas those who played well could expect larger congregations.[23] Score cards of matches between village teams printed in *The Sussex Express* show that most village teams in East Sussex did not include a cleric, whilst only three reverends played for the 14 village teams from Kent and Surrey whose matches were reported on in *The News Chronicle* by Arthur Gilligan in 1931. Bolton and its surroundings in Lancashire were an area where league cricket of high quality was played and where a very high number of churches and Sunday schools had cricket clubs, yet even here the number of clerics who played regularly was low. A Catholic priest and a Congregationalist minister seem to have been the only clerics who played regularly for clubs at the higher levels of league cricket. Oral evidence has shown that the minister played regularly for the Stand Unitarian team which played at a far humbler level of league cricket, but generally clerics played only in emergencies when the teams associated with their churches were short of players.[24] In 1939, however, *The Sports Argus* shows that each team playing in the Birmingham Methodist League usually included a reverend. Clerics were often the presidents of village clubs in Sussex and of church or Sunday school clubs in the Bolton area, and in both areas took the chair at annual meetings and prize-giving events.

CHURCH TEAMS AND RECREATIONAL CRICKET

In many parts of the North the number of church-based cricket clubs was high. For most northern towns and industrialised villages the number of such teams was higher in the 1920s than at any other time in the twentieth century. Samples from the cotton towns of Lancashire show that over a half in the 1920s and more than a third in the 1930s of those who played regularly did so for church teams. In 1922, 70 of the 134 teams playing each week in the Bolton area, 107 out of 129 in the Burnley area and 79 out of 132 in the Oldham area were church teams. In 1939, when the numbers of church teams had fallen, 62 out of 155 teams playing in Bolton, 54 out of 101 in Burnley and 64 out of 140 in Oldham were church teams. In 1935 more than 40 per cent of the 288 teams from Bradford and its surroundings in the West Riding of Yorkshire mentioned by *The Yorkshire Sports and Cricket Argus* were church teams. In other northern towns such as Barnsley, Halifax, St Helens and Wigan, the proportion of church teams was not so high but for much of the inter-war period formed more than ten per cent of all teams playing regularly.

Church teams were less common in other parts of England. In 1925 only one club out of the first hundred of an alphabetical listing of clubs affiliated to the London and Southern Counties Club Cricket Conference was based on a church. In 1939 only four of the Club Cricket Conference's 157 clubs from Essex and 11 of the 430 from Middlesex were church clubs. Only five of the 104 cricket clubs from the eastern half of Sussex mentioned by *The Sussex Express* in 1939 were church clubs. In 1930 the 65 teams mentioned by *The Hereford Times* included only two connected with churches and one of these was that of the YMCA. In parts of the Midlands numbers of church teams were higher than in much of the South but lower than in the textile districts of the North. In 1922 around a third of the 190 teams from Birmingham and perhaps just beyond its boundaries were church teams, but by 1939, when the total number of teams was over 300, only around 12 per cent of them were church teams. These totals of teams for Birmingham do not include those which were playing in the internal competitions of large firms, such as the 14 teams which in 1930 were playing in the BSA cricket league. The city of Worcester was far from being a stronghold of cricket playing. In 1922 less than 20 teams from Worcester played regularly and only three were connected with churches. By 1939, when between 30 and 40 teams were playing each week, the number of church teams was still three. In 1930, however, nine teams had played in the Worcester Sunday School Union Cricket League but this had collapsed by 1939. *The Mansfield and North Notts Advertiser* shows that around 80 teams were playing regularly in the Mansfield district of north Nottinghamshire in 1922, 1930 and 1939. The number of church teams fell from ten in 1922, to seven in 1930 and two in 1939.

Many towns and villages in the North had Sunday school cricket leagues. These were leagues for men, not children, though often youths played. In Lancashire the Burnley and District Sunday Schools League was probably that with most teams. In 1922 it had 83 teams and there were also Sunday school leagues in the neighbouring towns of Padiham and Nelson. In Yorkshire the Bradford Mutual Sunday School Cricket League had 80 teams in 1935. In the 1920s Oldham had four separate cricket leagues for church and Sunday School teams – the Pleasant Sunday Afternoon League, the Sunday school Alliance League, the Primitive Methodist League and the Congregational League. Church teams were not restricted to Sunday school leagues. In 1924 14 of the 20 teams playing in the two divisions of the Oldham and Ashton League were based on churches. In 1929, 32 of the 59 teams playing in the second division of Bolton and District Cricket Association and in the Junior Second Teams Association, in effect the BDCA's third division, were church teams as were 20 of the 24 teams in the Walkden Amateur League, which drew its clubs from the area between Bolton and Salford. In locations with a high number of church teams, the greatest concentrations of church clubs were found at the humblest levels of recreational cricket. In Lancashire, no church club between the wars played in the Lancashire League or the Central Lancashire League, which were usually regarded as the county's most prestigious leagues. Pudsey St Lawrence was the only church club to play in the Bradford League between the wars. In 1929 two church clubs played in the first division of the BDCA, but neither was invited to join the 12 clubs that seceded from the BDCA during the winter of 1929–30 and formed the Bolton League, which immediately became the most prestigious league in the Bolton area. Many church clubs severed their links with churches when they progressed to the higher levels of league cricket. This may have been because becoming an open club made it easier to attract players of the standard required to compete successfully at the higher levels of league cricket. In 1924, for instance, Walkden Congregational CC of the first division of BDCA, opted to become Walkden CC[25] and was invited to be one of the founder members of the Bolton League. Because the church presence was strongest at the lowest levels of recreational cricket, church clubs often played with very poor facilities, but some talented cricketers emerged from such humble leagues. Five players from the Bacup and District Sunday School in Lancashire went on to play county cricket and one played for England.[26]

Most church and Sunday school leagues were inter-denominational. In the early 1920s five Methodist churches had teams in the Oldham Primitive Methodist League but they were not all Primitive Methodist. The Oldham Congregational League was open to clubs of all denominations. Halifax had a Nonconformist Cricket League which played throughout the inter-war period. The Church Institute League in Sunderland seems to have been restricted to Anglican teams but had only four teams in 1922 and had collapsed by the mid 1920s. In the early 1920s there was an Anglican Birmingham Diocesan Federation Cricket League but this was not mentioned by the local press in 1930. Birmingham had a Wesleyan Cricket League consisting of two divisions in 1930 and by 1939 this may have become the Methodist Cricket League. In Lancashire and Yorkshire the Church of England, the differing branches of Methodism, Unitarians and Congregationalists were usually the denominations with most teams, but some sects were stronger in some areas than others. No Baptist teams played in Bolton and its surroundings, whereas six Baptist churches from Burnley had cricket teams between the wars. Only one Catholic church from the Bolton area had a cricket club, but Catholic churches had cricket teams in other Lancashire towns such as Burnley and St Helens. Catholic teams, however, did not usually belong to Sunday school leagues, preferring to play in leagues not based on religious organisations. In the words of one priest the Catholic church 'did not go in for mixed bathing' and tended to remain aloof from inter-denominational sports organisations.[27]

The strength of the church presence within recreational cricket in the North before 1914 does much to explain its continued strength after the First World War. Many Sunday school cricket leagues had been formed before 1914 and the church presence was equally pronounced in association football. Indeed many parts of the North and Midlands had more church football than cricket teams.[28] This colonisation of recreational sport by the churches before 1914 had created an assumption that it was natural for cricket teams to be grafted on to churches or Sunday schools, whilst the frequent assertions before and after the First World War that cricket was an expression of Christian morality helped to confirm beliefs that it was appropriate for cricket clubs to be connected with churches. The paucity of evidence about the establishment of church cricket teams means that it is difficult to be sure whether clerics or laymen took the lead in their

149

formation. Extensive searches in north of England newspapers have not uncovered statements from clerics or superintendents of Sunday schools condemning cricket or wishing to sever the connections between cricket and churches, although in 1928 the chairman of the Bolton Sunday Schools Social League, which organised competitions for a wide range of sports but not cricket, and which had probably more registered players than any similar organisation in the country, complained about the 'antagonism or lack of encouragement on the part of clergy and the heads of some of the Sunday schools'.[29] Clerics were often prepared to be the presidents of church clubs, attended the annual prize-giving ceremonies of clubs and became vice-presidents of Sunday school cricket leagues. Most Sunday school leagues and most church clubs had rules insisting that all players attended church or Sunday school regularly, and although such rules were not always observed, the possibility of cricket teams encouraging church attendance may have occurred to some clerics. In 1922 the Reverend W. Popplewell in Bolton declared that he 'testified in no uncertain manner to the value of cricket in connection with parochial work',[30] but such statements in local newspapers are rare. More common were statements by clerics that cricket promoted qualities which could reinforce Christian morality. The Reverend A.W. Nye, treasurer of the Bolton Junior Second Teams Association, said in 1921 that 'from the disciplinary point of view' cricket was 'a good thing because it helped to school one to success or defeat' whilst 'if sport was clean, conducted properly and entered into in the right spirit, it tended to develop character'.[31] In *The Bolton Congregationalist* Dr Albert Peel, a prominent Congregationalist minister, claimed that 'Modesty and patience, intellect and harmony, these are the things that make for success on the cricket field – and also in the game of life'.[32]

The attitude of most clerics towards church cricket teams seems to have been closer to indifference than to fervent enthusiasm. Weekly columns by clerics in local newspapers hardly ever mentioned cricket or any other sport. Two national Methodist newspapers, *The Methodist Times* in 1926 and *The Methodist Recorder* in 1935, did not have articles by ministers about cricket, but printed photographs of Methodist cricket teams which suggests that the playing of cricket was not considered contrary to Methodist teachings. These newspapers had little to say about other sports except to condemn gambling and to oppose calls for the playing of sports on Sundays. Reports of the annual meetings of Sunday school unions held in Bolton, Wigan and St Helens did not discuss sport as a means of attracting support. Interviews with five clerics who worked in the Bolton area before 1939 showed that one was an enthusiastic club cricketer but had not thought of forming a team at his church and another had occasionally played for the team at his church when it was short of players, but the other three admitted having no interest in cricket.[33] The scale of the numbers of church teams in the North at least suggests that whilst most clerics may not have been enthusiastic supporters of church cricket, they did feel that it was appropriate for cricket to be played under the auspices of churches.

The strength of the church presence within recreational cricket did much to determine who played cricket in the North. Oral evidence from the Bolton area shows that the great majority of those who played for church teams were working-class, the majority of players having blue-collar occupations though many teams also included two or three clerks or teachers.[34] But church cricket clubs were not entirely working-class cultural institutions. Clerics were often the presidents of the clubs attached to their churches and many clubs had middle-class patrons. Local worthies were also prominent as patrons of Sunday school cricket leagues. A mill-owner, for instance, donated the trophies of the Horwich Sunday School League.[35] In the 1920s Captain Lloyd, a Conservative councillor and director of the United Thread Mills, was the president of the Bolton Junior Second Teams Association, whose member clubs were almost all church clubs. The vice-presidents included his father-in-law, the industrialist Colonel E.W. Greg, and the owner of one of Bolton's bleach works.[36] It would seem that the association of cricket with churches helped to make cricket clubs social institutions which could draw support from different social classes. Interviews reveal that the church presence within cricket discouraged the involvement of certain groups with cricket in the Bolton area. Those who played for church teams tended to belong to what they believed were the 'respectable' sections of the working class. 'Roughs' are not remembered as playing for church clubs. Only one player of the Stand Unitarian Church CC in the late 1920s and 1930s has been remembered as a 'boozer', 'the black sheep of the club'.[37] Most who played for church team teams attended church regularly and as church attendance was often seen as mark of respectability, church teams reinforced assumptions about the respectability of cricket.

The strength of the church presence within cricket may have discouraged the formation of cricket clubs based on pubs. Several first-class cricketers were heavy drinkers. Socially exclusive cricket clubs in all parts of England and some league clubs had bars. Pub cricket clubs were rare, though players at some clubs may have met regularly in a particular pub. Burnley had a licensed houses cricket league in 1900 and Halifax one in 1922 but neither lasted for long. Tom Harrisson's *The Pub and the People*, based upon evidence collected by Mass-Observation in Bolton during the late 1930s, does not mention cricket playing as a recreation for frequenters of Bolton pubs or cricket being among their common topics of conversation. The belief that cricket represented Christian values, and the strength of church and Sunday school cricket before 1914, seems to have created an assumption that it would be inappropriate to graft cricket clubs on to pubs, whilst the rarity of pub cricket clubs strengthened perceptions of cricket as a respectable activity.

SABBATARIANISM AND CRICKET

Church support for Sabbatarian attitudes restricted opportunities to play cricket, though this varied between denominations and between localities and over time. In the south of England, and especially the London area, playing cricket on Sundays became more extensive between the wars. In 1937 Sir Home Gordon wrote that 'One post-War innovation is the multiplicity of Sunday club cricket. Some may remember how long ago those playing for the Thespids furtively carried their cricket bags to some remote field to encounter a rather conscious-stricken scratch side … Now many clubs, both peregrinatory and domiciled, exist more for Sabbatarian games than others.'[38] In 1925, only one in a sample of 100 clubs from the Home Counties affiliated to the Club Cricket Conference played on Sundays, but in 1933 over half of the Conference's 208 clubs from Surrey played on Sundays, though only three clubs played only on Sundays. The LCC first allowed cricket and other team sports to be played on its recreational land in 1922, but no Sunday games could be cup-ties or league matches.[39] Outside the south-east little cricket was played on Sundays even in 1939. The first match to be played on a Sunday in County Durham took place in 1936.[40] League matches do not seem to have been held on Sundays in the North between the wars. In the Bolton area the conviction that cricket was not played on Sundays was so deeply entrenched that one respondent has recalled that organising matches on Sundays 'was just not thought about'.[41]

Playing county cricket on Sundays was only occasionally suggested as a means of increasing the gate receipts of county clubs. In 1930 Bev Lyon, the captain of Gloucestershire and one of the tiny number of Jews who played county cricket, called for county matches to be played on Sundays. 'Let us go to Church in the mornings and acknowledge the Sabbath. In the afternoon let us play the clean, honest, wholesome game.' He added: 'If I am going too fast in suggesting that first-class cricket be played on Sunday afternoons, why should we not let the county grounds be used on Sundays by clubs.' The church-going Jack Hobbs declared himself to be 'dead against' county cricket being played on Sundays, but had no objection to cricket being played on Sundays by those who could not play during the week.[42] In the early 1920s Hobbs had refused to play cricket on Sundays when touring India, but other English professionals had agreed to play. In 1937 Sir Home Gordon argued in *The Cricketer* for county matches to be played on Sundays, but a few months later in the editorial notes to *The Cricketer Annual* Pelham Warner, who just after the First World War had advocated the playing of recreational sport on Sundays, pointed out there was 'still a strong body of opinion in this country against organised Sunday sport, and we think that that opinion should be respected'.[43] Omission of any reference to Sunday play in the report of the Findlay Commission which was issued in 1937 suggests that the degree of support for county cricket to be played on Sundays was no more than minimal.

In the south-east of England demands for cricket and other sports to be played on Sundays grew in the years just after the First World War. In April 1919 the Sunday Games Association was launched in London at a meeting where Pelham Warner, then captain of Middlesex CCC, took the chair. He argued that during the First World War, games had been played by the troops after they attended church on Sundays and claimed that those who had played games on Sundays during the war, would grumble if they had no games after the war and that the country could not 'afford too much grumbling'. Warner wanted a 'Merrie England'.[44] What became of the Association is unclear as the press ignored whatever subsequent meetings it may have held. At the Canterbury Diocesan Conference in 1922 Lord Harris spoke in favour of Sunday sports. Accepting that Sunday ought to be a day of rest and recreation for tired minds and bodies, he challenged anyone to say that young men would be better employed in their own homes than in God's air playing manly games under proper control. In his view exhibition matches played by professional cricketers on Sundays would 'advantage the great mass of the population not only physically but mentally and morally'.[45] In 1922 an editorial in *The Times* supporting the decision of the LCC to permit Sunday matches on its recreational land argued that 'Young people must have an outlet for their abounding energies'. If denied the opportunity to play sport, it feared that 'many of them may be driven, at best to idle loafing, and at worst to pursuits more definitely harmful ... To deny to young people of the middle and working classes in London those facilities for healthy recreation which are enjoyed every Sunday as a matter of course by the sons and daughters of the richer classes is obviously inequitable.'[46] A year later, *The Times* noted that there had been less gambling on the LCC's playing fields at Wormwood Scrubs since the introduction of Sunday games and that therefore, 'For moral, as well as for physical reasons, we sincerely hope that the LCC will not be moved to undo the good work which they have set on foot'.[47] In the year following the LCC decision to allow games on Sundays, 36 borough and district councils, including those for such large towns as Birmingham, Brighton, Bristol, Hastings, Leeds, Leicester, Liverpool, Northampton and Swansea voted against games being played on Sundays upon municipal land, whilst only six had decided to permit Sunday games.[48]

Clerical responses to the playing of cricket and other sports on Sundays were divided on denominational and regional lines. Nonconformist ministers were prominent in the opposition to Sunday games from organisations such as the Imperial Sunday Alliance and the United Council for Sunday Protection. *The Methodist Times* and *The Methodist Recorder* opposed the playing of sports on Sundays. Anglican clerics were found among the supporters and opponents of sports being played on Sundays, but it is difficult to be sure what the majority of Anglican clergy thought or whether their opinions changed between the wars. At the meeting of the Canterbury Diocesan Conference in 1922 where Lord Harris had spoken in favour of Sunday sport, the Archbishop of Canterbury appeared to be steering a middle course, arguing that all would have to think for themselves whether Sunday sports would impair the principle of Sunday worship.[49] Other Anglicans were more outspoken in their opposition to Sunday sport. Frank Gillingham, the rector and rural dean of Bermondsey, who played county cricket as an amateur for Essex from 1903 until 1928, feared that the playing of recreational cricket on Sundays would lead to league and county cricket being played on Sundays and the opening of cinemas on Sundays. The Bishop of Chelmsford found the LCC's decision 'deplorable'.[50] In January 1923 the bishops of Barking and Willesden and two canons attended a meeting of the United Council for Sunday Protection arranged to protest against the LCC's decision to permit Sunday games.[51] But press reports of Anglicans defending the playing of sports on Sundays are equally common. In 1920 H.R. Gamble, the Dean of Exeter, claimed that recreation on a Sunday afternoon 'violated no Christian principle'.[52] In 1922 the Reverend Basil Bourchier of Hampstead wrote to *The Times* in support of Sunday sport and argued that that the church would gain immensely by making Sunday a 'healthy and happier day'.[53] In 1923 the Oxford Diocesan Conference carried by a large majority a resolution that where games on Sundays did not involve paid labour, they were not incompatible with Christian practice, but emphasised that worship was the first duty of all professed Christians.[54] In 1926 the Church Commissioners allowed the playing of some sports on their land on Sundays, but not cricket because the preparation of pitches required some to work on Sundays.[55]

Opposition to Sunday games was expressed more forcefully among Anglicans in the North than in the South. Press reports of Anglican clerics in the North speaking in favour of Sunday sport are rare. In 1922 J.E.C. Welldon, who had become the Dean of Durham in 1918, wrote that he was not opposed to games on Sundays.[56] Dr Henson, the Bishop of Durham, argued that whilst Sunday games were not necessarily inconsistent with the observance of Sunday duties, Sabbatarianism was probably less harmful to society than the 'laxity now carrying all before it' but in 1926 he called Sunday games a 'misuse, or even a profanation of the Lord's day'.[57] Temple, the bishop of Manchester, was one of the few Anglicans in the North to speak publicly in favour of Sunday games. At a meeting of the Church Assembly in 1926 he declared that he had voted for the decision of the Church Commissioners to permit the playing of games on their land on Sundays and would do so again, but added that they 'should all act together to see how they could protect Sunday', and that 'no question was more urgent than the proper observance of Sunday'.[58] Intensive searching in the local newspapers from Bolton and St Helens for the whole of the inter-war period and for selected years of newspapers from Barnsley, Burnley, Halifax, Oldham, Sunderland and Wigan have revealed condemnations but no support for Sunday sport from Anglican clerics. Anglican clerics seem to have done little to have weakened Sabbatarian restrictions upon the playing of cricket on Sundays in the North. The growth in the number of teams which played cricket on Sundays in the south-east suggests that Sabbatarianism, which owed much to the churches, had been a crucial factor in restricting the playing of cricket for recreation in other regions.

Apologists for cricket often claimed that levels of sportsmanship within cricket were higher than those found in other sports, and it is possible that the repeated expression of such views may have influenced how some played cricket. Evidence from Bolton and its surroundings, however, shows that the church presence within cricket did not discourage cheating and other forms of unsporting behaviour and that the levels of sportsmanship at church clubs were no higher than those of other clubs. Chapter 4 has shown that the most flagrant instances of unsporting behaviour in Bolton cricket involved church and Sunday school teams.

THE IMPACT OF CRICKET ON THE CHURCHES

The inter-war years have often been seen as a time when English society and culture became more secularised. John Stevenson has written of 'the decline of organised religion, judged both in terms of allegiance and membership of the Christian churches and their role as arbiters of public conventions and private morality ... Increasingly, Christianity and formal religious adherence of other kinds was becoming a marginal feature of British society, in which secular conventions increasingly dominated public and private life.'[59] The association of the churches with cricket, however, helped to resist this marginalisation of organised religion in English social and cultural life. The strength of Sabbatarian opposition, often led by clerics, to playing cricket and other sports on Sundays outside the south-east, and the very small number of calls for county cricket to be played on Sundays, are evidence that the influence of the churches was still a major force in English social and cultural life. The extensive church presence in recreational cricket in some parts of England shows that the churches were still important as providers of leisure. The number of church cricket teams, and church football teams, tended to be higher in the 1920s than in any other decade of the twentieth century. In the late 1930s, the number of church cricket teams did fall, but not as a result of a spreading conviction that the social role of churches should be restricted. The main reason for the reduction in the number of church teams was the loss of grounds to housebuilding. Very few church teams owned their grounds and the shortage of sports grounds meant that the termination of a ground tenancy usually resulted in the collapse of a club. Sixteen cricket clubs from Bolton county borough, for instance, disbanded as a result of being evicted from their grounds between 1924 and 1934. Fourteen of them were church clubs.[60]

Declining levels of church attendance have often been used to measure the growth of secularisation. Whilst church attendance does not prove acceptance of Christian teachings, clerics certainly felt that regular church attendance was essential for propagating Christian values and for ensuring that the churches had a central role in English national life. Church cricket clubs, and church teams playing other sports, encouraged church attendance. Church cricket clubs and Sunday school cricket leagues usually had regulations requiring players to attend church services or men's classes regularly. Oral evidence shows that not all who played for church teams were regular worshippers. Some clerics and Sunday school superintendents turned a blind eye to the playing of non-attenders when prohibiting them from playing would have made it difficult or impossible to have raised a team and so denied regular attenders of opportunities to play.[61] But oral evidence from the Bolton area shows that most of those who played for church teams did attend church regularly. Attending church on Sundays gave players the opportunity to mull over the previous day's match. Moreover the presence of young men at church persuaded young women to attend. All the interviewees, although a tiny sample of all of those who played for church teams in the Bolton area, had married women who attended the same church. The presence of young women at church also led young men who were not interested in sport to attend. Church cricket teams encouraged church attendance at a stage of life when attendance often ceased.

Church teams reduced the power of religious affiliation as a source of social division. It has already been mentioned that most Sunday School cricket leagues were interdenominational and that leagues not restricted to church or Sunday school teams often included teams from a variety of denominations. In the north and to a lesser extent the Midlands church teams can be seen as expressing interdenominational co-operation, which in many towns was also found in the 'walking days' and processions which included Anglican and Nonconformist churches, and which was also demonstrated by inter denominational church conferences such as the Conference of Christian Politics, Economics and Citizenship held at Birmingham in 1924. Many interdenominational Sunday school leagues were formed during the Edwardian period which shows that political animosities between Anglicans and Nonconformists stimulated by conflict over education reform were not so intense as to prevent co-operation in other areas of social activity. Playing cricket between Wesleyan, United Methodist and Primitive Methodist teams may have eased the path to the Methodist reunion in 1934. At the same time, church cricket emphasised the gulf between Catholics and those of other denominations. In some towns with very high numbers of church cricket clubs, very few Catholic churches had cricket teams and where they did play, they tended not to join inter-denominational cricket leagues. This does not seem to have been a result of an anti-Catholic prejudice so much as the desire of Catholic clerics to discourage contact with other denominations. When the Horwich Sunday School League was being established in 1922, all Horwich churches, including St Mary's, the Catholic church, were asked to join, but the invitation was declined. St Mary's joined the League in 1946.[62] Newspapers from a number of northern towns have not revealed the existence of a Catholic churches' cricket league. Anti-Catholicism was far from dead in the England between the wars, and whilst church cricket did not cause such sentiments, the small number of Catholic churches with cricket teams did help to define Catholics as a separate social grouping and had not the capacity to bridge the gulf between Catholics and non-Catholics.

The emphasis on the Christian character of cricket can be interpreted as the strongest evidence that cricket was retarding the advance of secularisation within England between the wars. It has already been shown that discourses on cricket celebrated it as a symbol of England and as an expression of English moral worth. Cricket rhetoric had a key role in how the English, especially those with social and economic power, imagined themselves and their moral status. It may have been the case that the supposed Christian character of cricket was more myth than reality, but the fact that it was felt necessary to stress the connections between cricket and Christianity indicates how widespread was the approval of Christian teaching. Belief that Christian morality was thought to be such an important constituent of an institution of such national significance as cricket shows that a respect for Christian ethics was still very much at the centre of English cultural values in the 1920s and 1930s.

NOTES

1. B. Darwin, 'British Sport and Games', in *British Life and Thought: An Illustrated History* (London: Longman Green for the British Council, 1940), p. 288.
2. *Cricketer*, 22 Aug. 1931, p. 517.
3. *Cricketer*, 5 Aug. 1922, p. 16.
4. F. Root, *A Cricket Pro's Lot* (London: Arnold, 1937), p. 178.
5. W.R. Inge, *More Lay Thoughts of a Dean* (London: Putnam, 1931), p. 178.
6. N. Cardus, *Cricket* (London: Longmans, Green, 1930), pp. 58–60.
7. R.C. Robertson-Glasgow, *46 Not Out* (London: Constable, 1985 reprint of the 1948 edition), p. 103.
8. K.A.P. Sandiford, *Cricket and The Victorians* (Aldershot: Scolar, 1994), Chapter 3.
9. For a detailed examination of the moral values associated with athleticism at the public schools, see J.A. Mangan, *Athleticism in the Victorian and Edwardian Public School* (Cambridge: Cambridge UP, 1981).
10. See, for instance, J.E.C. Welldon, 'The Value of Games', *The Cricketer Annual, 1922–23* (London: Cricketer Syndicate, n.d.), pp. 23–4, and *Forty Years On: Lights and Shadows (A Bishop's Reflections on Life)* (London: Nicholson and Watson, 1935), pp. 141–2.
11. G. Boyes, *The Imagined Village: Culture, Ideology and the English Folk Revival* (Manchester: Manchester UP, 1994), p. 69.
12. G. Howat, 'Local History, Ancient and Modern: Cricket and the Victorian Church', *Journal of the Cricket Society*, 9, 4 (Spring 1980), p. 61.
13. *The Times*, 26 Jan. 1922; J. Hill, 'League Cricket in the North and Midlands, 1900–1940', in R. Holt, ed., *Sport and the Working Class in Modern Britain* (Manchester: Manchester UP, 1990), p. 69.
14. *The Times*, 28 May 1934.
15. Ibid., 1 Sept. 1921.
16. *Farnworth Weekly Journal*, 7 Dec. 1934.
17. *Buff*, 21 Nov. 1925.
18. *Radcliffe Times*, 20 Oct. 1934.
19. *Buff*, 19 Jan. 1935.
20. The military, cricketing and clerical life of Parsons is described in G. Howat, *Cricketer Militant: The Life of Jack Parsons* (Oxford: Oxford and Cambridge Examination Board, 1980).

21. P. Bailey, P. Thorn and P. Wynne-Thomas, *Who's Who of Cricketers* (London: Guild, 1984), p. 320.

22. B. Green, ed., *The Wisden Book of Obituaries: Obituaries from Wisden Cricketers' Almanack 1892–1985* (London: Queen Anne, 1986), p. 310.

23. *Cricketer*, 12 May 1923, p. 21.

24. Interviews with Sir Robert Southern (retired bank official), Rev. J.W. Markham (Anglican cleric), Rev. F.A. Asprey (Congregational minister), Rev. G.L.W. Ridge (United Free Methodist minister).

25. *The History of Walkden Cricket Club* (n.p., n.d.), p. 15.

26. *Bacup and District Sunday School Cricket League Jubilee Souvenir Handbook, 1899–1949* (n.p., n.d.,), p. 19.

27. Interview with Father T. Gallagher (Catholic priest).

28. For the totals of church teams playing football in selected northern towns, see J. Williams, 'Churches, Sport and Identities in the North, 1900-1939', in J. Hill and J. Williams, eds., *Sport and Identity in the North of England* (Keele: Keele UP), p. 115.

29. *Farnworth Weekly Journal*, 10 Aug. 1928.

30. *Buff*, 18 Nov. 1922.

31. Ibid., 19 Nov. 1921.

32. *Bolton Congregationalist* (May 1925), p. 75.

33. Interviews with the Revs. V.J. Abernethy (Presbyterian minister), F.A. Asprey, P. Breen (Catholic priest), J.W. Markham, G.L.W. Ridge.

34. J.A. Williams, 'Cricket and Society in Bolton between the Wars', Lancaster University unpublished PhD thesis, (1992), Chapter 5.

35. J.A. Hester, E. Ward and L.E. Perry, *Horwich Churches Welfare League 1922–1972* (n.p., n.d.), pp. 18, 20–1.

36. G. Cleworth, *The Story of Eagley Cricket Club 1837–1987* (Bolton: n.d.), pp. 8, 15; lists of the office holders of the BDCA and of the Junior Second Teams Competition are provided in the annual handbooks of the BDCA.

37. Interviews with Mr A. Burnham (retired clerk) and Mr J. Pickstone (retired railway clerk) and with R. Southern.

38. *The Times*, 25 May 1937. For a discussion of how Sabbatarian restrictions upon the playing of some sports had begun to weaken before 1914, see J.R. Lowerson, 'Sport and the Victorian Sunday: The Beginnings of Middle-class Apostasy', *British Journal of Sports History*, 1, 2 (Sept. 1984).

39. Ibid., 24 July 1922. The LCC allowed league and knock-out games to be played on its recreational land in 1934, ibid., 14 July 1934.

40. Ibid., 25 May 1937.

41. Interview with A. Burnham and J. Pickstone.

42. *Halifax Daily Courier*, 12 April 1930.

43. *The Cricketer Annual 1937–38* (London: Cricketer Syndicate, n.d.), p. 4.

44. *Athletic News*, 28 April 1919.

45. *St Helens Newspaper*, 20 June 1922.

46. *The Times*, 10 July 1922.

47. Ibid., 7 July 1923.

48. Ibid., 25 June 1923.

49. *St Helens Newspaper*, 20 June 1922.

50. *The Times*, 7 Aug. 1922.

51. Ibid., 24 Jan. 1923.

52. Ibid., 4 Feb. 1920.

53. Ibid., 26 May 1922.

54. Ibid., 20 Oct. 1923.

55. Ibid., 21 April 1926.
56. Ibid., 15 July 1922.
57. Ibid., 17 July 1922, 3 May 1926.
58. Ibid., 19 Nov. 1926.
59. J. Stevenson, *British Society, 1914–45* (Harmondsworth: Penguin, 1984), p. 356.
60. *Bolton Playing Fields Association: Report and Statement of Accounts for the Period Ending 31st December 1934* (Bolton: Bolton Playing Fields Association, 1935), p. 4.
61. Interviews with Mr S. Webb (retired cotton mill manager, former cotton mill office worker) and J.W. Markham.
62. The letter inviting St Mary's to enter a team and the reply declining to join have been added to the Horwich Sunday School Cricket League minute book, Horwich Churches Welfare League; J.A. Hester, E. Ward and L.E. Perry, *Horwich Churches Welfare League*, p. 39.

8

Cricket and Commercialisation

Since the late 1970s there has been much discussion of whether English cultural values, especially among those from public schools, have been vital factors in Britain's relative decline in the twentieth century as one of the world's major economic powers. In *The Audit of War* Corelli Barnett argued that public schools had been a major cause of British economic decline by undervaluing technology and industry while emphasising that an education in the humanities, and imperial administration, the civil service, the financial world of the city or the professions were more appropriate forms of activity for gentlemen.[1] *English Culture and the Decline of the Industrial Spirit*, by Martin Wiener, claimed that British economic expansion in the first half of the nineteenth century had been spearheaded by a spirit of risk-taking entrepreneurship among industrialists, but that from the mid-nineteenth century, English literary culture, fostered by the public schools, had nurtured disdain for industrialism and that this had been the underlying cause of Britain's decline as an industrial power in the twentieth century.[2] This cultural critique of Britain's economic performance has not passed without challenge. Its critics have pointed out that any economic decline of Britain has been largely relative and that the national income has grown more or less without interruption since the mid-nineteenth century.[3] Although Barnett and Wiener were concerned primarily with industrial decline, debates surrounding this cultural critique have been broadened into discussion of whether English culture inhibited all forms of economic growth by not according in its scale of values high priority to a spirit of unbridled commercialism and a fervent desire to exploit to the utmost all opportunities for profit maximisation. James Raven's survey of these debates surrounding the cultural critique shows that they came to include discussion about the existence of 'a non-enterprise culture' in Britain and that in American business schools during the 1980s Britain was identified as a society whose performance suffered because its culture had encouraged 'a national rejection of business values'.[4] As cricket was held in such esteem by those social groups with established economic and political power, attitudes towards the commercialisation of cricket help to assess how far their cultural values were sympathetic to enterprise and a ruthless pursuit of profit.

THE ECONOMICS OF FIRST-CLASS CRICKET

First-class cricket was not highly commercialised between the wars. Neither the MCC nor any county club was a limited liability company with even a nominal obligation to make profits for shareholders. The grounds of Hampshire and Warwickshire were owned by companies formed before the First World War but their shares were held by supporters of the county clubs. Staging county cricket required money. Ground maintenance, salaries for administrative staff and wages for professional players were costly, but there were great differences in the expenditure and income of county clubs. Between 1927 and 1939, Worcestershire, always among those counties with the lowest annual incomes, had its lowest yearly income (£6,138) in 1928 and its highest (£8,926) in 1934, whereas that of Yorkshire, always among those with high incomes, only fell below £16,000 in 1931 when it amounted to £15,969.[5] Yorkshire's highest annual inter-war income was £39,387 in 1938 and the figure for 1934 was almost as high. Variations in income between seasons were greatest at those counties with the highest levels of income. For much of the inter-war period, county cricket was financially ailing. Worcestershire's regular income exceeded expenditure only in 1934. Essex had losses in 12 of the seasons from 1920 to 1939.[6] In 1932 and 1937 the Leicestershire club organised special meetings of members to discuss whether the club should drop out of the county championship for financial reasons.[7] Kent, whose highest income between the wars was £16,332 in 1926, made a loss in seven seasons.[8] Even Yorkshire recorded losses in three seasons and Lancashire, another of the wealthier counties, made a loss in six seasons. By 1937 the finances of so many counties were in such a parlous state that the MCC and the Advisory Committee appointed the Findlay Commission to investigate the financial basis of county cricket. This found that in 1934 only Middlesex and Leicestershire had made a loss, but that only five counties in 1935 and three in 1936 had recorded profits.[9]

Members' subscriptions and gate receipts were the two major sources of regular income for county clubs. In most seasons almost all counties' gate receipts were higher than subscription revenue. At Surrey, a club with a very high number of members, subscription revenue exceeded that of gate receipts in only three seasons between 1922 and 1939. The Findlay Commission established that for the seasons 1934, 1935 and 1936 gate receipts of all counties were higher than subscription revenue.[10] Gate receipts, however, were at the mercy of the weather and a wet summer could cause them to fall. In 1921, an exceptionally hot and dry summer, 284,677 paid to watch Yorkshire's home matches. In 1922, when only two home matches were not affected by rain, the number of spectators at Yorkshire's home matches was nearly 60,000 lower.[11]

The profits from test matches played in England and those made by the MCC on its overseas tours when test matches were played formed another vital source of income for the county clubs. Counties on whose grounds test matches were played received a larger proportion of the profits from test matches played in England than did other counties. Test matches played against Australia always produced higher profits than those against other countries. In 1934, for instance, they resulted in £45,569 being distributed among the counties compared with £5,344 for the series against the West Indies in 1933 and £15,698 against South Africa in 1936.[12] The Findlay Commission found that had it not been for the share of test match profits, only four counties would have recorded a surplus in 1934 and none in 1935 and 1936.[13] Some counties had far greater reserves than others. In 1930 those of Surrey were over £43,000 but those of Worcestershire only £616.[14] Several counties needed overdrafts. In 1936 Gloucestershire had an overdraft of £1,994, Hampshire £1,707, Lancashire £3,924, Nottinghamshire £3,572 and Worcestershire £1,918.[15] Several counties required wealthy supporters to guarantee their debts and had patrons whose generosity helped them to overcome financial crises. In 1921 Alfred Cockerill, a Northampton businessman and chairman of the County Ground Company, made a gift of his shares to the club and persuaded others to do so and then leased the ground to the club at a peppercorn rent for a thousand years.[16] It was estimated that this and the improvements he made to the ground cost him over £10,000.[17] Lords Cobham and Doverdale guaranteed £1,000 of Worcestershire's overdraft of £1,746 in 1933.[18] In 1934 Sir Julian Cahn, a millionaire furniture manufacturer, gave £1,000 to Leicestershire and in 1935 paid the subscriptions of 800 new members for Nottinghamshire.[19] At the end of the First World War, Fry, the chocolate company, bought the ground of Gloucestershire and allowed the club to use it rent free, which had the effect of wiping out the club's debts.[20] Hard-pressed counties appealed for funds and arranged special fund-raising events. In 1923 Sir Thomas Beecham organised a concert which raised £645 for Northamptonshire.[21] In 1928, at a dance held in Mayfair, £800 was raised for Glamorgan when girls dressed in traditional Welsh costume collected donations from guests which were recorded on a cricket score board.[22] In 1933 Major Jewell, who played for Worcestershire from 1909 until 1933, offered to arrange a pierrot show to raise funds for the club.[23] An appeal by Warwickshire in 1936 to cover the losses incurred through wet weather raised £5,362.[24] Bazaars were a further means of raising money. In 1935 that of Leicestershire brought in £1,000 and one organised by Lady Cobham for Worcestershire in 1937 produced over £1,730.[25] In 1932 special fund-raising efforts converted what would have been a deficit of over £2,000 into a surplus of £250 for Northamptonshire.[26]

Economic analyses of sports organisations suggest that the extent to which a league acts as a cartel with the aim of maximising spectator revenue is a measure of whether a sports league should be seen as a fully commercialised organisation. Theories of cartelisation in sport claim that uncertainty about the outcome of matches stimulates spectator interest. In order to guarantee that the outcome of matches remains uncertain, leagues acting as cartels require a strong central authority to which member clubs surrender much of their independence and which has the power to ensure that playing talent is distributed more or less evenly between member clubs. Procedures to guarantee an even distribution of playing talent include allowing players to move between clubs and imposing maximum wages to prevent one club monopolising the best players. A transfer system, which in effect compensates a club when it loses a player and gives it the finances to buy an adequate replacement, is a further method of ensuring equal distribution of playing talent. The provision of additional competitions and changing the rules of a sport are other forms of cartelisation designed to encourage spectator interest. Clubs which fail to meet the playing standards of a league acting as a cartel are usually asked to leave the league.[27]

County cricket was very far from being a sports league acting as a commercial cartel. The limited authority of the Advisory Committee has been discussed in Chapter 2. The counties retained much independence. No central body superintended the arrangement of fixtures until 1929. The counties showed little interest in transforming the county championship into a genuine league competition. Counties had to play the same number of matches only from 1929 to 1932. Until 1922 they had to play a minimum of 14 matches, and from 1923 to 1928 and from 1933 to 1939, a minimum of 24 matches. One consequence of this was that often some counties played many more matches than others and this meant that the championship lacked credibility as a league competition. In 1922, for instance, Derbyshire, Glamorgan, Middlesex, Northamptonshire and Worcestershire played as few as 22 matches, whereas Lancashire, Sussex and Yorkshire played 30. The playing strength of some counties was far greater than that of others. In the 21 inter-war seasons Yorkshire won the championship 12 times, Lancashire five, Middlesex twice, and Derbyshire and Nottinghamshire once each. Yorkshire finished outside the top three positions in only two seasons and Lancashire outside the top six only twice. At the opposite extreme Glamorgan finished in the top ten only twice, Leicestershire five times and Somerset five times. In the 1920s Worcestershire always finished in one of the three bottom places of the championship table. Northamptonshire had the weakest playing record. Its highest inter-war position in the championship was thirteenth and from 1935 until 1939 it won only three out of 120 matches. There was no procedure for automatic dropping of the weakest counties. Finding a system of points scoring to determine placings in the championship table and also encourage attacking cricket proved elusive. Eight different systems of points scoring were introduced.[28] The strongest counties had agreed that from 1921 the maximum payment to be paid to a professional who played in 28 championship matches was to be £440 but that winning bonuses, talent money and payment for additional matches could be added to this. But this seems to have been a voluntary agreement and there was no compulsion to ensure that counties stood by it.[29] Residential qualifications for players added to the difficulties of trying to ensure that playing talent was distributed evenly between counties, although Yorkshire, the county with the strongest playing record, selected only those born in Yorkshire. All were qualified to play for the county of their birth. A cricketer wishing to change counties had to reside in a county for two years before he could play for it but in 1938 the period of residential qualification was reduced to one year. Many amateurs, however, played for counties for which they had no residential qualification. No additional competition was introduced into county cricket until the 1960s, though starting to play test matches against the West Indies, New Zealand and India may have been prompted in part by a hope that they would bring in additional income which could be divided among the counties. Changes were made to the laws of cricket, partly to stimulate spectator interest by encouraging less defensive batting and by helping bowlers. The ball was made smaller in 1927, the wickets larger in 1931 and in 1935 the LBW law was amended so that batsmen could be given out to balls pitching outside the off stump. In 1939 eight-ball overs were introduced in the hope of providing spectators with more play in one day. Except for the revision of the LBW law none of these changes was especially bold.[30]

The main aim of those who controlled county cricket was to find a means of making county cricket pay its way without introducing major changes to its ethos or structure. In the 1920s there were a few calls for the introduction of two divisions in the county championship. In 1923 Percy Fender, the Surrey captain, and Pelham Warner argued independently of each other in favour of two divisions and the following year T.A. Higson, the Lancashire chairman, suggested two divisions.[31] Such proposals found little support, partly because no county wished to play in a lower division and because of fears that few spectators would watch second division matches. Two-day matches would have enabled each county to play every other county twice in one season, but two-day matches were played only in 1919. Officials of the Lancashire club who had been the driving force behind the introduction of two-day matches in 1919 urged their restoration at various times between the wars, and in 1931 representatives of Leicestershire proposed two-day matches with each innings restricted to three and a half hours.[32] The Findlay Commission, however, rejected a return to two-day matches. The attitude of cricket authorities to the entertainment tax indicates their desire to see county cricket pay its way, but without making any drastic changes to its structure. In the 1920s the county clubs made repeated calls for the lifting of the entertainment tax, especially upon the subscriptions of members. In 1923 there was a partial success when the government conceded that only the part of a member's subscription which represented the cost of admission to matches should be liable to duty.[33] In the later 1930s the report of the Findlay Commission emphasised the burdens of the entertainment duty and in 1937 the MCC called for county cricket to be exempt from it. In 1935 the 13 counties which had recorded a combined deficit of £17,785 had paid £8,973 in entertainment tax.[34]

In 1937 Fred Root, the former England and Worcestershire professional fast bowler, wrote in his autobiography that 'First-class cricket is a business in these days. The people who run it and the people who play it have to treat it as such.'[35] But this seems to have been very much an exaggeration. Those who controlled county cricket showed no wish to see it become highly commercialised, dominated by a relentless quest for revenue. The Times claimed in 1936: 'No-one who loves the game wants it to be put on a strictly commercial basis.'[36] Little attention was paid to the marketing of county cricket, although its press coverage was in effect free advertising. It was feared that attempts to increase gate receipts of clubs by increasing the spectator appeal of cricket would transform its nature. In 1926 The Field claimed that if cricket were to adopt 'the newspaper interviews and public recriminations of Baseball, we shall lose something from the best of our English games'.[37] In 1932 The Times wrote that 'the spectator has come to expect something more exhilarating, something more in keeping with the competitive thrills of speedway racing, and, if disappointed, his inadequate understanding of cricket encourages him to say that it is a dull game'. It continued that the Advisory Committee had 'quite rightly refused to transform cricket grounds into some form of circus on which clowning is to be recognised for gate money'.[38] In 1937, in anticipation of the report of the Findlay Commission, the cricket correspondent of *The Times* commented that the demands for brighter cricket as a means of attracting spectators could see the 'game turned into a circus, with batsmen hitting wildly against a ball of good length. That would lead in the end to an exhibition of buffoonery in flood-light in a covered ground.'[39]

Unease over commercialising county cricket by increasing its spectator appeal was related to fears that this could undermine the sportsmanship of cricket by weakening the amateur presence. Amateurism was seen as the means of ensuring that cricket would continue to be played in a spirit of sportsmanship. League football, which had become played almost exclusively by professionals, was seen as less sporting than cricket, and an example of what county cricket should try to avoid. Before the First World War C.B. Fry, an amateur captain of Sussex and England, had described proposals to change cricket into a genuine league competition as 'mob rule'.[40] In 1913, W.H., writing in *Cricket*, had argued that 'if we yield to the clamour of the newspaper and the "mob", and institute a championship with two divisions and automatic promotion and relegation, it is to be feared that county cricket ... will become much less a sport and so much more a business, taking up so much more time, that the amateur will be driven out entirely. The county clubs will then steadily deteriorate into mere "firms", like the Football League clubs, who simply provide public entertainments by the medium of troupes of paid players. And thus true sport and real sportsmanship will be eliminated.'[41] After the First World War cricket discourses did not describe paying spectators as 'the mob', but the attitudes expressed by W.H. still pervaded the thinking of those who controlled county cricket. In 1930, a writer in *Athletic News,* a journal usually sympathetic to league football, urged: 'Let us endeavour to prevent first-class cricket from becoming contaminated with the pernicious influence of league football.'[42] In the same year a letter to *Athletic News* from a correspondent calling himself an artisan from Birmingham, complained of 'the take-it-or-leave-it air that county cricket affects' and mentioned that the artisan or labourer was 'really quite a decent sort you know, but he doesn't like getting wet through, and hates standing for hours outside the ground "waiting for the wicket to dry"'.[43] In addition to being thought the means of protecting the sportsmanship of cricket, the retention of the amateur presence may have related to the ailing finances of so many county clubs. Chapter 6 has shown that 32 per cent of appearances in the county championship for Kent in 1930, for instance, were made by amateurs but their expenses were less than 11 per cent of the total paid for amateur expenses, the wages of the professionals and the scorer.

FIRST-CLASS CRICKETERS AND COMMERCIALISATION

Attitudes towards the earnings of first-class cricketers help to determine how far cricket was dominated by commercial values. Although amateurs were supposed to receive no payment for playing cricket, they were permitted to receive expenses, but precise details of these are hard to find. Clear scales of reimbursement were laid down for test matches. In 1924 amateurs could receive up to £2 each day in expenses and the cost of first-class rail travel.[44] Some amateurs with businesses may have found that playing first-class cricket helped their businesses. In the 1943 edition of *Wisden* R.C. Robertson-Glasgow wrote that there were 'only a few, a very few amateurs who earned no money, directly or indirectly, from playing the game' and that some played cricket as amateurs because of the 'publicity which attracts clients to themselves or to the business for which they may be working'.[45] Some amateurs were shamateurs, determined to make a good living from cricket. In the mid 1930s, Arthur Carr, the amateur captain of Nottinghamshire, stated that some amateurs received over £500 in expenses, roughly equal to what the best professionals were paid.[46] Some payments to amateurs may not have been disclosed in balance sheets. Michael Marshall's *Gentlemen & Players* contains fascinating material about the payments made to amateurs between the wars. Nigel Haig, educated at Eton and a nephew of Lord Harris, played as an amateur for Middlesex. When another amateur was going to ask for expenses only to cover the cost of a bus ride, Haig said 'I'm not having you rock the boat. You can put in for expenses in coming up from your parents' place in Hampshire!' Another Middlesex amateur, R.W.V. Robins, who captained England in 1937, felt that if he had played as a professional he would have received two benefits and that this justified 'reasonable reimbursements' for playing cricket.[47] The true extent of shamateurism within first-class cricket can never be known, but it does seem to have been sufficiently widespread to indicate that despite the exaltation of the amateur tradition some amateurs had a commercialised approach to cricket. C.B. Fry and Pelham Warner, among the stoutest defenders of amateurism in first-class cricket, had no compunction about being paid for writing on cricket.

In 1920 the Advisory Committee had recommended that the maximum annual remuneration for a county professional should be £440 and in 1921 the 'big six' counties had also agreed that £440 would be the annual sum paid to a professional who played in 28 matches, but that winning bonuses, talent money and match fees for extra matches could be added to this.[48] At a meeting in November 1928 it was revealed that the six counties had differing methods of paying their professionals but all had observed the principle of not paying a professional more than £440 for playing in 28 matches. This meeting also agreed that the pay of a professional including bonuses, talent money and fees for additional matches should not exceed £500,[49] but in 1931 it was found that in 1930 Kent had paid Freeman £501.10s, Middlesex had paid Hearne and Hendren £515, and Yorkshire, whose players had appeared in more matches, had paid several professionals between £522 and £544.[50] In 1931 the six counties again agreed that no professional would be paid more than £500 but also decided that each county could manage its own affairs.[51]

Ric Sissons' analysis of the pay of professional county players shows that levels of payment for capped or established players varied between counties. Most paid a higher weekly wage in summer than winter, though Surrey paid its leading professionals £4.10s a week throughout the year.[52] Usually players were paid for each match in which they played, with more being paid for away than for home matches. Match fees and weekly wages varied between counties and some counties guaranteed that the annual earnings of their capped players would reach a given figure. The annual guarantee at Hampshire was £200, £315 at Lancashire, £250 at Nottinghamshire and £400 at Surrey. In 1938 one Kent professional was guaranteed that his pay would not fall below £400, three had a guarantee of £375, one £350 and another £250.[53] A capped player who played in ten home matches and ten away matches in one season would have earned in one year £342.10s with Hampshire, £325 at Kent, £382 at Lancashire, £330 at Nottinghamshire.[54] These figures probably underestimate the earnings of many professionals. Winning bonuses and talent money need to be added. The bonus for winning a match was usually £1. Talent money varied between counties. In some seasons Kent distributed among its players more than £400 in talent money. In 1927 'Tich' Freeman received nearly £90 and Frank Woolley almost £80.[55] Lancashire, Nottinghamshire and Yorkshire for part of the inter-war period limited the total amount paid in talent money to £200, though this did not apply to years when the championship was won. In 1927, when Lancashire were champions, no player received more than £31 in talent money but each player also received a bonus of £40 for winning the championship.[56] For the year ending April 1933, Essex, almost always among the most hard-up counties between the wars, paid one professional £432 and another £427. Six received sums between £348.10s and £395.10s. Except for one who received £108.10s, the remaining five professionals received under £100.[57] For the same season Worcestershire, another of the perennially hard-up counties, would have paid a professional who had played in all 28 county championship matches £258, but this did not include winning bonuses, talent money or fees for playing in non-championship matches.[58] Fred Root claimed that when Worcestershire were paying him under £300 per season, at least four other counties paid their professionals less.[59] The pay of capped professionals compared favourably with that of most manual workers, but professionals had to pay for their accommodation and travel when playing away matches. Cricketers pointed out the insecurity of their employment. Injuries, loss of form and age could affect earnings and most were retained upon annual contracts. The 1930s, however, with high levels of unemployment in many areas, were hardly a time of great security for many workers and capped professional players had the prospect of a benefit or of seeking employment in league cricket.

The most talented players earned more from cricket than run-of-the-mill professionals. In 1924 professionals received £27 per match when playing for England against South Africa. By 1930 the pay for playing against Australia was £40, but £20 for a test match against the West Indies, India or New Zealand. In 1938 the professionals who played against Australia received £50 per match plus the cost of accommodation provided that they stayed at the hotel chosen by the selection committee.[60] On the tours to Australia in 1928–29 and 1932–33 the professionals were paid £400 with the possibility of earning an extra £300 in bonuses, but in 1938 the MCC's finance sub-committee recommended that on the next tour to Australia professionals would be paid £450 with the possibility of earning up to £255 in bonuses.[61] On tour professionals did not have to pay for travel and accommodation. Jack Hobbs was given a five-year contract by Surrey in 1919, which was extended in 1922 and 1927.[62] In 1924 Lancashire agreed to pay Ted McDonald who had been playing as a professional in the Lancashire League £500 and guaranteed a benefit after five instead of the usual ten years.[63] Not all big name cricketers were treated with such generosity. Dick Tyldesley had been one of Lancashire's main spin bowlers in the 1920s and played for England seven times. In 1930 he asked Lancashire to guarantee annual earnings of £400 for five years plus £80 to cover expenses and after five years two-thirds of a benefit match or £1,000. The county refused to meet these demands and Tyldesley was obliged to sign another one-year contract, though the committee did say that at its discretion a bonus might be paid. Tyldesley had a successful season in 1931, but was not offered a contract for the following season.[64] Seven players between the wars had benefits which exceeded £2,500, the highest being the £4,016 which Roy Kilner of Yorkshire received. Generally benefits were highest at counties which had the greatest levels of income and at most counties players who received the highest benefits were usually those with the best playing records. At Lancashire the average inter-war benefit was over £1,500, but they tended to be higher in the 1920s than the 1930s. The lowest inter-war benefit at Lancashire was £1,000 for Bill Farrimond in 1939. At Hampshire two players had benefits of less than £800, but £800 was still a considerable sum of money in the 1920s and 1930s.[65] Players had to meet the expenses of organising-benefit and some lost money on benefits. One Worcestershire player refused a benefit because of the risk of losing money.[66]

A few of the big name professionals were able to supplement what their counties paid them. Some were invited to coach overseas during the winter. Outstanding playing achievements could attract considerable financial rewards. When Jack Hobbs scored his hundredth hundred in 1923, the Surrey committee gave him 100 guineas and 250 guineas in 1925 for passing W.G. Grace's record of 126 centuries.[67] In 1938 a well-wisher gave Len Hutton £1,000 for breaking the world record test score.[68] A few prominent players advertised products. In 1925 Jack Hobbs promoted Waterman's pens and Saxony Virginia cigarettes in *Athletic News*, although in the second of his autobiographies he mentioned that he did not smoke cigarettes. The same cigarettes were also promoted in 1925 by Maurice Tate and Andy Sandham. A small number of players were paid for recommending cricket equipment. Some prominent England players, amateurs as well as professionals, published their autobiographies, but details of what these earned for them are hard to find. Autobiographies of Jack Hobbs were published in 1924, 1930 and 1934. These were ghost-written, but the fact that three were published suggests that the first had sold reasonably well. Jack Hobbs also put his name to two novels. Some cricketers earned extra income by writing for newspapers while they were still playing. In the summer of 1929 Harold Larwood had a regular column in *The Sunday Chronicle*. In 1933 Larwood was paid around £50 by *The Sunday Express* for an interview about the bodyline tour and was expecting to receive £500 from *The Sunday Dispatch* for the serial rights of a book about bodyline which was being ghosted for him.[69] Given the excitement generated by the bodyline tour, it is probable that these sums represent the highest amounts which cricketers could expect to receive for writing for newspapers. During the tour of Australia in 1920–21, the amateurs Percy Fender of Surrey and Rockley Wilson of Yorkshire sent back regular reports for English newspapers, but there was unease in England about their criticisms of Australian umpires. Individual counties also restricted the opportunities of professionals to write for newspapers. In 1929, the Lancashire committee, for instance, decided that its players could write for the press only in the close season and that all articles had to be submitted to it for approval before publication.[70] Ric Sissons believes that Patsy Hendren earned around £1,500 a year from playing cricket and activity related to cricket during his inter-war playing days. Jack Hobbs probably earned at least as much as Hendren.[71]

Some of the most successful cricketers made more than a comfortable living out of cricket, but few seem to have made a determined effort to seek out all possible avenues for exploiting their popularity. They do not appear to have realised how their status could have been exploited and it is unlikely that any professional cricketer employed an agent to discover ways of maximising earning potential which in itself indicates that the culture of English professional cricketers and English culture in general had not become saturated with commercial values. J.M. Kilburn, cricket correspondent for *The Yorkshire Post*, claimed that 'the professional was a paid player not through a conscious assessment of comparable financial rewards but because there was no other way of exploiting his cricketing talents and satisfying his cricketing longings'.[72] Sir Home Gordon wrote that county professionals were like the senior service in not grousing about their earnings and for their uncomplaining acceptance of their lot.[73] Though there may be an element of self-delusion about these comments, very few professionals at the peak of their powers abandoned county cricket for higher earnings in league cricket, which suggests that most professionals placed great value upon exercising their playing skills at the highest level. Most professionals must have known that many county clubs were strapped for cash and would have found it hard to pay them more. Fred Root was one of the few professionals who suggested how county cricket could be re-organised to boost its income and consequently the earnings of professionals, but he did this after his retirement from county cricket. No trade union or association for professional cricketers was set up between the wars, which may mean that professionals did not imagine that collective pressure could improve their earnings. The structure of authority within first-class cricket made it difficult for professional cricketers to develop an aggressive determination to exploit their fame and skills. The great majority of professionals were employed on one-year contracts and residential qualifications made it almost impossible to increase earnings by moving to another county. Long-serving players could be awarded benefits, but as there was no automatic entitlement to them, benefits or the prospect of a benefit could be an indirect method of disciplining professionals.

LEAGUE CRICKET AND COMMERCIALISM

Clubs playing at the highest levels of club cricket in the south of England were very far from being imbued with a spirit of commercialism. Almost all accepted the ruling of the Club Cricket Conference that they should not play professionals and no club seems to have been organised as a profit-making concern. The highest levels of league cricket were played in those areas which had traditionally been associated with industrialisation and hard-headed businessmen intent upon maximising all opportunities for profit. League cricket was expensive but leading clubs were no more committed to an ethic of out-and-out commercialisation than county clubs. Clubs had to hire a professional and a skilled groundsman was a necessity. In some leagues illicit payments were made to amateurs. Ground facilities had to be maintained to the level expected by spectators. The turnover of Nelson CC in the Lancashire League must have been among the highest of league clubs between the wars. In 1921, a season of very high gate receipts in league cricket, its income was just under £3,400, more than half that of a poorer first-class county such as Worcestershire.[74] As with county clubs the two major sources of income for league clubs were gate receipts and members' subscriptions. The attractions of the Australian fast bowler Ted McDonald as its professional from 1922 to 1924 and of the West Indian all-rounder Learie Constantine from 1929 to 1937 meant that Nelson had unusually high gate receipts for much of the inter-war period. Nelson's gate receipts were £2,452 in 1929, £1,715 in 1932 and over £1,400 in 1922, 1933 and 1934. Nelson's lowest gate receipts were in 1927, a very wet year and one when the gate receipts of most Lancashire League clubs were very low. The subscription revenue of Nelson was highest in 1936 when it reached £826 but it never fell below £632.[75] Drink and refreshments were other important sources of income. In 1921 the income of the refreshment tent, which sold alcoholic drink, came to £541, but in 1922 the profit from this was only £139. The largest annual profit of the Nelson club was £1,115 in 1929 but the next highest profit was £332 in 1930 and in no other year was there a profit of more than £300. The club recorded losses in 1920, 1924, 1926, 1927, 1928 and from 1935 until 1938. The biggest loss, £506, was in 1920.[76] A portion of the losses, however, could have been described as investment. In 1920 the club bought a house for £380, which may have been intended to attract a 'big name' professional, but this was sold a year later. In this same year, expenditure of £118 on converting the former pavilion into a tea room, £90 on ground repairs and £85 on painting and decorating the pavilion were intended to increase revenue in subsequent years. For much of the 1920s, the club had a growing burden of debt. After the 1920 season its overdraft came to £288 and by the start of the 1929 season it exceeded £2,900.[77]

East Lancashire CC from Blackburn had a turnover comparable to that of Nelson. From 1929 until 1934 the gate receipts of East Lancashire were below those of Nelson, but in 1935, a season when Constantine missed several matches, East Lancashire's gates were £967 and those of Nelson £919.[78] Like Nelson, expenditure for the East Lancashire club often exceeded income. From 1923 until 1927 East Lancashire recorded losses and had to take an overdraft. In 1927, £2,290 was owed on the ground purchase account. In 1929 East Lancashire spent £850 on a new stand, a new score box and a shelter for spectators.[79]

Other Lancashire League clubs had much lower turnovers than Nelson or East Lancashire. In 1927, when gate receipts and subscriptions at Nelson came to £1,245 and £1,483 at East Lancashire, these were less than £400 at Rishton and just over £450 at Enfield.[80] The turnover of Rochdale CC, one of the biggest clubs in the Central Lancashire League, was similar to that of the bigger Lancashire League clubs. League cricket in the Bolton area was not on a level with that of the Lancashire League or the Central Lancashire League, but the First Division of the Bolton and District Association in the 1920s and the Bolton League in the 1930s seem to have been at least on a par in terms of club support and prestige with all leagues in Yorkshire except for the Bradford League. Apart from two colliery clubs, Farnworth CC was the only league club in the Bolton area with a licensed bar and for this reason its income was far greater than that of other clubs around Bolton. Farnworth's income was £2,201 in 1921, £1,621 in 1922, £1,280 in 1924, £1,325 in 1926 and £1,408 in 1927.[81] In 1921, a year when club income tended to be high, the average income of nine other leading clubs from the Bolton area was only £419. The income of Heaton CC was usually higher than that of most clubs in the Bolton area. In 1920 this was £634 and £708 in 1933; 1938 was probably the first inter-war season when Heaton's income dropped below £400.[82] Radcliffe left the Bolton League to join the more prestigious Central Lancashire League in 1937. In 1938 the income of Radcliffe was £1,283, but its highest reported figure for the 1920s had been £585.[83]

League clubs were not regarded as institutions whose primary purpose was to produce profits. Playing success was their overriding aim. All their financial activity was designed to achieve playing success or to guarantee the survival of the club. In 1926, Olympian wrote in *The Buff*: 'Everybody associated with the game is aware ... that clubs in leagues as we have in Bolton are not run for profit. Indeed, they cannot make money out of cricket ... [They] are doing a valuable service in providing recreation and exercise

174

for young people.'[84] Extensive trawls through local and sporting newspapers from the North and Midlands between the wars have not revealed a desire for league clubs to be converted into profit-maximising concerns. Burnley CC of the Lancashire League provides the only instance which has been found of a league club being converted into a limited company between the wars, but this seems to have been a means of reducing the burden of debt rather than an attempt to produce a source of profit, the club's creditors receiving shares equal in value to what the club owed them. The club did not pay a dividend to its shareholders before the Second World War.[85] The strategies employed by league clubs to ensure their survival were very similar to those of county clubs. Bazaars were organised to bring in large sums to eradicate debts. The bazaar of Rawtenstall CC in 1926 raised £2,400.[86] In 1929 a bazaar organised by East Lancashire CC raised £4,000 which paid off debts of £2,500 and provided for ground improvements costing £1,200.[87] In 1927 *The Nelson Leader* organised a shilling fund for Nelson CC and by 1928 this had produced £906.[88] Establishing bowls and tennis sections were other methods of raising additional income. Sports days and gala days were often organised by league clubs and became important events in the entertainment calendar of their localities. In 1937 that of Eagley CC from near Bolton included athletic races, a ladies' egg and spoon race, a display of motor cycle riding and a band concert.[89] Often gala days had dancing in the evening. The patronage of the local economic and social elite was important to clubs. In 1926, Harry Whitehead, the owner of a cotton firm and president of Rawtenstall CC, bought the ground of the club and gave it to the town corporation on the condition that the club would be able to rent it in perpetuity for a trifling annual sum.[90] In the Bolton area, Colonel Greg, the president of Eagley CC, allowed the club to rent its ground for only a shilling a year, a practice which Greg's firm continued after his death. In 1920, Colonel Hardcastle, another industrialist, made a gift of Bradshaw's ground to the village of Bradshaw as a war memorial, which relieved the cricket club of any threat of its ground being sold.[91] On occasions league clubs could take bold action to improve their financial position, but their aim was usually to achieve the financial security required to play cricket to a particular standard. In the winter of 1929–30, for instance, 12 of the leading clubs left the First Division of the Bolton and District Association to set up a new league, the Bolton League. Their action was motivated in part by a belief that having a league with fewer clubs and requiring all clubs to engage an established professional would boost gate receipts.[92]

Some groups had a commercial approach to league cricket. Oral evidence has shown that many business people became members of league clubs because they felt that such clubs were local institutions which expressed pride in a locality. But some small business people, such as shopkeepers and self-employed tradesmen, also feared that their business could suffer if it became known that they had refused to support a local institution. In 1925 Radcliffe CC launched a public appeal to raise £400 for a new tea room. For five weeks *The Radcliffe Times* listed the names of subscribers to this appeal and the amounts which they had subscribed.[93] Nearly all local firms seem to have subscribed and the publication of the list in a local paper could have been a means of shaming some businesses into making donations.

Some league professionals had a highly commercial attitude to league cricket and were determined to make as much money as possible out of 'proing'. A few were paid more or as much as capped county players, but the exact amounts of professionals' pay are hard to establish. Clubs and professionals had an interest in not making public the details of such payments and as a result annual balance sheets of league clubs often disguised the amounts paid to professionals by lumping payments to the professional, groundsman and bar staff under the heading of 'wages'. The professional with Rochdale CC of the Central Lancashire League in 1938, Learie Constantine, thought that he was perhaps the best paid professional cricketer in the world. For playing for 20 weeks he was paid £800 and collections could have been added to this.[94] Gerald Howat believes that Constantine was paid £1,200 during his first two seasons with Nelson but this included money from collections.[95] In 1936 Constantine's benefit was £500.[96] In 1934 another league club had offered Constantine £1,100 to play for one season.[97] The sums paid to Constantine were unusually high for league professionals. In Yorkshire, clubs did not usually pay sufficient for 'proing' to become a full-time job and almost all their professionals had another occupation. The highest weekly wage paid to a professional in the Bolton area between the wars was £20 by Radcliffe in 1934, but the officials of this club complained that the reluctance of other Bolton League clubs to engage equally illustrious players meant that insufficient spectators were being attracted to fund these wages.[98] Farnworth paid W. Blackburn only £39 for the 1926 season and £40 in 1927.[99]

Weekly wages do not reveal the full extent of professionals' earnings. Clubs often organised seasonal benefit matches for professionals with a promise to make the receipts up to a given sum should the takings prove disappointing. Collections for such feats as scoring 50 runs or taking five wickets were an additional form of income for many professionals, and the prospect of bigger collections at a club which attracted higher gates could persuade professionals to change clubs. In the Lancashire League collections of over £20 were common. In the Bolton area, collections tended to be lower, but could still be substantial. In 1921, a season of record gate receipts, 95 collections were taken at matches in the First Division of the Bolton and District Cricket Association. Not all of these were for professionals, but the professional Ernest Dickens received the largest collection, £10.16s. which easily exceeded his weekly pay.[100]

Many professionals moved from one league to another every two or so seasons, it has been suggested, in order to ensure that their playing skills, and potential earnings did not decline as players became more familiar with their skills. Where a professional had boosted the playing success and gate receipts of a club, he often demanded better terms and there could be intense negotiations between professionals and club committees. In the 1920 season Heaton CC paid Ernest Dickens £6 per week for 24 weeks and he was allowed to arrange a benefit match but the club did not guarantee to make this up to a particular level. In July 1920 the club offered him the same terms for 1921, but perhaps because he was aware that his great playing success in 1920 had put him in a stronger position, Dickens refused them. A week later the club committee resolved to allow a deputation to offer him £7 per week with the option of raising this to £8.[101] The career of C.B. Llewellyn who had played test match cricket for South Africa demonstrates how the earning potential of a professional declined as he aged. In 1928 the Radcliffe club paid him £9 per week plus talent money for outstanding performances. By 1931 his pay had dropped to £5.5s per match plus ten shillings for a night's coaching and £1 for taking five wickets or scoring 50 runs.[102]

Some amateurs at the highest level of league cricket had a commercial attitude to playing cricket. Most prestigious leagues permitted amateurs to receive collections for outstanding playing performances, but it was often alleged that this caused some to put the prospect of a collection before the interests of their team and to change clubs in the hope of receiving larger collections. In the Bolton area illicit payments were made to amateurs, but it has not been possible to establish whether this also occurred in other strongholds of league cricket. As the scales of shamateurism and of playing for collections are unknown, the proportion of league amatuers with a commercial approach to cricket – and whether their number varied over time – cannot be calculated.

CRICKET AND A CULTURE OF COMMERCIALISM

It has been argued earlier that much of the respect accorded to county cricket stemmed from the pastoral tradition in English culture and the associated belief that the town and especially the city represented moral degeneration and money grubbing. Although the grounds of all county clubs were situated in towns, the organisation of clubs based on counties, with their connotations of a pastoral, pre-industrial England, would seem to resonate with the animus against industrialism and urban life found in the novels of Hardy and Lawrence, and in the taste for pastoral poetry, the retreat to suburbia, mock Tudor architecture and enthusiasm for folk song and dance. All these cultural forces seemed to express an unease with urban life and its accompanying industrialisation and commercialism. Through its association with the historic shires and the connotations of pre-industrial England, county cricket can be seen as an expression of a culture which tried to hold commercialism and the industrial world at bay. League cricket, of course, was primarily a form of sport organisation based on industrial towns and villages. The popular image of a league cricket ground was one surrounded by industrial grime and factory chimneys. In northern towns in particular, the growth of industry was a source of great local pride and often associated with a spirit of determined, profit-maximising entrepreneurship. Yet despite being essentially urban and set in an industrial context, league cricket was no more suffused with a spirit of out-and-out profiteering than county cricket. League clubs certainly wanted to make ends meet and playing success usually went to the wealthiest clubs, but playing success always came before profit maximisation.

The limited extent of commercialism within cricket and the determination to keep this within bounds, when related to the great cultural and moral significance accorded to cricket, suggest that English culture, especially that of the public schools, was not dominated by a spirit of unbridled commercialism or a belief that making money was a measure of moral worth. It is likely that many felt that cricket, and especially county cricket, offered few opportunities for risk-taking or profiteering but the importance extended to a sport which was barely economically viable is further evidence that English culture was far from being governed by values sympathetic to the remorseless accumulation of profit. The determination to maintain a strong amateur presence at the highest levels of cricket shows how keenly it was felt that cricket should not be consumed by commercial values. Some amateurs were in effect shamateurs and in some cases made a rich living out of cricket, but the fact that they felt constrained to play as amateurs and to keep hidden what they made out of cricket indicates the pervasiveness of the view that county cricket would become morally contaminated by a greater degree of commercialisation. It is highly probable that the most famous professional cricketers were not aware of how their status could have been exploited, but the limited degree to which professional cricketers were able to cash in on their fame suggests that few others had realised the economic potential of sport stars. This in itself suggests that English culture was not consumed with a desire to make profits from all possible sources. No doubt many businessmen who were committee members or subscribers of county and prominent league clubs ran their businesses as profit maximisers, but their reluctance, or rather determination to ensure that the moral stature of cricket was not compromised by the introduction of commercial practices, shows that they were very far from adopting the view that the pursuit of profit should be extended to all spheres of activity. Baseball, so often regarded as America's national sport, was far more imbued with business values than was cricket in England,[103] which says much about how cultural assumptions in America differed from those in England.

Cricket between the wars can be seen as a narrative through which the English, and especially those from the wealthier classes, told themselves what it meant to be English. The version of Englishness associated with cricket was one which stressed Englishness as a moral force, but much of the morality of cricket was related to the limited degree of commercialisation within cricket. Discourses about the need to keep cricket free from the contamination of commercialism stemmed most often from those educated at public schools, but there was no strong desire for league cricket to be converted into profit-maximising businesses. Most of the major sports in Britain with professional practitioners have been seen to have been utility, rather than profit, maximisers but none of them was regarded as a totem of Englishness to the same extent as cricket. The perspective which cricket provides of English culture, and particularly of those educated at public school, is that it did not put fervent seeking of profit first or see making profit a supreme virtue. In this respect cricket between the wars supports the argument that English culture did not encourage a spirit of bold, risk-taking entrepreneurship or a belief that the principle of making profit should be extended to all forms of activity.

NOTES

1. C. Barnett, *The Audit of War* (London: Macmillan, 1986).
2. M.J. Wiener, *English Culture and the Decline of the Industrial Spirit* (Cambridge: Cambridge UP, 1981).
3. See, for instance, N. McKendrick, '"Gentlemen and Players" Revisited: The Gentlemanly Ideal and the Professional Ideal in English Literary Culture' in N. McKendrick and R.R. Outhwaite, eds., *Business Life and Policy: Essays in Honour of D.C. Coleman* (Cambridge: Cambridge UP, 1986); B. Collins and K. Robbins,

eds., *British Culture and Economic Decline* (London: Weidenfeld and Nicolson, 1990); W.D. Rubinstein, *Capitalism, Culture and Decline in Britain, 1750–1990* (London: Routledge, 1993); H. Berghoff, 'Public Schools and the Decline of the British Economy 1870–1914', *Past & Present*, 129 (Nov. 1990).

4. J. Raven, 'Viewpoint; British History and the Enterprise Culture', *Past & Present*, 123 (May 1989), p. 190.
5. Annual balance sheets of Worcestershire CCC, Worcestershire County Cricket Club; the annual balance sheets of Yorkshire are provided in annual issues of *Yorkshire County Cricket Club*.
6. Annual reports of Essex CCC, Essex County Record Office D/Z 82/1/29.
7. D. Lambert, *The History of Leicestershire County Cricket Club* (London: Christopher Helm, 1992), p. 118; *Buff*, 23 Jan. 1937.
8. The annual handbooks of Kent CCC include balance sheets.
9. Findlay Commission, schedule II, Nottinghamshire CCC library.
10. The annual balance sheets included in the annual handbooks of Surrey CCC state subscription and gate receipt income.
11. The annual issues of *Yorkshire County Cricket Club* state the number of paying spectators at each of Yorkshire's home matches.
12. Findlay Commission, schedule IV.
13. Ibid., schedules II and III.
14. Balance sheets of county clubs include details of their reserves.
15. Findlay Commission, schedule XI.
16. M. Engel and A. Radd, *The History of Northamptonshire County Cricket Club* (London: Christopher Helm, 1993), pp. 96–7.
17. *Northamptonshire CCC Yearbook 1931* (Northamptonshire CCC, n.d.).
18. D. Lemmon, *The Official History Worcestershire County Cricket Club* (London: Christopher Helm, 1989), p. 88.
19. *Buff*, 24 Feb. 1934, 6 Feb. 1937.
20. *Athletic News*, 13 Jan. 1919.
21. M. Engel and A. Radd, *History of Northamptonshire*, p. 100.
22. *Times*, 24 Mar. 1928.
23. D. Lemmon, *History of Worcestershire*, p. 83.
24. *Times*, 11 Feb. 1937.
25. *Buff*, 22 Feb. 1936; minutes of Worcestershire CCC AGM, 24 Jan. 1938, Worcestershire CCC.
26. *Buff*, 23 March 1933.
27. For a discussion of the theories underlying the contention that leagues act as cartels, see J. Cairns, *Economic Analysis of League Sports – A Critical Review of the Literature*, and J. Cairns, N. Jennett and P.J. Sloane, 'The Economics of Professional Team Sports: A Survey of Evidence and Theory', *Journal of Economic Studies*, 12, 1 (1986).
28. E.W. Swanton, G. Plumptre and J. Woodcock, eds., *Barclays World of Cricket: The Game from A–Z* (London: Guild, 1986), pp. 392–3, provides details of the changes in points scoring.
29. County Cricket Advisory Committee minutes, 30 Aug. 1920, Worcestershire CCC.
30. J.A. Schofield, 'The Development of First-class Cricket in England: An Economic Analysis', *Journal of Industrial Economics*, XXX, 4 (June 1984), argues that county cricket clubs in the twentieth century have acted as a profit-maximising cartel, but that this has been qualified by a desire to retain the traditions of cricket which often ran counter to profit maximisation. Most of Schofield's evidence concerning the cartelisation of county cricket is drawn from the period after the Second World War,

but he cites the limitation upon the number of first-class counties as a form of carletisation between the wars.

31. *Athletic News*, 30 July 1923; *Buff*, 7 July 1923, 28 June 1924.
32. *The Times*, 7 Aug. 1931, 20 Sept. 1934.
33. Ibid., 28 June 1923.
34. Ibid., 1 Dec. 1936, 20 Jan. 1937; Findlay Commission, schedules II, X.
35. F. Root, *A Cricket Pro's Lot* (London: Arnold, 1937), p. 168.
36. *The Times*, 9 Sept. 1936.
37. *Field*, 12 Aug. 1926.
38. *The Times*, 20 April 1937.
39. Ibid., 8 April 1937.
40. *C.B. Fry's Magazine* (1911–12), p. 461.
41. *Cricket*, 13 May 1913.
42. *Athletic News*, 4 Aug. 1930.
43. Ibid., 11 Aug. 1930.
44. *The Times*, 1 Dec. 1923.
45. *Wisden Cricketers' Almanack 1943* (London: Whittaker, 1943), p. 60.
46. A.W. Carr, *Cricket with the Lid Off* (London: Hutchinson, 1935), p. 70.
47. M. Marshall, *Gentlemen & Players: Conversations with Cricketers* (London: Grafton, 1987), p. 14.
48. Advisory County Cricket Committee minutes, 30 Aug. 1920; Kent CCC Managing Committee minute book, 10 Oct. 1922, Kent County Record Office Ch. 75 A2/4.
49. Kent CCC Managing Committee minute book, 6 Nov. 1928.
50. Kent CCC General Committee minute book, 30 Jan. 1931, Kent County Record Office Ch 75 A2/5.
51. Ibid.
52. R. Sissons, *The Players: A Social History of the Professional Cricketer* (London: Kingswood, 1988), p. 213.
53. Ibid., p. 206; Kent CCC Managing Committee minute book, 18 Mar. 1938, Kent County Record Office Ch. 75 A3/6.
54. This data about the earnings of professionals is calculated from the table of payments to capped players given in R. Sissons, *The Players,* pp. 206.
55. Kent CCC Managing Committee minute book, 15 Nov. 1927.
56. *Buff*, 14 Nov. 1931; R. Sissons, *The Players,* pp. 206–7.
57. Essex CCC Notes on Annual Salaries, Essex County Record Office D/Z 82/1/32.
58. This calculation is based upon the wages data provided by D. Lemmon, *History of Worcestershire*, p. 88.
59. F. Root, *Cricket Pro's Lot*, p. 52.
60. *The Times*, 1 Dec. 1923; R. Sissons, *The Players*, p. 209; Board of Control minutes, 19 Dec. 1937, Meetings at Lord's November 1934 to November 1948 volume, MCC Library.
61. R. Sissons, *The Players*, p. 209; MCC Finance Sub-committee minutes, 1 June 1938, MCC Cricket Minutes volume January 1938 to August 1952, MCC Library.
62. R. Sissons, *The Players*, p. 213.
63. Ibid., pp. 216–17.
64. Ibid., pp. 219–20; *Buff*, 14 Nov. 1931; P. Wynne-Thomas, *The History of Lancashire County Cricket Club* (London: Christopher Helm, 1989), p. 145.
65. E.W. Swanton, G. Plumptre and J. Woodcock, *Barclays World of Cricket*, p. 395; R. Sissons, *The Players,* p. 233; M.G. Lorimer, ed., *Lancashire Cricket Yearbook 1997* (Manchester: Lancashire CCC, 1997), p. 253.
66. F. Root, *Cricket Pro's Lot*, p. 45.

67. R. Sissons, *The Players*, p. 214.
68. G.M.D. Howat, *Len Hutton* (London: Heinemann Kingswood, 1988), p. 40.
69. H. Larwood and K. Perkins, *The Larwood Story* (London: W.H. Allen, 1965), p. 183.
70. *Buff*, 10 Dec. 1929.
71. R. Sissons, *The Players*, p. 215.
72. J.M. Kilburn, *Thanks to Cricket* (London: Stanley Paul, 1972), p. 40.
73. H. Gordon, *Background of Cricket* (London: Barker, 1939), p. 118.
74. *Nelson Leader*, 20 Jan. 1922.
75. Ibid., 12 Jan. 1923, 20 Jan. 1928, 3 Jan. 1930, 20 Jan. 1933, 12 Jan. 1934, 18 Jan. 1935, 1 Jan. 1937.
76. Ibid., 21 Jan. 1921, 20 Jan. 1922, 12 Jan. 1923, 7 Jan. 1927, 20 Jan. 1928, 17 Jan. 1936, 1 Jan. 1937, 14 Jan. 1938, 13 Jan. 1939.
77. Ibid., 21 Jan. 1921, 3 Jan. 1930.
78. Ibid., 17 Jan. 1936; *Blackburn Times* cricket scrapbooks, Blackburn Public Library.
79. *Blackburn Times* scrapbooks.
80. Ibid.
81. *Buff*, 24 Dec. 1921; *Farnworth Weekly Journal*, 19 Jan. 1923, 23 Jan. 1925, 28 Jan. 1927, 27 Jan. 1928.
82. J.A. Williams, 'Cricket and Society in Bolton between the Wars', Lancaster University unpublished PhD thesis (1992), pp. 120–1.
83. Ibid., p. 121; *Buff*, 30 Oct., 18 Nov. 1933, 26 Nov. 1938.
84. *Buff*, 19 June 1926.
85. Letter of J. Parker, secretary of Burnley CC, to Robert Aspinall, Painters and Decorators, 20 Oct. 1924, Burnley Public Library W126.
86. Rawtenstall CC press cuttings, Rawtenstall Public Library.
87. *Blackburn Times* scrapbooks.
88. *Nelson Leader*, 20 Jan. 1928.
89. Mass-Observation Worktown Survey: Box 2, File A, Sports: General.
90. *Rawtenstall Cricket Club Bazaar ... with a Brief History of the Cricket Club from 1868 to 1925* (n.p., n.d.), p. 101.
91. J.B. Taylor, *Bradshaw Cricket Club 1884–1984* (n.p., n.d.), p. 36; *Buff*, 22 Feb. 1936.
92. J.A. Williams, 'Cricket and Society in Bolton', Chapter 4; R. Wolstenholme, 'The Formation of the Bolton Cricket League', unpublished essay, provides a detailed chronology of the steps leading to the establishment of the Bolton League.
93. *Radcliffe Times*, 25 April, 2, 9, 16, 23 May 1925.
94. L. Constantine, *Cricket in the Sun* (London: Stanley Paul, n.d.), p. 131.
95. G. Howat, *Learie Constantine* (London: Allen and Unwin, 1975), p. 75.
96. *Buff*, 9 Jan. 1937.
97. L. Constantine, *Cricket in the Sun*, p. 65.
98. *Buff*, 8 Dec. 1934; *Radcliffe Times*, 8 Dec. 1934.
99. *Farnworth Weekly Journal*, 28 Jan. 1927, 27 Jan. 1928.
100. *Bolton Evening News* cricket notes, *Bolton Evening News* library.
101. Heaton CC minute book 18 June, 15 July 1919, 5, 13 July 1920, Heaton CC.
102. Radcliffe CC minute book, 29 Feb. 1928, 21 July 1930, Radcliffe Public Library.
103. See R.C. Crepeau, *Baseball: America's Diamond Mind 1919–1941* (Orlando: University Presses of Florida, 1983), Chapter 5, for a discussion of commercialisation within baseball and of how this reflected American values.

Conclusion

Cricket demonstrates the strength of social cohesion and cultural conformity in England between the wars. The scale of interest in cricket and the extent to which this crossed the boundaries of gender, class and locality are in themselves a register of how cricket expressed social and cultural harmony. Had England been a more bitterly fragmented society it seems unlikely that interest in cricket could have been found among such a wide spectrum of society.

Cricket discourses stressed that cricket was an expression of a distinctively English moral worth. The belief that cricket was a distillation of English morality was related to the association of cricket with the Christian churches, assumptions about the Empire being a moral trust, the English pastoral idyll, the limited degree of commercialisation within cricket, reverence for tradition and respect for accepted forms and manners. At the heart of this belief that cricket expressed moral values was the conviction that it was pervaded by a spirit of sportsmanship which the playing and watching of cricket could extend to other areas of social activity. The discourses which stressed that cricket was a register of English moral worth stemmed primarily from the economically and socially privileged. Indeed the rhetoric of sportsmanship, with its exaltation of selflessness, loyalty and putting the welfare of the team before oneself, can be seen as very much related to the assumptions which provided a moral validation for their exercise of social and political authority. The privileged classes' defence of sportsmanship and its moral value, and the ways in which the rhetoric of this drew parallels between cricket and politics, demonstrated, at least to their satisfaction, that they could be trusted to exercise political power for the general good. Of course, some from these classes thought that the moral elevation of cricket was largely humbug, that cricket was merely a game surrounded by much hypocrisy. Yet those who did think this seem to have kept their views very largely to themselves. Cricket did not generate an oppositional discourse which denied the essential sportsmanship of cricket.

183

Emphasis upon cricket as a reflection of morality is found most often in cricket discourses by those from privileged backgrounds, but statements about the special moral worth of cricket were made by those from other classes. In writings and public speeches professional cricketers often defended the sportsmanship of cricket. Professional cricketers with working-class backgrounds whose bowling tactics were criticised, such as Fred Root and Harold Larwood, were quick to claim that they were not violating cricket's tradition of sportsmanship. It is possible that professional cricketers expressed beliefs that cricket was pervaded by a spirit of sportsmanship because they believed that this was expected of them and perhaps suspected that criticising the received version of cricket could have harmed career prospects. But written and oral reminiscences do show that professional cricketers believed cricket was played in a sportsmanlike manner. Attacks in newspapers with large numbers of lower middle- and working-class readers on amateur privilege in cricket were rare, but, when made, they usually claimed that professionals could be trusted as much as amateurs to defend the tradition of sportsmanship. The general acceptance that cricket was a distillation of sportsmanship and morality is evidence of how cricket expressed cultural cohesion in England between the wars.

The spirit in which cricket was played reinforces the case for regarding it as an expression of cultural and social conformity. Objective measures of sportsmanship cannot be made. What one group or individual sees as cheating is thought to be quite acceptable by others. There is, however, sufficient impressionistic evidence to suggest that all levels of cricket were usually played in what was thought to be a sportsmanlike manner. Instances of cheating and sharp practice have been found in first-class cricket and localised studies have shown that they occured at other levels of cricket. The significance accorded to cricket and its supposed morality could have meant that cheating may have been under-reported, and when those who were involved with cricket are interviewed they may feel it is expected of them to confirm the view that cricket was played in a sportsmanlike manner. The defenders of friendly club cricket in the south of England such as E.A.C. Thomson of the Club Cricket Conference argued that league competitions encouraged a competitiveness which undermined the spirit of sportsmanship, but apologists for league cricket denied such claims and local newspapers and the archives of leagues usually show that instances of unsporting behaviour were not common. In both county and league cricket a blind eye was turned to some forms of sharp practice, such as the flouting of residential qualifications by some counties and the playing of unregistered players in leagues, but it seems that at the time such activities were not considered by those involved to be major transgressions of the spirit of sportsmanship. Whilst the association of cricket with other institutions such as the Empire and the public schools may have caused many of the economically privileged to have imagined that the level of sportsmanship within all levels of cricket was greater than was really the case, incidents of cheating never appear to have reached such a scale as to challenge the view that cricket was played in a sportsmanlike manner.

The forms of involvement with cricket among women can also be seen as evidence of cultural and social cohesion within England. Whilst very many more men than women played cricket, cricket playing among women expanded between the wars and probably no other team sport for women grew at a faster rate in the 1920s and 1930s. The emphasis of the Women's Cricket Association on not playing against men can be seen as a form of sports separatism and an expression of women's emancipation, as growing evidence that women believed that they should control the range of their social activity. But women playing cricket should not be seen as a form of antagonism to men. The playing ethos of the WCA was so close to that of men from the privileged classes that it can be claimed that playing cricket by women is a further example of cricket as an expression of shared cultural values. The WCA was committed to friendly rather than league cricket from a fear that over-competitive cricket could discourage sportsmanship. The dress code of the WCA implies a belief that cricket ought to be played with decorum. Playing cricket under the auspices of the Women's Cricket Federation, whilst limited to the West Riding and parts of eastern Lancashire, was administered by men, but it seems to have been dominated by the forms of organisation and values which existed in league cricket for men in these areas and can be seen as an acceptance by women of the values found in league cricket for men in these parts of the North. The social backgrounds of those who played for the WCA and WCF seem to have been different but matches between WCA and WCF representative sides in the North shows a degree of social and cultural cohesion in women's cricket. Some men scoffed at women's cricket and the MCC showed no desire to assume responsibility for women's cricket, but men's clubs did not discourage women playing cricket. As no women's cricket clubs, except for those based on girls' schools and women's colleges had their own grounds, many women's teams had to use the grounds of men's clubs. If men's clubs had refused to allow women to use their grounds, this would probably have restricted the growth of women's cricket. The co-operation between men's and women's cricket is a further instance of social harmony.

Many women would have been indifferent to men's cricket. Some must have found it boring. Others may have disliked it, but there is no means of estimating how many felt like this or whether their numbers fluctuated between the wars. Oral evidence shows that some men stopped playing cricket because of opposition from their womenfolk and it is probable that some men stopped watching cricket for the same reason, but the scale of this is never likely to be known. But what is also clear is that many women were interested in men's cricket and provided vital support for men's cricket. The number of women who watched those levels of cricket where spectators were charged for admission was lower than for men though usually considerably more than a negligible minority. Women formed a significant proportion of members of county and league clubs. Within recreational cricket women washed the kit of players and usually made and served the teas, which were considered a vital ritual of cricket. Ladies' committees made important contributions to the finances of league clubs. The support which women gave to men's cricket can be seen as a form of male exploitation of women, but oral evidence has revealed that women tended not to regard it in this light. Women seem to have enjoyed providing such help, partly because it allowed them to socialise with other women, but also because they did not see cricket as a threat to their interests. Certainly both sexes seem to have accepted that the performance of domestic tasks such as the preparation of teas was naturally a sphere of female expertise. It can be contended that the support which women provided for male cricket is evidence of how far the assumption that cricket was pervaded by morality had penetrated the general culture of England. Most women who have been interviewed have said that their menfolk could have done much worse than be involved with cricket, which suggests a measure of moral approval of cricket but also means that women saw cricket as distracting men from activities which women considered were likely to threaten their interests. Cricket shows that women and men inhabited different social worlds and perceived their social roles to be quite different, but in the context of cricket this does not seem to have provoked intense gender conflict. Within cricket, relations between the sexes seem to have been characterised by harmony and compatibility rather than animosity.

Cricket was riddled with social division and forms of exclusion. Few other social and cultural institutions can have made so obvious to individuals their place in the social hierarchy. In first-class cricket the amateur/professional divide can be seen as an illustration of class privilege and snobbery. As at other sporting venues, pavilions, grandstands and the popular sides of county grounds emphasised the differences in the social backgrounds of cricket spectators. Socially exclusive cricket clubs were found in many areas, and one reason why such clubs usually played only friendly cricket may have been a fear that the more competitive nature of league cricket would have led to sides being selected on playing ability, regardless of social background. Clubs affiliated to the Women's Cricket Association were largely for the better-off. Yet cricket discourse celebrated cricket as an expression of social harmony. Village cricket in particular was lauded for bringing together those from the opposite ends of the rural social spectrum and for promoting understanding and goodwill among them. Many of those from the wealthier classes seem to have been convinced that professional county cricketers with working-class backgrounds preferred sides to be captained by amateurs rather than by professionals.

Cricket, because it revealed the extent of economic and social inequalities, shows that England between the wars was a class society. Cricket helped to remind individuals and groups of their position in the social hierarchy. But the forms of class distinction within cricket do not seem to have provoked a great depth of resentment and antagonism between classes. Chapter 6 shows that professionals, who were by and large of working-class origin, did object to losing their places to amateurs and found some amateur captains to be overbearing. The fact that even Jack Hobbs, who usually accepted the practices of cricket with equanimity, expressed reservations about amateur captains suggests that many other professionals also did not agree entirely with the tradition of amateurs captaining county sides. Yet it would seem that most professional cricketers accepted the amateur presence and amateur authority within cricket as a fact of life, something which was beyond their power to change. The reminiscences of professionals show that they preferred to retain a measure of social distance between themselves and amateurs. Professional cricketers with strong political objections to privilege, such as the Gloucestershire bowler Charlie Parker, seem to have been rare. The reaction of professionals to most amateurs seems to have been based upon responses to them as men rather than as representatives of a class. It must also be recognised that many professionals were probably aware, as the example of Cecil Parkin had shown, that overt criticism of the power structure of first-class cricket could threaten career prospects. Some of those with strong resentments of class privilege may have felt it wiser not to seek employment as professional county cricketers.

Criticisms of amateur authority made by those outside cricket did occur and became most intense in the mid-1920s when Lord Hawke was criticised for his attacks on Cecil Parkin and his hopes that England would never be captained by a professional. In 1926 there were calls for the England team against Australia to be captained by a professional and in 1927 sections of the press welcomed the offer of the Yorkshire captaincy to the professional Herbert Sutcliffe. Yet none of these criticisms of amateur captaincy lasted for very long. For much of the 1930s *The Daily Herald,* the newspaper from which a campaign for a restriction of amateur privilege might have been most expected, said little about the matter. Although some village sides contained people from a wide variety of backgrounds, many clubs playing only friendly cricket were socially exclusive and played only against sides with similar backgrounds. As cricket was so often taken to be a symbol of much more than merely a game, the very limited degree of criticism directed at the forms of class privilege found in cricket suggests that whilst it would have helped to make clear the nature of class divisions within English society, these were not accompanied by a strong sense of class antagonism. Chapter 6 also shows that county and league cricket could stimulate county and town loyalties which crossed class boundaries. For many, support for the Yorkshire county side enjoined a hostility towards the South. Localised research into the lowest levels of league cricket in Lancashire and village cricket in Sussex shows that clubs playing at this level often enjoyed the patronage of the local elite. It is possible that those with the strongest sense of class antagonism may have felt that it was not worth protesting about class privilege within cricket. No doubt many Labour Party activists may have thought that low pay, unemployment and slum housing were more pressing matters than class privilege within cricket, but the rarity of attacks on class privilege in cricket, especially when it is remembered that cricket was taken to represent much more than a mere sport, suggests that class relations were not in general accompanied by a strong sense of class antagonism. When English society is observed from the vantage point of cricket, the perspective that emerges is one of a society in which class differences were clear to almost all, but the level of resentment which they stimulated was not very great. At the risk of sounding paradoxical, cricket suggests that England was a class society largely at ease with itself, a society of social inequality yet also characterised by a high level of social harmony.

The connections of the churches with cricket also indicate that it can be regarded as an expression of social cohesion. The congruence between cricket and Christian morality figured prominently in cricket discourse. It is possible that many who made such statements did so because they believed that this was expected of them, but this shows that many suspected that it was widely believed that there was a close connection between Christianity and cricket. It has been demonstrated that in the South clerics were often honorary officials of village clubs whilst in many parts of the North church and Sunday school teams formed a very high proportion of those playing at the lower levels of recreational cricket. The inter denominational nature of most church and Sunday school cricket leagues shows that inter-denominational animosities cannot have been so very strong and this can be seen as the expression of a form of social and cultural cohesion, though the small number of Catholic teams suggests a desire among the Catholic clergy and the laity to maintain a social distance between themselves and other denominations. Detailed localised research indicates that the strong church presence within recreational cricket encouraged church attendance. Most church and Sunday school teams and leagues required players to attend church regularly and oral evidence shows that most were regular attenders. In the North the high numbers of church teams and leagues, and similarly the supposition in the rural South that clerics should be associated with village teams, represented a belief that the churches should have had a role in cultural life. The strength of the churches' involvement with cricket can be seen as an obstacle to the increasing secularisation of English society and suggests that in the North in particular claims about the marginalisation of churches in cultural life require qualification.

First-class cricket was in many respects a business. Staging county cricket was expensive. By 1939 the majority of appearances in county cricket were made by professionals and higher than those made before 1914 which could be taken to mean that English society had become infused with a stronger spirit of commercialism. But county cricket was never between the wars dominated by commercial values. There was a strong desire to maintain an amateur presence in cricket and for authority to be exercised by amateurs. Many amateurs may have been shamateurs, but their desire to give the appearance of being amateurs shows the strength of the determination to maintain an amateur presence. Many county clubs struggled to make ends meet, but there was great resistance to increasing the commercial appeal of county cricket. To a degree, opposition to the greater commercialisation of county cricket may have owed something to beliefs that it could never be made financially viable but there is much to suggest that the root cause of opposition to proposals for easing the financial worries of county clubs by increasing the attractions of cricket for spectators was a fear that this could change the nature of cricket. Greater commercialisation, it was thought, could undermine sportsmanship and fair play. The veneration accorded to cricket, a sport in which the commercialism was kept at arm's length and in which many county clubs were financially ailing, suggests that the cultural values of those who controlled first-class cricket were not dominated by commercialisation and a ruthless desire to gather profits from almost any possible source. Professional cricketers were interested in their contracts and, as interviews with surviving professionals show, most felt that their cricket salaries were better than those they could have earned in other jobs. They were interested in their contracts but there was no concerted or sustained campaign from county players for a higher level of pay. At some counties in the early 1930s, capped players agreed to accept wage cuts. It can be argued that the attitude of professional cricketers towards their remuneration shows that they too did not subscribe to an ethic of overtly aggressive pursuit of profit. Those who controlled the most successful league clubs did not see them as commercialised undertakings. Hardly any league clubs were limited companies. Some league 'amateurs' moved from club to club for illicit payments and in the hope of obtaining bigger collections for playing well, but the scale of this cannot be measured with accuracy. Those who ran league clubs seem to have done so largely as a labour of love and valued club income primarily as the means of promoting success on the playing field. Cricket suggests a widespread reluctance at many levels of society to extend commercial values to as many aspects of social life as seem to be current today or as occurred in America between the wars.

England in the 1920s and 1930s faced severe social and political problems. World trading conditions were not as favourable as before the First World War. Much of the industrial North experienced heavy unemployment in 1926 and in the first half of the 1930s. The economic crisis of 1931 was considered sufficiently serious to justify the formation of a coalition government. Labour disputes occurred in coal mining in 1921 and 1926 and led to the General Strike. A protracted strike occurred in the cotton in industry in 1932. The Empire was challenged by granting independence to the Irish Free State and the growth of support for the Congress Party in India. The Labour Party eclipsed the Liberals as an electoral force in politics. For many who had fought in the First World War, post-war England had not proved to be a land fit for heroes. On the other hand, real wages for those in work in most occupational groups rose slightly between the wars. New forms of manufacturing were located in the South and Midlands. English society showed much stability. The major forms of feminist agitation did not so much call upon women to challenge the social and political authority of men as to press for greater recognition of women's expertise in areas such as motherhood and caring. Unlike in much of Europe, support in England for political extremism of the left and the right was limited. The reformist nature of the Labour Party and its acceptance of parliamentary politics cast doubts upon how far electoral support for Labour meant that political allegiances were becoming based upon class identities and a conviction that the interests of classes were in conflict. The social and cultural world of cricket does much to make clear the degree of stability within English society in the 1920s and 1930s. Cricket was characterised by social harmony and cultural cohesion, but it was also a sport which made very obvious the inequalities and snobberies

190

found in English society. Had a strong awareness of social animosity existed in other areas of English life, it seems unlikely that the social distinctions of cricket would have provoked so little protest or criticism. Without such a wide measure of cultural and social harmony in England, there could not have remained such widespread acceptance of cricket as a symbol of England and of English moral worth. The social and cultural harmony found in cricket was not restricted to cricket. It both reflected and strengthened cultural and social harmony in England.

Bibliography

MANUSCRIPTS AND UNPUBLISHED MATERIALS

Advisory County Cricket Committee minutes (Surrey County Record Office).

Board of Control minutes (Meetings at Lord's December 1900–December 1926, January 1927–October 1934, November 1934–November 1948, MCC).

Bolton CC scrapbooks (Bolton Public Library)

Bolton Cricket League Executive Committee minute book (Bolton Cricket League).

Essex CCC Committee minute book 1929–35 (Essex Country Record Office).

Essex CCC annual reports and statements of accounts (Essex County Record Office).

Farnworth Social Circle CC minute book (Farnworth Social Circle CC).

Findlay Commission Schedules I–XI (Nottinghamshire CCC library).

First-class County Captains Meetings minutes (Meetings at Lord's December 1900–December 1926, January 1927–October 1934, November 1934–November 1948, MCC)

Heaton CC minute book (Heaton CC).

Henfield CC minute book 1926–39 (Sussex CCC)

Horwich Sunday School Cricket League minute book (Horwich Churches Welfare Cricket League).

Kent CCC General Committee minute book 1919–39 (Kent County Record Office).

Kent CCC Managing Committee minute book 1913–48 (Kent Record Office).

Lancashire CCC List of New Members 1914, 1922 (Lancashire CCC).

Lancashire CCC Annual Accounts 1919–21, 1924–39 (Lancashire CCC)

Little Hulton CC minute book (Little Hulton CC).

MCC Cricket minutes January 1938–August 1952 (MCC).

MCC Daily Receipts (MCC).

MCC Members Registers 1920–26, 1934–41 (MCC).

Mass-Observation Worktown Survey (University of Sussex).

Meeting of seven umpires with the secretary and assistant secretary of MCC 11 October 1934 (Meetings at Lord's January 1927–October 1934, MCC).

Radcliffe CC minute book and finance ledger (Radcliffe Public Library).

Surrey CCC extraneous minute book vols. 2, 16 May 1932–6 Sept. 1962 (Surrey County Record Office).

Surrey CCC Match Receipts (Surrey County Record Office).

Sussex CCC Executive Committee minute books 1919–39 (East Sussex County Record Office)

Sussex CCC Annual Reports 1926–39 (East Sussex County Record Office).

Walkden Amateur Cricket League minute book (Salford Record Office).

Westhoughton CC minute book and account book (Westhoughton CC).

Worcestershire CCC Manager's Report 1934 (Worcestershire CCC).

Worcestershire CCC Annual Financial Statements 1927–39 (Worcestershire CCC).

Wolstenholme, R., 'The Formation of the Bolton Cricket League', unpublished essay (Bolton Cricket League).

Yorkshire Cricket Federation minute book 1929–39 (West Yorkshire Archive Service).

INTERVIEWS

Mr. A. (college lecturer, played for Burnley CC).

Ms. A. (librarian, played for Yorkshire Women's Cricket Association).

Ms. C. Airey (woollen mill warper, later restaurant proprietor, played for Standard Fireworks CC, Lectern Highlanders CC, Pennine Nomads CC, Yorkshire WCA and Yorkshire WCF teams).

Rev. V. J. Abernethy (Presbyterian minister).

Rev. F.A. Asprey (Congregationalist minister, played for Farnworth Social Circle CC).

Mr. J. Ashton (colliery yard sawyer, later colliery electrician, played for Astley and Tyldesley Collieries CC).

Mr. J. Billinge (clothing factory cutting room manager, played for Walkden CC).

Mr. B. Blackburn (tannery operative, played for Walker Institute CC).

H. Blundell (engineer, later instructor of apprentices, played for Horwich RMI CC).

Mr G.S. Bown (railway clerk, later school teacher, played for St Peter and Paul CC, Radcliffe CC, Farnworth CC).

Rev. P. Breen (Catholic priest).

Mr. G. Bromilow (moulder, played for Little Hulton CC).

Mr. A. Burnham (clerk, played for Radcliffe Parish Church CC, St John's CC, Unsworth CC).

Mr. G.O. Dawkes (Leicestershire professional cricketer).

Mr. C.S. Elliott (Derbyshire professional cricketer).

Rev. T. Gallagher (Catholic priest).

Mr. J.A. Gledhill (grammar school teacher, played for Farnworth CC).

Mr. S. Greenhalgh (dye works operative, played for Eagley CC, professional league cricketer with Delph Hill Wesleyan CC, Egerton CC).

Ms. L. Hall (office worker, later school teacher, secretary, played for Bolton Ladies CC).

Mr A Hargreaves (towel designer, played for Barlow and Dobson CC).

Ms. M. Lockwood (school teacher, England wicket-keeper, played for Meltham Mills, Leeds Women's CC).

Rev. J.W. Markham (Anglican cleric).

Mr T. B. Mitchell (Derbyshire and England professional cricketer)–radio interview with Mr. I.W. Hall, 19 Jan. 1993.

Mr. T. Needham (groundsman, played for East Lancashire Paper Mill CC).

Mr. W. Place (Lancashire professional cricketer).

Mr. J. Pickstone (railway clerk, played for Stand Independents CC).

Rev. G.L.W. Ridge (United Free Methodist minister).

Mr. E.P. Robinson (Yorkshire professional cricketer).

Mr. S. Rowland (colliery clerk, later colliery accountant, played for Astley and Tyldesley Collieries CC).

Mr. H. Scholes (school teacher, played for Bolton CC).

Mr. A. Smale (paper factory worker, Little Lever CC).

Sir Robert Southern (bank official, chairman Radcliffe Sunday School Cricket League, played for Stand Unitarian CC).

Mr. E. Tatlock (glass manufacturer's warehouse labourer, played for St Helens Recs CC).

Mr. G. Tildesley (engineer, later engineering works manager, played for Farnworth Social CC).

Mr. S. Webb (cotton mill office worker, later mill manager, played for Brunswick United Methodist CC).

Mr. N. Wilcock (glass manufacturers' invoice clerk, later departmental manager, played for St Helens Recs CC).

NEWSPAPERS AND PERIODICALS

Athletic News
Barnsley Chronicle
Barnsley Independent
Berrow's Worcester Journal
[Birmingham] Sports Argus
Blackburn Times cricket scrapbooks (Blackburn Public Library).
Bolton Congregationalist
Bolton Evening News
[Bolton Evening News] Buff
[Bolton Evening News] Cricket and Football Field
Bolton Journal and Guardian
Bradford Telegraph and Argus
Burnley Express
C.B. Fry's Magazine
Cricket
Cricketer
Daily Express
Daily Herald
Daily Mail
Daily Mirror
Daily Telegraph
Farnworth Weekly News
Field
Fortnightly Review
Guardian
Halifax Daily Courier and Guardian
Hereford Times
Huddersfield Weekly Examiner
Keighley News
Lancashire Evening Telegraph
Leigh, Tyldesley and Atherton Journal
Liverpool Weekly Post
Liverpool Echo
Liverpool Football Echo
Manchester Guardian
Mansfield and North Notts. Advertiser
Methodist Recorder
Methodist Times
Ministry of Labour Gazette

BIBLIOGRAPHY

Ministry of Labour Local Unemployment Index
Nelson Leader
New Statesman and Nation
News Chronicle
Nineteenth century and After
Observer
[Oldham Evening News] Green Final
Quarterly Review
Radcliffe Times
Rawtenstall CC press cuttings (Rawtenstall Public Library)
Rochdale Observer
Sunday Chronicle
Sunday Times
St Helens Newspaper
St Helens Reporter
Sporting Chronicle
Sunderland Daily Echo
Sussex Express
The Times
Time and Tide
Weekly Dispatch
Wigan Observer
Women's Cricket
Worcester Evening News & Times
Worcester Herald
Worcester Sports News
Yorkshire Sports and Cricket Argus
Yorkshire Sports and Football Argus

ANNUALS AND YEARBOOKS

Bolton and District Cricket Association Annual Handbook
Calendar of All Grants of Probate and Letters of Administration
*City of Liverpool Education Committee Report on the Medical Inspection
    of School Children Cricketer Annual*
Cricketer Spring Annual
Cricketer Winter Annual
Colliery Yearbook and Coal Trades Directory
The Directory of Directors
Kent County Cricket Club

Lancashire Cricket League Handbook
Lancashire County and Manchester Cricket Club Yearbook
Lancashire Schools' Cricket Association Handbooks
London and Southern Counties Cricket Conference: Cricket Clubs' Annual and Secretarial Directory–from 1927 *The Official Annual Handbook of the Club Cricket Conference: Cricket Clubs' Annual and Secretarial Directory*
Northamptonshire County Cricket Club
Somerset County Cricket Club Yearbook
Surrey County Cricket Club
Warwickshire County Cricket Club
Who's Who
Who Was Who
Wisden Cricketers' Almanack
Yorkshire County Cricket Club

BOOKS AND ARTICLES

A County Cricketer, *A Searchlight on English Cricket* (London: Robert Holden, 1926).

Alasuutari, P., *Researching Culture: Qualitative Method and Cultural Studies* (London: Sage, 1996).

Altham, H.S., *A History of Cricket from the Beginnings to the First World War* (London: Allen and Unwin, 1962).

Ames, L., *Close of Play* (London: Stanley Paul, 1953).

Andrews, B., *The Hand That Bowled Bradman* (London: Macdonald, 1973).

Bacup and District Sunday School Cricket League Jubilee Souvenir Handbook, 1899–1949 (n.p., n.d.).

Bailey, P., Thorn, P. and Wynne-Thomas, P., eds., *Who's Who of Cricketers* (London: Guild, 1984).

Baldwin, F., *A Century at Castle Hill: Tonge Cricket Club 1876–1976* (n.p., n.d.).

Baldwin, S., *On England and Other Addresses* (London: Philip Allan, 1926).

Baldwin, S., *Our Inheritance: Speeches and Addresses* (London: Hodder and Stoughton, 1928).

Baldwin, S., *Service of Our Lives: Last Speeches as Prime Minister* (Hodder and Stoughton, 1938).

Bale, J., 'Cricket Landscapes and English Eternalism', paper presented at

25th. meeting of the Eastern Historical Geography Association, Codrington College, Barbados, 3–9 February 1994.

Bannister, J. and Graveney, D., *Durham C.C.C.: Past, Present and Future* (Harpenden: Queen Anne, 1993).

Barker, E., *National Character and the Factors in Its Formation* (London: Methuen, 1927).

Barker, E., ed., *The Character of England* (Oxford: Clarendon, 1947).

Barnett, C., *The Audit of War* (London: Macmillan, 1986).

Bearshaw, B., *From the Stretford End: The Official History of Lancashire County Cricket Club* (London: Partridge, 1990).

Beckles, H. McD. and Stoddart, B., *Liberation Cricket: West Indies Cricket Culture* (Manchester: Manchester UP, 1995).

Berghoff, H., 'Public Schools and the Decline of the British Economy 1870–1914', *Past & Present*, 129 (Nov. 1990).

Birley, D., *Playing the Game: Sport and British Society* (Manchester: Manchester UP, 1995).

Birley, D., *The Willow Wand: Some Cricket Myths Explored* (London: Queen Anne, 1979).

Bolton Cricket Club: 100 Years at Green Lane (Bolton: n.d.).

Bolton Playing Fields Association: Report and Statement of Accounts for the Period Ending 31st December (Bolton: Bolton Playing Fields Association, 1935).

Bolton Sports Federation Centenary Booklet 1890–1990 (Bolton: Bolton Sports Federation, n.d.).

Bourdieu, P., *Distinction: A Social Critique of the Judgement of Taste* (Cambridge: Harvard UP, 1984).

Bowes, B., *Express Deliveries* (London: Stanley Paul, 1949).

Boyes, G., *The Imagined Village: Culture, Ideology and the English Folk Revival* (Manchester: Manchester UP).

Bradley, J., 'The MCC, Society and Empire: A Portrait of Cricket's Ruling Body, 1860–1914', *International Journal of the History of Sport*, 7, 1 (May 1990).

Bradley, J., 'Inventing Australians and Constructing Englishness: Cricket and the Creation of a National Consciousness, 1860–1914' *Sporting Traditions*, 11 (1995).

Brailsford, D., *British Sport: A Social History* (Cambridge: Lutterworth, 1992).

Brailsford, D., *Sport, Time and Society: The British at Play* (London: Routledge, 1991).

Brodribb, G., *The English Game: A Cricket Anthology* (London: Hollis and Carter).

Brodribb, G., *Next Man In: A Survey of Cricket Laws and Customs* (London: Putnam, 1952).

Brodribb, G., *Maurice Tate: A Biography* (London: London Magazine Editions, 1976).

Brookes, C., *English Cricket: The Game and its Players through the Ages* (London: Weidenfeld and Nicolson, 1978).

Brookes, C., *His Own Man: The Life of Neville Cardus* (London: Methuen, 1985).

Brown, I., *The Heart of England* (London: Batsford, 1935).

Cairns, J., *Economic Analysis of League Sports–A Critical Review of the Literature* (Aberdeen: University of Aberdeen, Department of Political Economy Discussion Paper 83 –01, 1983).

Cairns, J., Jennett, N. and Sloane, P.J., 'The Economics of Team Sports: A Survey of Evidence and Theory', *Journal of Economic Studies*, 12, 1 (1986).

Cardus, N., *Autobiography* (London: Collins, 1948).

Cardus, N., *Cricket* (London: Longmans, Green, 1930).

Cardus, N., *A Cricketer's Book* (London: Grant Richards, 1922).

Cardus, N., *Days in the Sun: A Cricketer's Book* (London: Cape, 1929).

Cardus, N., *The Summer Game: A Cricketers' Journal* (London: Cape, 1935).

Cardus, N., *Good Days: A Book of Cricket* (London: Cape, 1934).

Cardus, N., 'Idle Thoughts on Cricket' *Listener*, 2 May 1934.

Carr, A.W., *Cricket with the Lid Off* (London: Hutchinson, 1935).

Cavanagh, R., *Cotton Town Cricket: The Centenary History of Lancashire's Oldest Cricket League* (Bolton: n.p., n.d.).

Central Lancashire League: Centenary Year 1892–1992 (n.p., n.p.).

Cleworth, G., *Cricket at Eagley: The Story of Eagley Cricket Club, 1837–1987* (Bolton: Eagley Cricket Club, 1987).

Cohen-Portheim, P., *England, the Unknown Isle* [translated by A. Harris] (London: Duckworth, 1930).

Coldham, J.D., *Lord Harris* (London: Allen and Unwin, 1983).

Collins, B. and Robbins, K., eds., *British Culture and Economic Decline* (London: Weidenfeld and Nicolson, 1990).

Cook, T., *Character and Sportsmanship* (London: Williams and Norgate, 1927).

Cox, R.W., *Index to Sporting Manuscripts in the UK* (Frodsham: British Society of Sports History, 1995).

Cox, R.W., *Sport in Britain: A Bibliography of Historical Publications, 1800–1988* (Manchester: Manchester UP, 1991).

Crepeau, R.C., *Baseball: America's Diamond Mind, 1919–1941* (Orlando:

University Presses of Florida, 1983).

Currie, R., Gilbert, A. and Horsley, L., *Churches and Church-goers: Patterns of Church Growth in the British Isles since 1700* (Oxford; Oxford UP, 1977).

Darwin, B., 'British Sport and Games' in *British Life and Thought: An Illustrated History* (London: Longman, Green, 1940).

Darwin, B., *The English Public School* (London: Longmans, Green, 1929).

Darwin, B., *Pack Clouds Away* (London: Collins, 1941).

Davis, A.E., *First in the Field: A History of the Birmingham and District Cricket League* (Studley: Brewin, 1988).

Dintinfass, M., *The Decline of Industrial Britain 1870–1980* (London: Routledge, 1992).

Duckworth, L., *Holmes and Sutcliffe: The Run Stealers* (London: Hutchinson/Cricketer, 1970).

Duckworth, L.B., *Cricket My Love* (Birmingham: Cornish, 1946).

Egerton Cricket Club: Souvenir Brochure, 1864–1989 (Bolton: Egerton Cricket Club, 1989).

Dunning, E. and Sheard, K., *Barbarians, Gentlemen and Players: A Sociological Study of the Development of Rugby Football* (Oxford: Martin Robertson, 1979).

Eley, S., and Griffiths, P., *Padwick's Bibliography of Cricket, Volume II* (London: Library Association, 1991).

Elias, N. and Dunning, E., *Quest for Excitement: Sport and Leisure in the Civilising Process* (Oxford: Blackwell, 1986).

Ellis, C., *C.B.: The Life of Charles Burgess Fry* (London: Dent, 1984).

Engel, M. and Radd, A., *The History of Northamptonshire County Cricket Club* (London: Helm, 1993).

Fishwick, N.B.F., *English Football and Society 1910–1950* (Manchester: Manchester UP, 1989).

Foot, D., *Cricket's Unholy Trinity* (London: Stanley Paul, 1985).

Foot, D., *Wally Hammond: The Reasons Why: A Biography* (London: Robson, 1996).

Ford, J., *Cricket: A Social History, 1700–1835* (Newton Abbot: David and Charles, 1972).

Fraser, D., *'The Man in White is Always Right': Cricket and the Law* (Sydney: Institute of Criminology, 1993).

French, G., *The Cornerstone of English Cricket* (London: Hutchinson, 1948).

Frindall, B., ed., *The Wisden Book of Cricket Records* (London: Book Club Associates, 1981).

Fry, C.B., *Life Worth Living* (London: Eyre and Spottiswoode, 1941).

Gannaway, N., *A History of Cricket in Hampshire* (Marsh Barton: Hampshire Books, 1990).

Genders, R., *League Cricket in England* (London: Laurie, 1952).

Gilbert, A.D., *The Making of Post-Christian Britain: A History of the Secularization of Modern Society* (London: Routledge, 1980).

Gilligan, A.E.R., *Sussex Cricket* (London; Chapman & Hall, 1933).

Gordon, H., *Background of Cricket* (London: Arthur Barker, 1939).

Gordon, H., 'Cricket Problems Today' *Fortnightly Review*, 109 (Jan.–June 1921).

Gover, A., *The Long Run* (London: Pelham, 1991).

Green B., *The Wisden Book of Obituaries: Obituaries from Wisden Cricketers' Almanack 1892–1985* (London: Queen Anne, 1986).

Hammond, W., *Cricket's Secret History* (London: Stanley Paul, 1952).

Hargreaves, A., *Cricket in My Life: A Story of Cricket in the Bolton District, 1917–83* (Swinton: Neil Richardson, 1984).

Hargreaves, Jennifer, '"Playing like Gentlemen while Behaving like Ladies": Contradictory Features of the Formative Years of Women's Sport', *British Journal of Sports History*, 2, 1 (May 1985).

Hargreaves, Jennifer, ed., *Sport, Culture and Ideology* (London: Routledge, 1982).

Hargreaves, Jennifer, *Sporting Females: Critical Issues in the History and Sociology of Women's Sports* (London: Routledge, 1994).

Hargreaves, John, *Sport, Power and Culture: A Social and Historical Analysis of Popular Sports in Britain* (Cambridge: Polity, 1986).

Harris, Lord, *A Few Short Runs* (London: Murray, 1921).

Harrisson, T., *The Pub and the People. A Worktown Study of Mass-Observation* (Welwyn Garden City: Seven Dials, 1970, re-issue of the 1943 edition).

Hawke, Lord, *Recollections and Reminiscences* (London: Williams and Norgate, 1924).

Haynes, B. and Lucas, J., *The Trent Bridge Battery: The Story of the Sporting Gunns* (London: Collins Willow, 1985).

Hester, J.A., Ward, E. and Perry, L.E., *Horwich Churches Welfare League, 1922–1972* (n.p., n.d.).

Hignell, A., *A 'Favourit' Game: Cricket in South Wales before 1914* (Cardiff: University of Wales, 1992).

Hignell, A., *The History of Glamorgan County Cricket Club* (London: Christopher Helm, 1988).

Hill, A., *Hedley Verity: A Portrait of a Cricketer* (London: Guild, 1986).

Hill, J., '"First Class" Cricket and the Leagues: Some Notes on the Development of English Cricket, 1900–40' *International Journal of the*

History of Sport, 4, 1 (May 1987).

Hill, J., 'League Cricket in the North and Midlands, 1900–1940', in Holt, R.J., ed., *Sport and the Working Class in Modern Britain* (Manchester: Manchester UP)

Hill, J., *Nelson: Politics, Economy and Community* (Edinburgh: Keele UP, 1997).

Hill, J., 'Reading the Stars: A Post-modernist Approach to Sports History' *Sports Historian*, 14 (May 1994).

Hobbs, J.B., *Between the Wickets: A Novel of Public School Life* (London: A. & C. Black, 1927).

Hobbs, J.B., *My Cricket Memories* (London: Heinemann, 1924).

Hobbs, J., *My Life Story* (London: Hambledon, 1981).

Hobbs, J., *Playing for England; My Test-cricket Story* (London: Gollancz, 1931).

Hobbs, J., *The Test Match Surprise: A Romance of the Cricket Field* (London: Readers Library, 1926).

Hobsbawm, E.J. and Ranger, T., eds., *The Invention of Tradition* (Cambridge: Cambridge UP, 1983).

Hobson, J.W. and Henry, H., *The Hulton Readership Survey 1947* (London: Hulton, 1947).

Hollis, C., *Oxford in the Twenties: Recollections of Five Friends* (London: Heinemann, 1976).

Holmes, E.R.T., *Flanneled Foolishness: A Cricketing Chronicle* (London: Hollis & Carter, 1957).

Holt, R.J., 'Cricket and Englishness: The Batsman as Hero', *International Journal of the History of Sport*, 13, 1 (March 1996).

Holt, R.J., 'Heroes of the North: Sport and the Shaping of Regional Identity', in Hill, J. and Williams, J., eds., *Sport and Identity in the North of England* (Keele: Keele UP, 1996).

Holt, R.J., *Sport and the British: A Modern History* (Oxford: Clarendon, 1989).

Holt, R.J., 'Sport and History: The State of the Subject in Britain', *20 Century British History*, 7, 2 (1996).

Howat, G., *Cricketer Militant: The Life of Jack Parsons* (Oxford: Oxford and Cambridge Examination Board, 1980).

Howat, L., *Learie Constantine* (London: Allen and Unwin, 1975).

Howat, G., *Len Hutton* (London: Heinemann Kingswood, 1988).

Howat, G., 'Local History, Ancient and Modern: Cricket and the Victorian Church' Parts I, II and III, *Journal of the Cricket Society*, 9, 2, 3, 4 (1979–80).

Howat, G., *Plum Warner* (London: Unwin Hyman, 1987).

Howkins, A., 'The Discovery of Rural England' in Colls, A. and Dodd, R., eds., *Englishness: Politics and Culture 1880–1920* (Beckenham: Croom Helm, 1986).

Hoy, M., 'Joyful Mayhem: Bakhtin, Football Songs and the Carnivalesque' *Text and Performance Quarterly*, 14 (1994).

Inge, W.R., *England* (London: Ernest Benn, 1926).

Inge, W.R., *More Lay Thoughts of a Dean* (London: Putnam, 1931).

Inge, W.R., *Our Present Discontent* (London: Putnam, 1938).

Inge, W.R., *A Rustic Moralist* (London: Putnam, 1937).

Jackson, W.W., *Worsley Cricket Club over One Hundred Years* (Worsley: Worsley Cricket Club, 1946).

James, C.L.R., *Beyond a Boundary* (London: Hutchinson, 1963).

Johnson, B., *Someone Who Wars* (London: Methuen, 1992).

Jones, S.G., *Sport, Politics and the Working Class: Organised Labour and Sport in Inter-war Britain* (Manchester: Manchester UP, 1988).

Jones, S.G., *Workers at Play: A Social and Economic History of Leisure, 1919–1939* (London: Routledge & Kegan Paul, 1986).

Joy, N., *Maiden Over: A Short History of Women's Cricket and a Diary of the 1948–49 Test Tour to Australia* (London: Sporting Handbooks, 1950).

Joyce, P., *Class* (Oxford: Oxford UP).

Joyce, P., *Democratic Subjects: The Self and the Social in Nineteenth-century England* (Cambridge: Cambridge UP, 1994).

Joyce, P., *Visions of the People: Industrial England and the Question of Class, 1840–1914* (Cambridge: Cambridge UP, 1991).

Kay, J., *Cricket in the Leagues* (Eyre and Spottiswoode, 1970).

Kearsley Cricket Club (n.p., n.d.)

Kilburn, J.M., *In Search of Cricket* (London: Arthur Barker, 1937).

Kilburn, J.M., *Overthrows: A Book of Cricket* (London: Stanley Paul, 1975).

Kilburn, J.M., *Thanks to Cricket* (London: Stanley Paul, 1972).

Kilburn, J.M. and Nash, J.H., *History of Yorkshire County Cricket 1924–1949* (Leeds: Yorkshire CCC, 1950).

Kircher, R., *Fair Play: The Games of Merrie England* [translated by R.N. Bradley] (London: Collins, 1928).

Kirk, N., 'History, Language, Ideas and Post-modernism: A Materialist View', *Social History*, 19, 2 (May 1994).

Kirk, N., ed., *Social Class and Marxism: Defences and Challenges* (Aldershot: Scolar, 1996).

Lambert, D., *The History of Leicestershire County Cricket Club* (London: Christopher Helm, 1992).

Larwood, H., *Body-line?* (London: Elkin, Mathews and Marrot, 1933).

Larwood, H. and Perkins, K., *The Larwood Story* (London: W.H. Allen, 1965).

Lee, F., *Cricket, Lovely Cricket* (London: Stanley Paul, 1960).

Lee, H.W., *Forty Years of English Cricket with Excursions to India and South Africa* (London: Clerke & Cockeran, 1948).

Lemmon, D., *For the Love of the Game: An Oral History of First-class Cricket* (London: Michael Joseph, 1993).

Lemmon, D., *Johnny Won't Hit Today: A Cricketing Biography of J.W.H.T. Douglas* (London: Allen and Unwin, 1983).

Lemmon, D., *The Crisis of Captaincy* (London: Christopher Helm, 1988).

Lemmon, D, *The Official History of Middlesex County Cricket Club* (London: Christopher Helm, 1988).

Lemmon, D., *The Official History of Worcestershire County Cricket Club* (London: Christopher Helm, 1989).

Lemmon, D., *Percy Chapman: A Biography* (London: Queen Anne, 1985).

Leveson Gower, H., *Off and On the Field* (London: Stanley Paul, 1953).

Lewis, A.R., *Double Century: The Story of MCC and Cricket* (London: Hodder and Stoughton, 1987).

Lodge, D., *After Bakhtin: Essays on Fiction and Criticism* (London: Routledge, 1990).

Looker, S.J., ed., *Cricket: A Little Book for Lovers of the Game* (London: Simpkin, Marshall, Hamilton, Kent, 1925).

Lowerson, J., *Sport and the English Middle Classes, 1878–1914* (Manchester: Manchester UP, 1993).

Lowerson, J., 'Sport and the Victorian Sunday: The Beginnings of Middle-class Apostasy', *British Journal of Sports History*, 1, 2 (Sept. 1984).

Lucas, E.V., *Cricket All His Life: The Cricket Writings of E.V. Lucas* (London: Pavilion, 1989).

Lyon, M.D., *Cricket* (London: Eyre and Spottiswoode, 1932).

Lyttelton, E., 'Sport and Sportsmanship', *Quarterly Review*, 481 (Oct. 1924).

Macartney, C.G., *My Cricketing Days* (London: Heinemann, 1930).

M'Connachie and J.M.B.: Speeches by J.M. Barrie (London: Davies, 1938).

McCrone, K.E., 'Emancipation or Recreation? The Development of Women's Sport at the University of London', *International Journal of the History of Sport*, 7, 2 (Sept. 1990).

McCrone, K.E., *Sport and the Physical Emancipation of English Women, 1870–1914* (London: Routledge, 1988).

McKendrick, N., '"Gentlemen and Players" Revisited: The Gentlemanly Ideal, the Business Ideal and the Professional Ideal in English Literary

Culture', in McKendrick, N. and Outhwaite, R.B., eds., *Business Life and Public Policy: Essays in Honour of D.C. Coleman* (Cambridge: Cambridge UP, 1986).

Mailey, A., *10 for 66 and All That* (London: Phoenix Sports, 1958).

Mais, S.P.B., *Oh! To Be in England: A Book of the Open Air* (London: Grant Richards, 1932).

Mangan, J.A., *Athleticism in the Victorian and Edwardian Public School* (Cambridge: Cambridge UP, 1981).

Mangan, J.A., ed., *Pleasure, Profit and Proselytism: British Culture and Sport at Home and Abroad 1700–1914* (London: Frank Cass, 1988).

Mangan, J.A. and Park, R.J., eds., *From Fair Sex to Feminism: Sport and the Socialization of Women in the Industrial and Post-industrial Eras* (London: Frank Cass, 1987).

Mangan, J.A. and Walvin, J., eds., *Manliness and Morality: Middle-class Masculinity in Britain and America, 1800–1940* (Manchester; Manchester UP, 1987).

Marqusee, M., *Anyone but England: Cricket and the National Malaise* (London: Verso, 1994).

Martin-Jenkins, C., *The Wisden Book of County Cricket* (London: Queen Anne, 1981).

Marshall, M., *Gentlemen & Players: Conversations with Cricketers* (London: Grafton, 1987).

Mason, R., *Batsman's Paradise: An Anthology of Cricketomania* (London: Hollis and Carter, 1955).

Mason, R., *Sing All A Green Willow* (London: Epworth, 1976).

Mason, R., *Walter Hammond: A Biography* (London: Hollis & Carter, 1962).

Mason, T., *Association Football and English Society, 1863–1915* (Brighton: Harvester, 1980).

Mason, T., *Sport in Britain* (London: Faber and Faber, 1988).

Massey, J., *A Condensed History of Radcliffe Cricket Club* (n.p., 1958).

Midwinter, E., *The Illustrated History of County Cricket* (London: Kingswood, 1992).

Midwinter, E., *W.G. Grace: His Life and Times* (London: Allen and Unwin, 1981).

Moore, A., 'The "Fascist" Cricket Tour of 1924–25', *Sporting Traditions*, 7, 2 (May 1991).

Moore, D., *The History of Kent County Cricket Club* (London: Christopher Helm, 1988).

Moult, T., ed., *Bat and Ball: A New Book of Cricket* (London: Sportsman's Book Club, 1960).

'Moral Influence of Sport', *New Statesman and Nation*, 17 June, 1933.

'What is Sport?', *New Statesman and Nation*, 3 July 1926.

Nauright, J. and Chandler, T.J.L., eds., *Making Men: Rugby and Masculine Identity* (London: Frank Cass, 1996).

Noble, M.A., *The Game's The Thing* (London: Cassell, 1926).

Noel, E.B., *Winchester College Cricket* (London: Williams and Norgate, 1926).

Norman, E.R., *Church and Society in England, 1770–1970: A Historical Survey* (Oxford: Clarendon, 1976).

Oldfield, W.A., *The Rattle of the Stumps* (London: Newnes, 1954).

Padwick, E.W., *A Bibliography of Cricket* (London: Library Association, 1984).

Parkin, C., *Cricket Reminiscences: Humorous and Otherwise* (London: Hodder and Stoughton, 1925).

Parkin, C., *Cricket Triumphs and Troubles* (Manchester: C. Nicholls, 1936).

Peebles, I., *'Patsy' Hendren: The Cricketer and His Times* (London: Macmillan, 1969).

Peebles, I., *Woolley: The Pride of Kent* (London: Hutchinson, 1969).

Planemen's Cricket: British Aerospace Cricket Club. 50 Years of Cricket at Lostock (n.p., n.d.).

Pollard, M., *Cricket for Women and Girls* (London: Hutchinson, 1934).

Pollock, W., *The Cream of Cricket* (London: Methuen, 1934).

Porter, R., ed., *Myths of the English* (Cambridge: Polity, 1993).

Pridham, C.H.B., *The Charm of Cricket Past and Present* (London: Herbert Jenkins, 1949).

Pullin, A.W., *History of Yorkshire County Cricket 1903–1923* (Leeds: Chorley & Pickersgill, 1924).

Pugh, M., *Women and the Women's Movement in Britain* (London: Macmillan, 1992).

Rawtenstall Cricket Club Bazaar...with a Brief History of the Cricket Club from 1868 to 1925 (n.p., n.d.).

Raven, J., 'Viewpoint: British History and the Enterprise Culture', *Past & Present*, 123 (May 1989).

Report of the Royal Commission on the Press, 1947–1949, Appendix III (London: HMSO Cmd. 7700, 1948–49).

Riordan, J., 'The Social Emancipation of Women through Sport', *British Journal of Sport History*, 2, 3 (May 1985).

Robertson-Glasgow, R.C., *The Brighter Side of Cricket* (London: Arthur Barker, 1933).

Robertson-Glasgow, R.C., *46 Not Out* (London: 1985 re-issue of the 1948 edition).

Roe, W.N., ed., *Public Schools Cricket, 1901–1950* (London: Max Parrish, 1951).

Roebuck, P., *From Sammy to Jimmy: The Official History of Somerset County Cricket Club* (London: Partridge, 1991).

Rogerson, S., *Wilfred Rhodes: Professional and Gentleman* (London: Hollis & Carter, 1960).

Root, F., *A Cricket Pro's Lot* (London: Edward Arnold, 1937).

Ross, A., *Blindfold Games* (London: Collins Harvill, 1986).

Rubinstein, W.D., *Capitalism, Culture, and Decline in Britain 1750–1990* (London: Routledge, 1993).

Russell, D., 'Amateurs, Professionals and the Construction of Social Identity', *Sports Historian*, 16 (May 1996).

Russell, D., 'Sport and Identity: The Case of Yorkshire County Cricket Club, 1890–1939', *20 Century British History*, 7, 2 (1996).

Sandiford, K.A.P., *Cricket and the Victorians* (Aldershot: Scolar, 1994).

Sandiford, K.A.P., 'The Professionalisation of Modern Cricket', *British Journal of Sports History*, 2, 1 (May 1985).

Sandiford, K.A.P. and Vamplew, W., 'The Peculiar Economics of English Cricket before 1914', *British Journal of Sports History*, 2, 3 (Dec. 1985).

Savage, M. and Miles, A., *The Remaking of the British Working Class, 1840–1940* (London: Routledge, 1994).

Schofield, J.A., 'The Development of First-class Cricket in England: An Economic Analysis' *Journal of Industrial Economics,* 30 (1982).

Scott, P., 'Cricket and the Religious World in the Victorian Period', *Church Quarterly*, III (1970).

Scowcroft, P.L., *Cricket in Doncaster and District: An Outline History* (Doncaster: Doncaster Library Service, 1985).

Sewell, E.H.D., *An Outdoor Wallah* (London: Stanley Paul, 1945).

Sewell, E.H.D., *From a Window at Lord's* (London: Methuen, 1937).

Sewell, E.H.D., *Who's Won the Toss* (London: Stanley Paul, 1944).

Shawcroft, J., *The History of Derbyshire County Cricket Club* (London: Christopher Helm, 1989)

Sissons, R., *The Players: A Social History of the Professional Cricketer* (London: Kingswood, 1988).

Sissons, R. and Stoddart, B., *Cricket and Empire: The 1932–33 Bodyline Tour of Australia* (London: Allen & Unwin, 1984).

Smith, D., and Williams, G., *Fields of Praise: The Official History of the Welsh Rugby Union 1881–1981* (Cardiff: University of Wales, 1980).

Squire, H.F. and Squire, A.P., *Henfield Cricket Club and Its Sussex Cradle* (Hove: Combridges, 1949).

Streeton, R., *P.H.G. Fender: A Biography* (London: Faber & Faber, 1981).

Stevenson, J., *British Social History 1914–45* (Harmondsworth: Penguin, 1986).

Sutcliffe, H., *For Yorkshire and England* (London: Edward Arnold, 1935).

Swanton, E.W., *Cricket Sort of Person* (London: Collins, 1972).

Swanton, E.W., *Gubby Allen: Man of Cricket* (London: Hutchinson/Stanley Paul, 1985).

Swanton, E.W., Plumptre, G. and Woodcock, J., eds., *Barclays World of Cricket: The Game from A–Z* (London: Guild, 1986).

Tabner, B., *Through the Turnstiles* (Harefield: Yore, 1992).

Tate, M., *My Cricketing Reminiscences* (London: Stanley Paul, 1934).

Taylor, J.B., *Bradshaw Cricket Club* (n.p., n.d.).

Tennyson, Lord, *From Verse to Worse* (London: Cassell, 1933).

Thomas, H.B.F., *Schoolboy Cricket in Manchester: A Short History of the Manchester Schools Cricket Association* (Salford: Manchester Schools Cricket Association, 1947).

Thompson, S.M., '"Thank the Ladies for the Plates": The Incorporation of Women into Sport', *Leisure Studies*, 9, 2 (May 1990).

Thomson, A.A., *Pavilioned in Splendour* (London: Museum, 1956).

Tomlinson, A., 'Good Times, Bad Times and the Politics of Leisure. Working-class Culture in the 1930s in a Small Working-class Community', in Cantelon, H. and Gruneau, R., eds., *Leisure, Sport and Working-class Cultures: Theory and History* (Toronto: Garamond, 1988).

Tozer, M., 'From "Muscular Christianity" to "Esprit de Corps": Games in the Victorian Public Schools of England', *Stadion*, 7, 1 (1981).

Tozer, M., 'Sport and the Mid-Victorian Ideal of Manliness' *Momentum*, 3, 4 (1986).

Trueman, F. and Mosey, D., *Fred Trueman Talking Cricket with Friends Past and Present* (London: Hodder & Stoughton, 1997).

29th Report of the Commissioners of Customs and Excise for the Year Ended March 31, 1938 (London: HMSO, 1938–39).

Trevor, P., *Cricket and Cricketers* (London: Chapman & Hall, 1921).

Vamplew, W., *Pay Up and Play the Game: Professional Sport in Britain, 1875–1914* (Cambridge: Cambridge UP, 1988).

Von Stutterheim, *Those English!* [translated by L.M. Sieveking] (London: Sidgwick & Jackson, 1937).

Walker, P.N., *The Liverpool Competition: A Study of the Development of Cricket on Merseyside* (Birkenhead: Countyvise, 1988).

Wallis, R. and Bruce, S., 'Secularization: The Orthodox Model' in Bruce, S., ed., *Religion and Modernization: Sociologists and Historians*

Debate the Secularization Thesis (Oxford: Oxford UP, 1992).

Walton, J.K., *Lancashire: A Social History* (Manchester: Manchester UP, 1987).

Walvin, J., *The People's Game: The History of Football Revisited* (London: Mainstream, 1994).

Warner, P.F., *Cricket: A New Edition* (London: Longmans, Green, 1920).

Warner, P.F., *Long Innings: The Autobiography of Pelham Warner* (London: Harrap, 1951).

Waugh, A., 'Village Cricket', *Fortnightly Review* (May 1923).

Welldon, J.E.C., *Forty Years On: Lights and Shadows (A Bishop's Reflections on Life)* (London: Nicolson and Watson, 1935).

Welldon, J.E.C., 'The Training of an English Gentleman in the Public Schools', *Nineteenth Century*, 60 (Sept. 1906).

'What is Sport?', *New Statesman and Nation*, 3 July 1926.

Wiener, M.J., *English Culture and the Decline of the Industrial Spirit* (Cambridge: Cambridge UP, 1981).

Williams, J., 'Churches, Sport and Identities in the North, 1900–1939' in Hill, J. and Williams, J., eds., *Sport and Identity in the North of England* (Keele: Keele UP, 1996).

Williams, J., 'Cricket', in Mason, T., *Sport in Britain: A Social History* (Cambridge: Cambridge UP, 1989).

Williams, J., 'Cricket and Christianity in Lancashire, 1900–1939', *Local Historian*, 25, 2 (May 1995).

Williams, J., 'Cricket and the Great War', *Stand To!*, 51 (Jan. 1998).

Williams, J., 'The Economics of League Cricket: Lancashire League Clubs and Their Finances since the First World War', *British Society of Sports History Bulletin*, 9 (1990).

Williams, J., 'Recreational Cricket in the Bolton Area between the Wars' in Holt, R., ed., *Sport and the Working Clas in Modern Britain* (Manchester: Manchester UP).

Williams, R., *Marxism and Literature* (Oxford: Oxford UP, 1977).

Woolley, F., *The King of Games* (London: Stanley Paul, 1936).

Woodhouse, A., *The History of Yorkshire County Cricket Club* (London: Christopher Helm, 1989).

Wyatt, R.E.S., *The Ins and Outs of Cricket* (London: Bell, 1936).

Wynne-Thomas, P., *The History of Hampshire County Cricket Club* (London: Christopher Helm, 1988)

Wynne-Thomas, P., *The History of Lancashire County Cricket Club* (London: Christopher Helm, 1989).

Wynne-Thomas, P., *The History of Nottinghamshire County Cricket Club* (London: Christopher Helm, 1992).

THESES

Arnold, J., 'The Influence of Pilkington Brothers (Glass Manufacturers) on the Growth of Sport and Community Recreation in St Helens', University of Liverpool M.Ed. (1977).

Bentley, C.A., 'Provision for Physical Education within Elementary Education in Bolton between 1870 and 1940', University of Manchester M.Ed. (1986).

Bradley, J., 'Cricket, Class and Colonialism, c1860–1914: A Study of two Elites. The Marylebone and Melbourne Cricket Clubs', University of Edinburgh PhD (1991).

Brook, M., 'A Study of Yorkshire Cricket between 1885 and 1925 and an Examination of the Relationship between Yorkshire Cricket and a Form of Yorkshire Cultural Identity', University of Warwick MA (1990).

Power, J., 'Aspects of Working-class Leisure during the Depression Years: Bolton in the 1930s', University of Warwick MA (1980).

Richards, H.G., 'Constriction, Conformity and Control: The Taming of *The Daily Herald*', Open University PhD (1992).

Ross, A.J., 'Cricket and the Establishment: A Social History of Cricket in Lancashire with Specific Reference to the Liverpool Competition, 1775–1935', Ohio State University PhD (1987).

Williams, G.A., 'A Socio-historical Analysis of the Development of Cricket in England since 1800: In Order to Investigate the Theories of Dunning and Sheard (1979), Hargreaves (1986) and Guttmann (1978)', Sheffield City Polytechnic M.Phil (CNAA) (1989).

Williams, J.A., 'Cricket and Society in Bolton between the Wars', University of Lancaster PhD (1992).

Index

advertising, 5, 171.
Advisory County Cricket Committee, 21–2, 24, 31, 80–1, 87, 162, 168
Ainscow, W.E., 33
Allen, Gubby, 81
Altham, H.S., 77
amateurism, xvi, 15–16, 39, 77, 82, 96, 114–31; commercialism, 167–8; criticism, 118, 136–7, 187–8; expenses, 68, 119–20; *see also* social class, sportsmanship
Ames, Leslie, 80
Andrews, B., 125–7
Anyone but England: Cricket and the National Malaise, xvii
association football, xvi–xvii, 45, 48–9, 67–8, 149
Association Football and English Society, xvi
Astill, W.E., 117–18
athleticism, 7
Athleticism in the Victorian and Edwardian Public School, xvi
Athletic News, 6, 12, 24, 57, 67, 80, 120, 128, 167, 171
Attlee, Clement, 137
Audit of War, The, 161
Australian Board of Control, 21–2, 81

Baden-Powell, T., 132
Baldwin, Lucy, 8
Baldwin, Stanley, 11, 13, 15, 23
Bale, J., 5
Barbarians, Gentlemen and Players: A Sociological Development of Rugby Football, xvi
Barker, Ernest, 12–13, 41
Barnett, Charles, 115
Barnett, Corelli, 161
Barratt, F., 130
Barrie, J.M., 8, 70
Barson, Frank, 93
Beasley, J.N., 119
Beecham, Sir Thomas, 163
Bencraft, Russell, 23

Beyond a Boundary, xviii
Birley, D., xvii
Blunden, Edmund, 70
Board of Control, 21
bodyline, xvii, 3, 14, 40, 81–2, 85, 93, 184
Bolton Congregationalist, 150
Bolton and District Cricket Association, 28, 32–3
Bolton Evening News, 77, 83
books, 68–71
Booth, J.J., 30
Bourchier, B., 154
Bourdieu, P., xiv
Bowes, Bill, 78, 85, 87, 129–30, 133, 144
Boyes, G., 9, 143
Bradford Evening Argus, 67
Bradford Telegraph and Argus, 97, 105
Bradman, Donald, 82, 87
Broadbent, Eileen, 98.
Brookes, Christopher, xviii
Brown, I., 1
Bryan, J.L., 16
Buff, The, 77, 83, 174
Burnley Express, 68

Cahn, Sir Julien, 119, 163
Canterbury Diocesan Conference (1922), 153–4
Cardus, Neville, xviii, 4, 8,12, 69, 104, 120, 134, 142
Carr, Arthur, 81, 117, 122, 128, 168
Central Lancashire League, 28–9, 60, 83–4, 174, 176
Chandler, T.J.L., 92
Chapman, Percy, 69, 80, 107, 118, 121
character-building, 1–3, 6, 150
Character and Sportsmanship, 74
cheating, 79–82
Chester, Frank, 87
Christianity, 142–58
Christian morality, xvi, 4–6, 142–4, 157–8, 188
church attendance, 150, 156–7, 189
Church Commissioners, 154–5

213